Children as Citizens

Children in Charge series

Children in Charge
The Child's Right to a Fair Hearing
Edited by Mary John
ISBN 1 85302 386 X
Children in Charge 1

Children in Our Charge
The Child's Right to Resources
Edited by Mary John
ISBN 1 85302 369 8
Children in Charge 2

A Charge Against Society
The Child's Right to Protection
Edited by Mary John
ISBN 1 85302 411 2
Children in Charge 3

The Participation Rights of the Child
Rights and Responsibilities in Family and Society
Målfrid Grude Flekkøy and Natalie Hevener Kaufman
ISBN 1 85302 489 9 hb
ISBN 1 85302 490 2 pb
Children in Charge 4

Children in Charge 5

Children as Citizens
Education for Participation

Edited by Cathie Holden and Nick Clough

Jessica Kingsley Publishers
London and Philadelphia

Figure 1.1 is reproduced from 'Issues of freedom and control' by J. Ruddock (1997). Figure 1.2 is reproduced form *Children's Participation: From Tokenism to Citizenship* by R. Hart (1992), by kind permission of the UNICEF International Child Development Centre. Table 4.1 was adapted from *Exploring Alternative Futures: A Teacher's Interim Guide* by D. Hicks (1991). Table 5.1, from 'Organisation of schooling: achieving access and quality through inclusion' in *Prospects 25* (1995), was reproduced by kind permission of the Bureau International d'Éducation. Figures 6.2–6.4 are reproduced from 'Gedenkstaettenbesuche im historich-politischen Unterricht' by H.F. Rathenow and N. Weber in *Praxis der Gedenkstaettempaedogogik*, edited by A. Ehmann *et al.* (1995). Table 15.1 is reproduced from *Adding Value? Schools' Responsibility for Pupils' Personal Development*, edited by M. Buck and S. Inman (1995), courtesy of Trentham Books. Figures 17.1–17.5 have been reproduced from *Speaking for Ourselves: Listening to Others*, published by Leeds DEC. The extract quoted on pp.258–9 from *The Little Prince* by A. de Saint-Exupéry (William Heinemann 1945) was reproduced by kind permission of Reed Consumer Books Ltd. Permission to quote from *Changing Childhoods – Britain since 1930* by M. Brown and D. Harrison (1996), and from *Lima Lives* by D. Harrison (1993), was granted by the Save the Children Fund.

All rights reserved. No part of this publication may be reproduced in any material form (including photocopying or storing it in any medium by electronic means and whether or not transiently or incidentally to some other use of this publication) without the written permission of the copyright owner except in accordance with the provisions of the Copyright, Designs and Patents Act 1988 or under the terms of a licence issued by the Copyright Licensing Agency Ltd, 90 Tottenham Court Road, London, England W1T 4LP. Applications for the copyright owner's written permission to reproduce any part of this publication should be addressed to the publisher. Warning: The doing of an unauthorised act in relation to a copyright work may result in both a civil claim for damages and criminal prosecution.

The right of the contributors to be identified as authors of this work has been asserted by them in accordance with the Copyright, Designs and Patents Act 1988.

First published in the United Kingdom in 1998 by
Jessica Kingsley Publishers
116 Pentonville Road
London N1 9JB, UK
and
400 Market Street, Suite 400
Philadelphia, PA 19106, USA

Second impression 2000
Third impression 2003
Printed digitally since 2005

Copyright © 1998 Jessica Kingsley Publishers

Library of Congress Cataloging in Publication Data
A CIP catalogue record for this book is available from the Library of Congress

British Library Cataloguing in Publication Data
Children as citizens: education for participation. – (Children in charge ; 5)
1.Citizenship – Study and teaching
I.Holden, Cathie II.Clough, Nick
323.6'071

ISBN-13: 978 185302 566 2
ISBN-10: 1 85302 566 6

Contents

Editors' Acknowledgements 8
Preface by Mary John 9

Part One: Introduction

1. 'The Child Carried on the Back Does Not Know the Length of the Road': The Teacher's Role in Assisting Participation 13
   *Cathie Holden, University of Exeter,
   and Nick Clough, University of the West of England*

Part Two: Primary Pupils: Values and Action

2. Participation and Learning in Early Childhood 31
   Liz Wood, University of Exeter

3. Keen at 11, Cynical at 18? Encouraging Pupil Participation in School and Community 46
   Cathie Holden, University of Exeter

4. Emerging from the Tunnel: Some Dilemmas 63 in Environmental Education
   Nick Clough, University of the West of England

Part Three: Secondary Pupils: Values and Action

5. The Voices of Young People with Disability 81
   *Rhiannon Prys Owen, Somerset Inclusion Project,
   and Jane Tarr, University of the West of England*

6. Education After Auschwitz: A Task for Human Rights Education 95
   *Hanns-Fred Rathenow and Norbert H. Weber,
   Technical University of Berlin*

7. Conflicts, Controversy and Caring:
Young People's Attitudes towards Children's Rights 113
Audrey Osler, University of Birmingham

8. Citizenship Education through Literature 127
Chris Spurgeon, Hartshill School

Part Four: Teacher Thinking: Values, Knowledge and Action

9. Understanding the Role of Emotion in Anti-Racist Education 141
Phil Johnson, University of Melbourne

10. The Teacher's Role in Democratic Pedagogies 154
Doug Harwood, University of Warwick

11. Economics, Environment and the Loss of Innocence 171
Martin Ashley, University of the West of England

12. Questioning Identities: Issues for Teachers and Children 183
Ian Davies, University of York, and Micheline Rey, University of Geneva

13. New Teachers Talking Citizenship: Europe and Beyond 196
Veronica Voiels, Manchester Metropolitan University

Part Five: Case Studies from European Primary Schools

14. Children's Newspapers: Meeting Other Minds 209
Geoff Anderson, Westminster College, Oxford

15. Children and the Supermarché 222
*Jean Pierre Branchereau,
Institut Universitaire de Formation des Maîtres des Pays de la Loire, Nantes*

16. Consumers as Citizens:
Children Working Together Across Europe 228
*Marta Utset, Bellaterra Primary School,
Maria Villanueva and Carmen Gonzalo, Universitat Autonóma de Barcelona*

Part Six: Children's Voices in Learning Materials

17. Speaking for Ourselves, Listening to Others: Young Global Citizens Learning through the Study of Distant Places 243
    Julia Tanner, Leeds Metropolitan University

18. Children's Voices from Different Times and Places 258
    Margot Brown, University College of Ripon and York St. John, and Don Harrison, Council for Education in World Citizenship

The Contributors 271

Subject Index 275

Author Index 277

Editors' Acknowledgements

Much of the work of this book has arisen out of an Erasmus project. Teacher educators across Europe collaborated in a five-year programme: *Education for Citizenship in a New Europe: Teaching about Social Justice, Democracy, Human Rights and Global Responsibility*. The work of this group of teacher educators is reflected in this book, whilst other authors are involved in a parallel project being run in the UK by the World Studies Trust.

The editors are grateful to Hugh Starkey and Miriam Steiner for their able co-ordination of the above projects, and to Professor David Hicks and Robin Richardson whose early work and continuing support in this field have been significant. We would also like to thank all the teachers and children who contributed to the book by sharing their thoughts and experiences. It is their voices and actions which have made this book possible.

Preface

The Children in Charge series describes, in various ways, work that is going on around the world that relates to the achievement of the aims of the United Nations Convention on the Rights of the Child. The series was named 'Children in Charge' rather than 'Children's Rights' quite deliberately, in order to emphasise the stance adopted throughout the whole collection. The present volume is no exception to this stance: that children are significant actors, powerful players and determined advocates in the shaping and creation of the societies in which they live.

Claiming rights, however, as every marginalised group knows, is no easy matter – it involves recognition, facilitation, advocacy, partners, partnership and full participation in the processes of society. The series so far has looked at elements in these processes, first by means of the three volumes which sprang from our early World Conference on the theme in 1992. In these books, the implications of the United Nations Convention in practical and research terms were teased out, aided by the arguments and inside experience of our Young People's Evaluation Panel. Those volumes (*Children in Charge, Children in Our Charge, A Charge Against Society*) crystallised around the 'three Ps' of the Convention – Participation, Provision and Protection. It is the first of these three which has been the most challenging aspect of the Articles of the Convention, and which has been addressed warily by many researchers and practitioners around the world who value the freedom of child citizens of today, and realise that the responsibilities of tomorrow will be theirs.

We were, later in the series, skilfully introduced to the rights and responsibilities of families and society in this process, in Flekkoy and Kaufman's work on the theme of *The Participation Rights of the Child*. This book takes us through the evolving capacities of the child in development and provides a framework and many practical demonstrations from a variety of countries of children expressing themselves as part of everyday decision-making processes. The freedoms and constraints of independent learning by the child have been the focus of the volume on *Educational Citizenship* which describes Griffith's extensive study in a number of UK schools.

The present book concentrates on the child's educational experiences largely in comparative European settings, and demonstrates, through a variety of approaches, the ways in which children are facilitated in developing a sense of individual freedom, balancing this against their responsibilities as citizens. The cultivation of their sense of civic duties is set in a context of inducting them into a full appreciation of their individual rights. Teachers here are seen as allies in the process. Children are skilfully placed in contexts and situations where they become stakeholders in their own learning experiences as, increasingly, trust is placed in their evolving skills and competence. The book peels back the process right to its roots, not just in the teacher's entrainment of the child, but also to the training of teachers themselves. Only by breaking into the cycle in this way can we hope to produce an educational system that, through its policies, practices and materials, recognises children as full participants in the process of an education which perceives values, emotions, identity, gender differences and an informed consciousness about rights, as interlocking issues. This is a crucial book in that it recognises that children are being educated, not just for the here-and-now in the UK, but also as Europeans and world citizens for a future many of us will not see, and of which we hope they will be fully in charge.

Mary John, Series Editor

PART ONE

Introduction

CHAPTER ONE

'The Child Carried on the Back does not Know the Length of the Road'

The Teacher's Role in Assisting Participation

Cathie Holden and Nick Clough

The process of assisting children to become active citizens requires the teacher to keep a delicate balance between providing security and offering challenge. Within the metaphor of the Yoruba saying above we maintain that the child will need support on the road but that to be carried all the way denies opportunities to appreciate the challenges and to participate as a traveller on the journey. The metaphor is appropriate because it epitomises the current challenge for teachers in educating children to participate fully as citizens in the life of the school and wider community.

This chapter will focus on the role of the teacher in supporting children's social and moral development, on the potential within the curriculum for participatory citizenship education and will provide a rationale for the inclusion of this approach, advocating that it is for the benefit of both children and democratic societies.

There is already much debate in the UK about how this might be done with calls for 'specialist citizenship teachers' (*Times Educational Supplement* 1997b), a moral framework for teaching values (School Curriculum and Assessment Authority 1995) and involvement by all pupils in community work as part of the curriculum (*Guardian* 1996). Within the broader European context there are calls for young people to be educated in democratic processes and values in the light of increasing xenophobia and racism (Council of Europe 1993). Furthermore at a global level there are movements to involve young people in actions to address issues of social injustice and environmental degradation. We argue that the curriculum should address these challenges, allowing opportunities for participation at many levels. In so doing children will be prepared for the road ahead and ready for the responsibilities of adult life in a global society. The contribution of this book to the current debate is thus timely.

WHAT IS EDUCATION FOR PARTICIPATION?

Education for participation involves reflecting on values, assisting children to acquire the skills necessary for taking action and ultimately providing opportunities for them to become involved as active citizens. Such education is endorsed by the Convention on the Rights of the Child (1989) (Articles 12 and 13) where children are given the right to seek and impart information, to express their thoughts and feelings, to have these listened to, and to partake in decisions affecting them.

Integral to the acquisition of skills is the acquisition of a values base from which to make one's decisions and responses. We suggest that children are taught a framework of values based on the principles underpinning the United Nations Declaration of Human Rights (1948) which includes learning about social justice and global responsibility.

Education for participation thus becomes education for values-based participation, and involves children:

1. Developing an understanding of
    - the significance of individual and collective action
    - their own values and the relationship of these to behaviour and action
    - democratic systems and the individual's role within these
    - contemporary events and controversial issues
    - the causes of social and environmental problems
    - recent historical events and their relationship to the present/future.

2. Being encouraged to
    - explore issues of justice, rights and responsibilities within the taught curriculum
    - voice their own needs and concerns within a responsive framework
    - develop the skills of critical reflection through discussion
    - address the implications of their own behaviour with respect to social and environmental problems
    - participate in decision making and action at school, community or global level.

WHY IS EDUCATION FOR PARTICIPATION NECESSARY?

Children's voices in research findings indicate that they are already concerned about environmental destruction, growing crime and violence and social inequality both locally and globally (Hicks and Holden 1995). Furthermore they wish to be active in working towards effective change to ensure improved social and environmental conditions. Secondary pupils reflecting on their schooling comment that:

> it has given them an inadequate education in this area and that they would like more information, discussion and advice. They feel responsible as citizens of the future for what might happen but lack a clear vision of what their own part might be. (Hicks and Holden 1995, p.112)

Facilitating values-based participation answers the needs of children to feel involved, informed and prepared for taking responsibilities. It is thus of benefit to the child.

To exclude young people from participation and from the consultative process, is, as Rudduck argues, to contribute to the 'bracketing out of their voice [and] is founded upon an outdated view of childhood which fails to acknowledge children's capacity to reflect on issues affecting their lives'. Furthermore she maintains that the curriculum and school environment do not reflect the social maturity of children today (Rudduck, Chaplain and Wallace 1995, p.172). Griffith also warns of the danger of curriculum content unrelated to the experiences or interests of pupils and to the wider social world thus 'existing without external relevance' (Griffith 1996, p.209).

A second argument moves beyond discussion of the benefits to the child to recognise the benefits of education for participation to society. Such an approach which aims to develop critically and politically aware citizens ultimately strengthens the power of democratic societies to address both social and environmental challenges. Orr (1992) writes that through programmes of active citizenship, educational institutions can become 'potential leverage points for the transition to sustainability'. He argues that a successful democracy depends on the contribution of each and every citizen:

> I see no prospect whatever [of a successful democracy] without an active, engaged, informed and competent citizenry. ...Education is not just about society, it is about persons. At the individual level the goal is something like the Greek model of Paideia or that of the Renaissance person of wide understanding, competence and commitment to the common good. (Orr 1992, p.84)

Beck (1992) also identifies the need for competent citizens who, as consumers and workers, are able to critically evaluate the contribution of science and technology. He argues for a more open democracy in which all citizens are involved in consideration of the risks as well as the benefits of progress. Each new situation or challenge, he says, should be analysed with reference to:

> alternative evaluations, alternative professional practice, discussions within organisations and professions of the consequences of their own developments. (Beck 1992, p.234)

Whereas Beck and Orr have identified the need for competent citizens, Griffith reminds us that such competence includes a moral dimension. He argues that central to citizenship is 'corporate responsibility, which manifests itself in a moral concern for social justice' (1996, p.203).

A curriculum which develops the skills of critical reflection and assists values-based participation can begin to meet the identified needs of both children and society.

IMPLICATIONS FOR TEACHERS AND SCHOOLS

Such an approach has implications for teachers and others who work with children. If children are to be educated to participate, they will require a 'range of skills, including social skills and skills of communication and judgment' and of course the opportunity to practise and develop these skills (Osler and Starkey 1996, p.27). Introducing such opportunities may require the management of a school to rethink its approach to pupil participation and may involve its teachers in a reassessment of their role. There are implications for teachers in terms of the values they hold, the freedom and autonomy they give their pupils, and the choices they make within the curriculum.

Current measures to improve standards in literacy and numeracy can divert attention from such discussions about the broader aims of education which encompass social, moral and citizenship education. Fielding (1997) argues that there is a 'relative absence of challenge' in the school effectiveness movement which has failed to address the 'fostering of critically and politically aware citizens' (p.13). We should, he maintains, be asking a more fundamental question:

> How do we develop the personal, professional and pedagogic courage to ask hard questions about the nature of education and schooling in an unjust society? (Fielding 1997, p.23)

As indicated above, children themselves from a very young age are already asking hard questions about their own lives and the lives of others in an unjust society and fragile environment (Hicks and Holden 1995). The teacher's role is thus to have the courage to listen to children's concerns, engage them in debate and support their developing understanding of citizenship through assisting participation.

THE TEACHER'S ROLE IN ASSISTING PARTICIPATION

The concept of assisted performance has been established as a powerful way of understanding the relationship between the teacher and learner. This is based on a social constructivist view of the learning process and draws on the theoretical perspectives of Vygotsky (1978) and Bruner (1966) who argue that children's level of skill and understanding can be enhanced through interaction with a more knowledgeable other. The desired learning outcome is a reduced dependence on such supportive scaffolding and the achievement of a higher level of skill and understanding so that external assistance becomes unnecessary. We would argue that within the field of education for citizenship such a concept of assisted performance can be translated to one of assisted participation.

What kind of ethos do we want in our schools?

There are three steps in this process of assisting participation. The first step is for teachers to consider the kind of qualities and characteristics they wish to encourage in children and the relationship between these and the ethos/culture of the working environment. The diagram presented below identifies a range of possible responses by children to opportunities in education (Rudduck 1997).

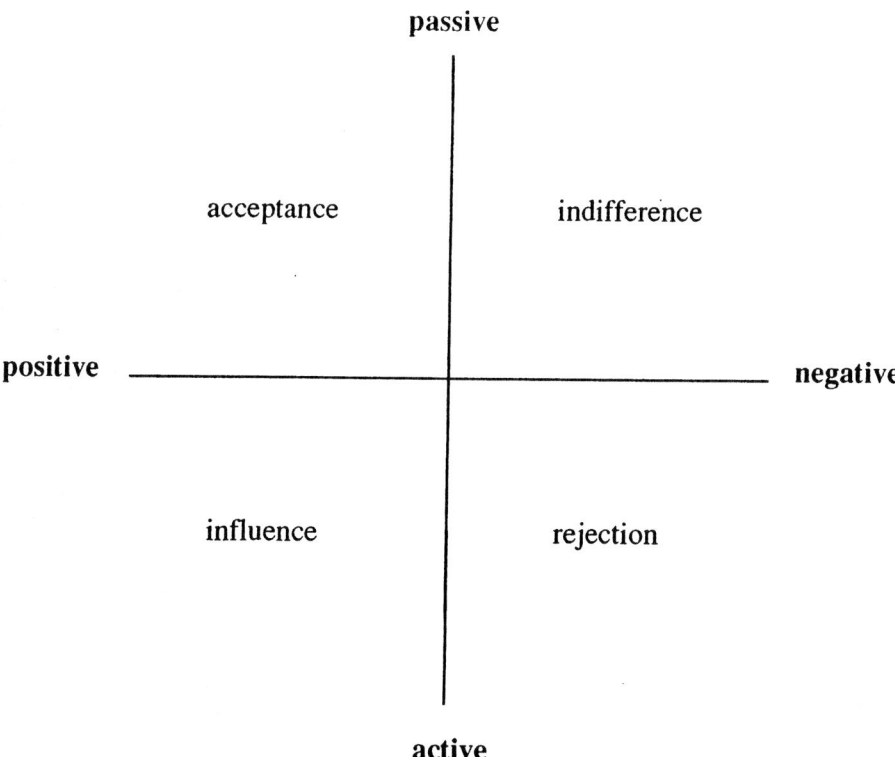

Figure 1.1 Pupil response
Source: Ruddock (1997)

Rudduck encourages us as educators to ask ourselves what kind of response we want from pupils. Do we want children who are positive and yet passive and who consequently comply and accept the status quo? Or do we want children who are positive and active and who are keen to have an influence on the life of the school, for example by participating in decision making? We also need to question our response to the child who is negative and rejecting. Do we ignore this or do we see it as a form of critical and constructive action? What about the indifferent child?

These are complex questions but necessary if we are to be responsive to the rights of all children to be listened to and thus to proceed to the next stage of assisting participation. We also need to acknowledge that this assistance will differ depending on the child. Whereas those children on the positive axis of the diagram will need both challenge and opportunity, those on the negative axis will need a different level of support and encouragement. What is required is a readiness to be open and responsive to the different challenges presented by children as they develop their own ideas about the way forward. Education for values-based participation thus involves consideration of our own responses and values as well as those of the children. This in turn involves consideration of the ethos, culture and moral framework of the school.

How do we prepare children for participation?

Having considered the kinds of responses we want from children and the context of the working environment, the second step is preparation for what we have called 'action competence'. This is the state of readiness pupils need to develop in order to be able to participate meaningfully. A pupil who is action competent is one who can argue, can reflect critically, can relate her opinions and action to a values framework. This requires the teacher to provide a responsive context in which the level of the learner's existing participatory skills and understanding of relevant concepts (rights, responsibilities, justice) can be extended. Without action competence the pupil is in danger of engaging in participation at a superficial level, with little understanding of the issues. Thus the role of the teacher is to provide opportunities for acquiring action competence, rather than 'saving the world'.

> It is not and cannot be the task of the school to solve the political problems of society. Its task is not to improve the world with the help of the pupils' activities. A school does not become green by conserving energy, collecting batteries or sorting waste. These (activities) must be assessed on the basis of...educational criteria. The crucial factor must be what the pupils learn from participating in such actions. (Jensen and Schnack 1994, p.6)

Trafford (1993) gives a very honest account of work in his own school to create action competent children who are able to make choices about their own learning and participate in the school's decision-making processes. Genuine power sharing requires courage on the part of both teachers and children and necessitates the learning of key skills by both groups. One child on the newly set up school council comments 'You cannot just dump a load of kids into a big room and expect them to form an effective school council'. So again, participation *per se* does not lead to competent citizens; action competence must be developed before participation can be effective.

What might this participation look like?

At a third stage teachers also need to consider the level at which they are promoting participation. We have found Hart's (1992) model particularly useful in

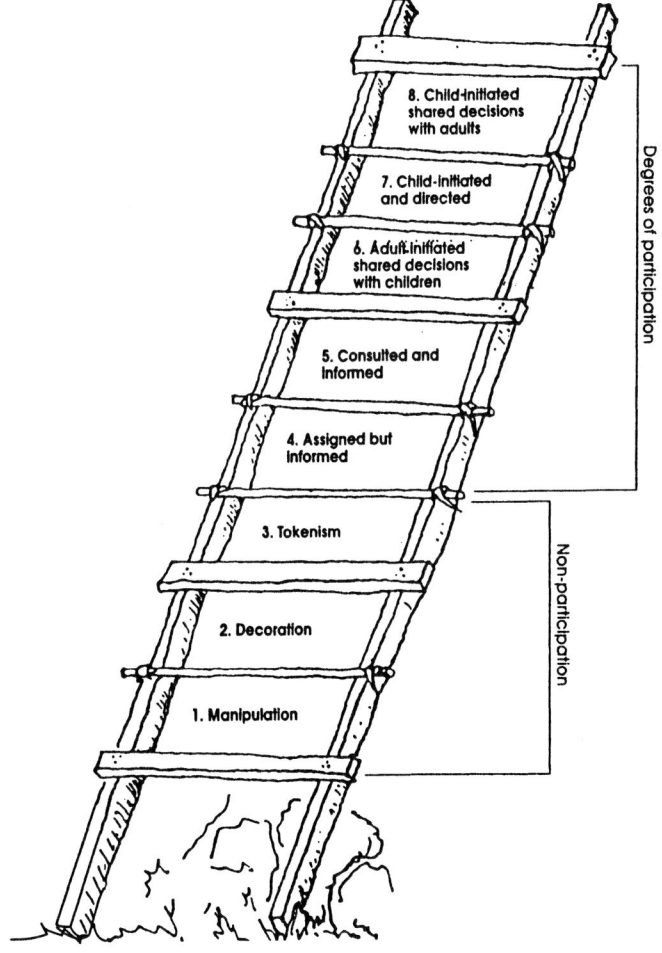

Figure 1.2 Ladder of participation
Source: Hart (1992)

trying to differentiate between the various levels of participation which teachers and those in the community might offer to young people.

A respect for democratic processes is a basic principle underpinning Hart's approach. He writes:

> Many western nations think of themselves as having achieved democracy fully, though they teach the principles of democracy in a pedantic way in classrooms which are themselves models of autocracy. (1992, p.5)

Hart's ladder starts with manipulation, where for example pre-school children carry political placards. Tokenism, he says, is particularly common in the West where children are apparently consulted (for example being asked to sit on a panel) but have no idea about the processes and no consultation with those they are meant to represent.

His contention is that genuine participation begins at level 4:

> There are a number of important requirements for a project to be truly labelled as participatory:
>
> i) the children understand the intention of the project
>
> ii) they know who made the decisions concerning their involvement and why
>
> iii) they have a meaningful role, rather than a decorative one
>
> iv) they volunteer for the project *after* the project was made clear to them. (Hart 1992, p.12)

Of course it is not necessary that children should always operate at the highest level: different levels are appropriate at different times, depending on the ability of child and the situation. One of Hart's main contentions is that we must give children the opportunity and encouragement to work alongside adults in school and community projects. At the highest level, adults and children work together on projects initiated by children and learn from each other, each group offering 'the special energies and perception of their generations' (1992, p.44).

Thus at one level pupils become action competent through engaging in assisted participation, and this in turn provides them with the skills and knowledge for more extended participation at higher levels. Hart usefully reminds us that the activities in which pupils participate may need to be differentiated according to gender:

> In designing programmes for girls, we will need to recognise the different ways girls are treated in different cultures and discover how to address the barriers to their effective participation in family, school and community. For example, in many societies it is still assumed that boys will be decision-makers and girls will not. (1992, p.40)

Many of the authors in this book also acknowledge that gender is an important consideration in the process of educating for participation. When the youngest children in Chapter Two exhibit gender-stereotyped behaviour, Wood discusses ways of challenging this; and in Chapter Three Holden reports on the differing responses of boys and girls to making the world a better place. Osler identifies different value systems at work in older pupils and Spurgeon cites the particular needs of some less able white males in relation to values and racism. It appears, then, that teachers must be sensitive to the differing responses of boys and girls if they are to be able to prepare both sexes for effective participation.

Thus education for values-based participation involves three stages:

1. Identifying the kind of responses the teacher or school wants from its children, and what ethos facilitates such responses.

2. Listening to and understanding pupil perspectives and providing appropriate opportunities for children to develop the skills, knowledge and values necessary for action competence.

3. Providing opportunities for genuine participation in school and community.

This book demonstrates how this process can be managed in the classroom with a particular focus on the role of the teacher in assisting pupils in the various stages of participation.

PRIMARY PUPILS: VALUES AND ACTION

The first section of the book demonstrates how even the youngest of children can become action competent. Throughout this section the authors stress not only the abilities of primary school children to make sense of difficult issues and to engage in values-based discussions, but also the crucial role of the teacher in providing opportunities for such participation.

Liz Wood, in Chapter Two, challenges the romantic view of early childhood and argues that underestimating the ability of young children can lead to a 'baby-safe' curriculum which denies the real experiences of childhood. Wood advocates an early years curriculum where children are assisted to attain social and interpersonal skills including those of conflict resolution. The role of the teacher is to move beyond 'protecting and providing to including, enabling and empowering' children. She gives many examples from the early years classroom where children's concerns have been listened to, where their perspectives have been taken into account and where teachers have challenged children to develop their thinking. To return to the Yoruba saying, Wood argues that to carry even the youngest child is patronising and inappropriate in today's world.

The second chapter in this section draws initially on research by the author into children's concerns for the future. Holden details the action young people from age 7 to 18 take in working for change and the part their schools play in enabling and encouraging such involvement. She argues that it is possible for schools to be more proactive than is currently the case by introducing innovative approaches into the curriculum and by facilitating involvement in school and community projects. Three examples are given: introducing a 'futures perspective' where children are encouraged to think through the implications of alternative futures, the setting up of school councils where even the youngest children participate, and community projects where children learn skills of advocacy and participation. It is evident that education for active citizenship involves more than encouraging children to give money to charity or plant trees (two examples mentioned initially of actions encouraged by schools): it is rather to do with providing opportunities for debate, decision making and participation and in so doing assisting action competence.

The final chapter in this section reiterates the importance of the role of the teacher, this time in the context of controversial environmental issues. Clough focuses on the dilemmas which can arise in environmental education, taking cars as an example. Case study material draws on children's experience of a curriculum project about a controversial road-building scheme in the locality of the school and on the views of student teachers learning about education for citizenship. A survey of the latter indicates that the majority believed some direct action (and even law breaking) to prevent environmental damage was acceptable, and most placed a relatively low value on democratic processes. The teachers in the school affected by the road construction were at pains to give children a balanced view, and the resulting play which the children enacted showed the viewpoints of councillors, residents, protesters and even animals. The children emerged at the end of the process with apparent confidence in democratic processes, unlike the students. What is important, however, is that the teachers did not ignore a local issue which was controversial but assisted the children to clarify their own values and to understand the debate.

SECONDARY PUPILS: VALUES AND ACTION

The chapters focusing on pupils in secondary education (aged 11–18) provide further examples of the role of the teacher in preparing young people for action competence and the response of pupils to school and community participation.

In Chapter Five, we have another example of the positive benefits a school council can bring to a school for children with disability. Prys Owen and Tarr maintain that it is very important for young people with disability to understand their rights and to learn the skills of advocacy if they are to overcome prejudice and gain access to the environments and conditions they will need. The initiation of a school council in difficult circumstances (a merger of two schools) is documented along with the work arising from this council. Not only was the physical environment improved, but also issues of unacceptable behaviour (verbal and physical abuse and bullying) were addressed. Whilst these pupils needed some adult support, the principle of pupils being actively involved in decision making and consultation was central as is evidenced by the voices of the children. As a result of the work of the school council these young people obtained a better learning environment but more importantly, learnt about their own vulnerable situation and how to argue their case for appropriate action.

With Chapters Six and Eight, we move to a curriculum focus. In Chapter Six, Hanns-Fred Rathenow and Norbert Weber provide an important contribution to the dilemmas faced by history teachers who teach about events in the past which are emotionally sensitive. This chapter is particularly important in the light of 'a resurgence of Holocaust denial...in Sweden, Britain, Canada and France' among today's young people (*Times Educational Supplement* 1997a). Whilst their chapter refers to Holocaust education with pupils in Germany, the dilemmas they describe and the classroom activities advocated are relevant to other situations and other countries. What is particularly interesting in the context of this book is the opportunity for participation. The authors describe a number of classroom activities which allow pupils to understand their own emotional responses to this subject. They also describe projects where pupils have worked together on conservation tasks in Jewish cemeteries and memorial sites. The chapter indicates how participation can be at many levels, and that each level makes its own contribution to pupils' understanding of history and citizenship.

Osler's chapter reports on a small-scale research project designed to assess young people's levels of support for human rights. Rather than merely assess their commitment to abstract principles she explores their responses when rights are in conflict. The choice of the 16–18-year-old age group is significant in that, having completed their compulsory schooling, their responses reflect the education they have received for participatory citizenship. Findings indicate that although these young people had a broad general commitment to the rights of others and to equality of rights within the community, this principle of universality of rights was, in practice, subject to specific restrictions. Young women were generally more supportive of human rights than young men, particularly with regard to the rights of gays and lesbians. Both sexes had lower levels of commitment to legal and child protection rights than they did to social/economic or participatory rights, indicating a need for more explicit teaching and learning about these issues in schools. Given the current debate about the teaching of morals in schools, Osler's work usefully reminds us of the value of human rights education.

Chapter Eight assesses the potential of literature in the classroom to raise awareness of racism and political structures and to help pupils clarify their own values. Chris Spurgeon describes pupil responses to a number of literary texts and demonstrates how variables such as class, gender and academic ability influence their attitudes towards 'reponsible citizenship'. In particular the racist attitudes of some of the less able white boys present a challenge for teachers. Interestingly, many of Spurgeon's pupils strongly support democratic structures and feel that outsiders should conform, reflecting the views of the primary pupils in Chapter Four. The ambivalence expressed by some pupils and the prejudiced attitudes of others indicate the importance of providing space in the curriculum for debate and critical reflection of moral and political issues. Spurgeon advocates that such opportunities need to be provided as part of a whole school policy if young people are to leave school as informed citizens, prepared to uphold and respect the rights of others.

TEACHER THINKING: VALUES, KNOWLEDGE AND ACTION

Part Four includes chapters which focus in particular on the importance of teachers' own knowledge and values to the process of assisting participation.

Johnson argues that teachers should pay more attention to the role of emotion in learning about tolerance, particularly between different ethnic groups. In his chapter he claims that the emotional commitment to prejudices formed early in life causes children to fail to respond and learn from programmes of social and moral education in school. He draws on observations of social divisions in Australian society and on data gathered from children in schools which indicate the prevalence of racist and negative attitudes towards other groups. One of the difficulties, he observes, is that children usually conceal such feelings from teachers by making statements of the kind they think they would like to hear. Having identified emotion as fundamental to the processes of decision making and self-justification he advocates that the teacher's role should be to help children become aware of their own emotions so that they can reconsider their attitudes to others. He concludes by providing a brief description of a programme for primary-aged pupils to reduce racist attitudes through developing their understanding of their emotional responses.

In Chapter Ten Harwood considers the range of alternative roles for the teacher wishing to promote democratic processes. Drawing on transcripts of discussions about controversial issues in classrooms he examines the effects of the teacher's management style on the contributions made by children. He outlines some advantages and disadvantages of these different roles and provides evidence of the relative effectiveness of the teacher who participates as an impartial chairperson. Importantly for this book he draws on comments from children about their own preference for teachers who encourage children to listen to each other rather than 'just standing there talking about it'. It is a chapter about the realities of developing critical thinking and promoting appreciation of democratic processes.

Ashley's chapter contributes to the debate about the role of the teacher. His contention is that for too long teachers have separated environmental education from economic and citizenship education and that this has left children with a superficial understanding of environmental issues. He argues that they are in danger of perceiving these as single issue campaigns, unrelated to economic and ethical factors. Ashley reports on research with pupils aged 11 and 14 into their knowledge of two issues (transport and waste recycling), their scientific understanding of these two issues and their intention to act in response to this knowledge and understanding. He concludes that the operative values of these pupils is a result of what he calls the 'nul curriculum', that is a curriculum which purports to be value free but in effect omits to give pupils an ethical base and an understanding of economic issues. Ashley thus recommends that teachers incorporate an economics and ethical perspective in their teaching about the environment so that children can develop the skills and understanding necessary to become active environmental citizens. Without this children may participate on a superficial level while at primary school, may become disillusioned at secondary school and may become unethical consumers of the environment as adults.

Davies and Rey explore ways in which teachers and children can develop understandings about identity, at personal and national levels. They argue for the acceptance of a broad view of identity to include multiple identities and post-national citizenship. This argument is developed through reference to work undertaken with student teachers in which they shared their experiences of migration and reflected on the effects of this on their personal identities. The writers argue that such migrations and their outcomes are common to many children in Europe and so teachers need to be able to understand these processes. The chapter also offers guidance for teachers on using history as a medium for pupils learning about national and cultural identity with suggestions which question traditional perspectives. This chapter stresses the significance of the teacher's personal understanding of identity: a concept which is at the basis of all education for citizenship.

Voiels develops further the argument that teachers' knowledge and beliefs directly affect their professional behaviour. Other researchers before have already noted the relationship between teacher thinking and classroom practice in the teaching of reading and mathematics, and this chapter raises similar questions about teachers' understanding of citizenship and identity. The chapter describes an enquiry with student teachers from the UK and the Netherlands conducted before and after a training course on citizenship education. The students from the Netherlands indicated that they felt more included as Europeans and reflected greater knowledge of citizenship issues world-wide. The British students, on the other hand, were less confident in discussing democracy, social justice and human rights. Voiels draws conclusions about the need to develop the focus on citizenship education in teacher training programmes and in the school curriculum.

CASE STUDIES FROM EUROPEAN PRIMARY SCHOOLS

The three chapters in this section all show at a practical level how children can participate in learning with those in other countries about issues of concern to themselves. The authors are not afraid to engage children in debate about citizenship issues such as social and economic injustice, environmental issues or consumer rights. Comments from the children indicate their ability to deal with complex issues and how such participation has assisted them to become action competent.

Anderson describes the participation of children from Russia, England, Scotland, France and the Gambia in two unusual newspaper projects. Information about different lifestyles was exchanged as well as ideas and opinions on pollution, conservation, bullying, friendships and stereotypes. The importance of the teacher's role is evident: she may need to assist children to rethink their perceptions of other cultures and lifestyles and in so doing help them understand the perspectives of others. Current advances in technology mean that possibilities for such international linking will be greater over the next few years and it behoves all teachers to think through the potential (and possible pitfalls) of this kind of communication before undertaking such work. Anderson's contribution to global participation through the use of such media is thus helpful.

The other two case studies both focus on food. Branchereau describes a project where children from a French primary school visited a supermarket and collected data about the origins of the products on sale. They then returned to the classroom to sort and analyse the information using maps of France, Europe and the world. Whilst they learnt something of the basis of trade between France and other European countries and began to understand the conditions of mutual dependency between developing and developed countries, Branchereau warns of the danger of pupils seeing this as the norm or status quo. This reflects points made by Ashley. Both maintain that education for citizenship must involve giving children an understanding of economic issues and their ethical basis.

Utset, Villanueva and Gonzalo follow this theme of economic awareness and food and describe a project where children and teachers from primary schools in Spain, Italy, France and Finland worked together. This work was made possible by funding from the European Union and is an example to teachers across Europe of what can be achieved. The teachers used the topic of food to prepare children for their role as informed consumers, both now and in the future. Thus the project covered the methods of production of foodstuffs, the effect of these methods on the environment, the use of additives and the effects of various foods on health. Comments from the children revealed that at the end of the first year of the project many were already exercising consumer rights based on their new-found knowledge: they had become active and informed participants. As with Anderson's newspapers, this chapter demonstrates the potential for collaboration across cultures where children debate difficult questions and in so doing learn more about each other and their own abilities.

CHILDREN'S VOICES IN LEARNING MATERIALS

The final two chapters of the book look at how children can learn through materials which include the voices and images of other children. Participation in the production of learning materials is seen both as an endorsement of the rights of children to be heard and also as a means to making children's voices more accessible.

Hart (1992) lends support to this view:

> Children are undoubtedly the most photographed and the least listened to members of society. There is a strong tendency on the part of adults to underestimate the competence of children while at the same time using them in events... (1992, p.8)

Tanner's chapter focuses on an international project which involved children and their teachers producing materials about their local area and using resources similarly created by other children in a distant place. In so doing, the children began to develop the ability to critically interpret visual and written sources of information about other places. The chapter raises questions about the creation and use of such teaching materials as well as exemplifying best practice in the field. Brown and Harrison also discuss the value of using children's personal experiences as a powerful motivating force for learning. They illustrate how the teaching of history and geography can be enhanced through knowledge of other children's lives in the 'long ago and far away', and give specific examples of education for citizenship.

The chapters in this book demonstrate in various ways the need for teachers to think carefully about their role in educating children as future citizens. We have argued that this should involve assisting children to participate in school and community at a variety of levels, and that in preparation for this children need particular skills and a values-based framework. This may require those concerned to rethink their conceptualisation of childhood, so that children are acknowledged as citizens and trust is placed in their evolving competence. Such an education would facilitate the global citizen who is:

> not merely aware of her rights but able and desirous to act upon them with an autonomous and inquiring critical disposition...her decisions and actions tempered by a moral concern for social justice and the dignity of human kind. (Griffith 1996, p.204)

REFERENCES

Beck, V. (1992) *Risk Society: Towards a New Modernity.* London: Sage Publications.

Bruner, J. (1966) *Towards a Theory of Instruction.* Cambridge, MA: Harvard University Press.

Council of Europe (1993) *Vienna Declaration.* 9 October. Strasbourg: Council of Europe.

Fielding, M. (1997) 'Beyond the school effectiveness movement: lighting the slow fuse of possibility.' *The Curriculum Journal 8*, 1, 7–27.

Guardian, The (1996) 'Citizens at the cutting edge.' 12 November.

Griffith, R. (1996) 'New powers for old: transforming power relationships.' In M. John (ed) *Children in Our Charge: The Child's Right to Resources.* London: Jessica Kingsley Publishers.

Hart, R. (1992) *Children's Participation: From Tokenism to Citizenship.* Innocenti Essays No. 4. Florence: UNICEF International Child Development Centre.

Hicks, D. and Holden, C. (1995) *Visions of the Future: Why We Need to Teach for Tomorrow.* Stoke-on-Trent, Trentham.

Jensen, B. and Schnack, R. (eds) (1994) 'Action competence as an educational challenge.' *Didaktiske Studier: Studies in Educational Theory and Curriculum 12*, 5–18. Royal Danish School: Copenhagen.

Orr, D. (1992) *Ecological Literacy: Education and the Transition to a Post Modern World.* Albany: State of New York University Press.

Osler, A. and Starkey, H. (1996) *Teacher Education and Human Rights.* London: David Fulton.

Rudduck, J., Chaplain, R. and Wallace, G. (eds) (1995) *School Improvement. What Can Pupils Tell Us?* London: David Fulton.

Rudduck, J. (1997) 'Issues of freedom and control.' Paper given at University of Exeter, February.

School Curriculum and Assessment Authority (SCAA) (1995) *Spiritual and Moral Development, Discussion Paper No. 3.* London: SCAA.

Times Educational Supplement (1997a) 'Extremists "manipulate teaching of history".' 4 July.

Times Educational Supplement (1997b) 'Plea for citizenship specialists.' 24 October.

Trafford, B. (1993) *Sharing Power in Schools: Raising Standards.* Ticknall: Education Now.

Vygotsky, L. (1978) *Mind in Society.* Cambridge, MA: MIT Press.

PART TWO

Primary Pupils
Values and Action

CHAPTER TWO

Participation and Learning in Early Childhood

Liz Wood

This chapter is concerned with how participation can be seen as integral to the early childhood curriculum, and can be linked to empowering children as learners. The years from birth to age eight represent the most formative period in children's lives in the rate of their physical growth, learning and development. A long period of childhood in humans is essential preparation for the complexities of adult life so that children gradually learn to take their place independently in society. But children are not just adults-in-waiting. Essentially they need time to be children, and the education they receive in and out of the home should focus on their current state of being, as well as the process of becoming.

From birth children participate in many different social groups, activities and communities including the home, preschool and school settings, clubs, health and recreation groups, with family, friends, educators, and other significant adults in their lives. In order to participate successfully in these communities they need to learn a wide variety of complex roles and behaviours, and to acquire social skills and understanding. It can be argued that children are citizens in their own right, and their relative immaturity and inexperience should not be confused as incompetence. Learning to participate successfully is a fundamental underpinning to the development of a positive sense of self, enabling children to express their opinions, ideas and make informed choices.

WHAT DOES PARTICIPATION MEAN?

The concept of children as citizens, who can participate actively in these various communities is relatively recent, and not unproblematic. The nature and extent of their participation is controlled largely by adults, and is dependent on how children are regarded in society. The concept of childhood itself has changed over the centuries and varies between cultures. One consistent factor is that children are highly dependent on the adults around them for love, care, support and for making decisions on their behalf. Such decisions are inevitably based on a variety of beliefs, assumptions, ideals, traditions and cultural practices. For example, in western societies there is a belief in childhood innocence, and allowing children the freedom to indulge their childish ways without the responsibilities of adulthood. However, romantic, sentimentalised views potentially undermine their status as people whose opinions, perspectives and choices should be taken seriously (Pollard, Theissen and Filer 1997). Such views also underestimate the powerful nature of children's thinking and learning and their abilities to form opinions and ideas about themselves and their experiences.

Osler (1996) argues that there are different levels of participation in community activities, based on a model devised by Hart (1992). This model includes eight levels, beginning with the manipulation of children by adults in issues which may not be understood, for example giving young children placards to carry in rallies or demonstrations. Consultation at the lower levels may be only tokenistic, with little appreciation by children of the underlying issues and causes. At a higher level, children may be assigned, but not informed, and with little real empowerment.

In Hart's model, authentic efforts at encouraging participation involve negotiation, planning, consultation, informed awareness and shared decision making between adults and children. Essentially, children have a voice and know that their opinions and perspectives will be taken seriously. Adult involvement will probably continue to be necessary, but this is characterised as supportive and enabling, for example teaching children specific skills such as collaborative research, interviewing, presenting a case, resolving conflict. Encouraging children to participate in more sophisticated ways also demands that they learn about rights, roles and responsibilities so that empowerment is genuine and not tokenistic.

High levels of participation are not a pipe dream and can be achieved in schools by teachers with vision and commitment, and with the support of parents and other adults. For example, a group of primary schools collaborated to form a pupil parliament to help teach about democracy and genuine participation (*Times Educational Supplement* 1997). Collectively the children mounted successful campaigns to tackle issues inside and outside school, including racist name-calling, bullying, graffiti and vandalism in the local park, pollution and animal welfare issues. Their efforts were supported by the local community including businesses and the council.

Clearly issues relating to children's needs and right to be heard, to participate successfully in communities, and to develop self-efficacy are of concern across all phases of schooling. So how can levels of participation be increased for all children from the early years right through into adulthood? First, the romantic view of childhood needs to be challenged, as concepts of freedom and innocence have been used as an excuse for benign and patronising learning environments. Second, childhood should be valued as a period in its own right as well as part of a complex continuum of learning and development. The knowledge, skills and attitudes children acquire should enable them to achieve their potential in this critical phase as well as in the future. Third, young children should be regarded as powerful thinkers and learners who are active citizens in diverse communities, capable of learning about their rights and responsibilities.

LEARNING TO PARTICIPATE

From birth, children are active, social and curious. Far from being passive recipients of knowledge and culture, they are active participants in making sense, constructing meaning, and in the creation of their self-identities. In the process they are engaged in citizenship. They are learning about themselves as individuals, and in relation to other people, in order to function successfully within various communities.

Everything children learn is influenced by these social, historical and cultural factors. Much of their early learning will be positive and enabling, but they also have to deal with negative and potentially disabling experiences. They learn about and experience bias and prejudice in class, gender and ethnicity through media images, the opinions and perceptions of their family, friends, and other significant adults. Negative learning experiences can result in anti-social behaviour towards others, and the impact of such behaviour can in turn lead to low self-esteem and a poor self-image. So the nature of children's early learning experiences can have a lasting influence on their identity into adulthood.

A wide repertoire of appropriate behaviours and skills associated with social responsibility has to be acquired to enable children to adapt to different social and cultural contexts. At the same time they learn to deal with difficult emotions such as fear, conflict, jealousy, love, hate, and with the frustration borne of powerlessness within an adult-dominated world. Educators who underestimate children's abilities may provide a 'baby-safe' curriculum which stresses positive behaviours and feelings in an 'all's right with the world' ethos. This may ignore negative and often damaging experiences such as family breakdown, death, bullying, racism and child abuse. Lack of maturity should not be equated with the inability to feel such grievances deeply. A baby-safe curriculum patronises children by denying the impact of such experiences and their ability to deal with them.

Young children have opinions and ideas and quickly learn the principles of social justice in the family and wider educational settings. They understand when something is not fair and often expect adults to intervene as advocates on their behalf to address a problem, listen and take them seriously. For example, in a Year Two class, the children were asked how to make their school a better place. Their answers revealed many serious concerns, ranging from developing interpersonal skills, to the school curriculum and wider social responsibilities.

Things the school could do:
- get some showers
- make a bigger environmental area
- don't burn the chips
- don't let any more children in our school
- do more fun stuff
- have more outings
- have separate classes for girls and boys.

Things the children could do:
- don't drop litter
- don't be horrible to the cats
- don't be stupid or other people will think that's right
- don't hurt other people's feelings.

Things our school of the future would have:
- a friendly room where you go to learn to be friendly
- a children's room for when it's wet
- a pond with ducks
- lots of bike racks so you could all cycle to school
- only space for a few cars
- a speed limit of 20 mph on all roads near the school.

Many of these concerns could be addressed collaboratively between the children, parents and teachers, according to Hart's model of participation. But the issue of separate classes for boys and girls raises an interesting dilemma. To what extent are adults able to respond to children's expressed needs and concerns where these challenge institutional practices and values? It was not possible to introduce such a policy in the school, but it was the teachers' responsibility to enable the children to discuss this issue openly in order to get to the root of the problem. Children develop preferences for same-sex friendships and groupwork at an early age and often find it difficult to play and work alongside each other. There can be conflict, competition and hostility between girls and boys, which derives from gender socialisation processes, and the drive to establish self and gender identities. These identities are usually firmly grounded in the children's conceptions of masculinity and femininity, and the differences rather than the commonalities between them.

These influential social, cultural and emotional factors can create difficulties for teachers in the amount of social engineering they undertake in order to encourage greater collaboration and understanding. However, listening to children can help educators to understand their perceptions and experiences, and to use these as a basis for curriculum development which includes participation and empowerment. At one level, institutional practices need to be examined and adapted. At another level, children need to learn social and interpersonal skills, and conflict resolution strategies to address problems. Such skills are essential for active citizenship in school and wider communities.

Children's concerns range widely across different issues which have social, emotional and cognitive content. These include developing a sense of self; building relationships with family, friends and other adults; their need for belonging in different communities and for positive self-affirmation; and their concerns about environmental issues at local, national and global levels. Through such concerns they develop knowledge and interests which often extend far beyond the bounds of formal schooling, but which may not be valued in the legislated and overloaded curriculum. Adults have a significant role to play in helping children to learn about participating as citizens in a democratic society, by harnessing their motivations and interests, and providing positive models of social justice and cohesion. So what principles and strategies might underpin this broader vision of the curriculum in the early years, and beyond?

EMPOWERING YOUNG CHILDREN AS LEARNERS

Nutbrown (1996) argues that early childhood educators (including parents and carers) must bear some responsibility for teaching children about the responsibilities that accompany rights and help them to learn how to shoulder those responsibilities. Thus the role of adults can be argued to go beyond that of protecting and providing to include enabling and empowering children. In order for this to become a reality in children's daily experiences, certain strategies and conditions are necessary. These can be categorised broadly into three areas: the role of the educator, children's learning, and the curriculum offered, each of which will now be examined.

It may seem ironic to place the role of the educator first in any discussion about participation and empowerment. However, this can be seen as fundamental to the nature and quality of children's experiences. Research has shown that teachers' beliefs, values, ideals, principles and knowledge influence teaching and learning, and the design of learning environments, activities and experiences (Bennett, Wood and Rogers 1997). Feinburg and Mindess (1994) consider that teachers have a responsibility to empower children, and this requires them to be intellectually vibrant, informed, responsive to ideas, imaginative, generative and stimulating:

> The teacher's capacity to embrace and understand differences in culture and learning, ability to model certain skills and techniques, and strength in communicating and interacting with children – describing, questioning, elaborating, using analogies, providing support and praise – all are important. In addition, the teacher must extend these values to children so that they too feel in charge of their own learning and acquire some of the rudimentary skills and attitudes central to becoming an alert and responsive person intellectually. (1994, p.147)

So educators need to have a commitment to the concepts of participation and empowerment, the pedagogical knowledge to teach children the requisite skills and strategies, and the ability to create learning opportunities in which these can be used. They need to recognise their responsibilities to be proactive in encouraging children to understand issues within their own communities, and in the wider world.

In the second area of children's learning, it is widely acknowledged that children should be encouraged to become independent and autonomous learners, able to think creatively, make decisions and plan their own activities. Independence is often fostered in the context of play where children are allowed varying degrees of choice of activities, materials, and play partners or groups. In the following example, a group of Year Two children were discussing their plans for designing a board game for younger children to 'sell' in the class toy shop. Their idea was for a jungle theme with frogs jumping on lily pads until they reached 'home'.

Jenny: What we could do is a little game for young children and put little sums on lily pads and they've got to add up the sums and they've got to jump on the next lily pad.

Lee: I like Jenny's idea.

Paul: It could be just like Jenny's but…you could go along with a dice and a counter and you throw the dice and if you land on a square that's got writing on then you've got to do what it says.

Jenny: That sounds good, like forfeits.

Betty: I think Paul's is quite good 'cos it's fun.

Jenny: What happens if it's really shy children, they might begin to cry with forfeits.

Paul: We could have easy sums like 1+1.

Lee: Easy peasy.

Jenny: That's easy for you but not for little children.

Betty: They put two fingers up and count with them.

Lee: Why don't we have both ideas on it?

Betty and Paul: Yes.

Jenny: Why don't we have sums and forfeits? And what did you say about the jungle, Lee?

(Wood and Attfield 1996, p.45)

These children were skilled learners who were able to listen, negotiate and pool ideas towards a common goal. They also revealed considerable understanding of younger children's social, emotional and cognitive skills. Later, the teacher helped them to reflect on their ideas and to design rules for the game which would be manageable for the players. This example demonstrates how high quality play experiences can support children's participation in constructing some elements of the curriculum, and can foster the development of decision making based on social and moral understanding.

It is often the youngest learners in the school system who are given substantial responsibility to plan their learning and participate in negotiating their own pathways in a structured learning environment. However, this approach has been shown to be problematic (Bennett, Wood and Rogers 1997). In a study of the relationship between teachers' theories of play and classroom practice, many assumptions were made about the capabilities of reception age children. Often they could not enjoy the degree of independence given in the curriculum because they lacked the requisite social, cognitive and manipulative skills. Some activities broke down because there was no adult available to support their learning, or help to resolve conflict.

Significant outcomes of this study were the teachers' recommendations that in the early years, children need to be taught the requisite skills and strategies for becoming independent, making choices and decisions, and becoming skilful players. They also perceived a need for balancing teachers' and children's intentions. For example, one teacher was dissatisfied with the repetitive and stereotypical nature of the children's role play in which the boys often engaged in themes based on superheroes, and the girls tended to dress up and play in the home corner. By using a variety of stories, the teacher helped the children to think more deeply about the roles and characters they wanted to develop, what resources they needed to support their imaginative play, how to extend their own story-making skills, and challenging gender stereotypical roles. In so doing the teacher modelled skills essential for citizenship such as the ability to question, to challenge stereotypes, and to think independently.

The third area which influences participation and empowerment is the curriculum offered. It is all too easy to pay lip-service to the concept of a child-centred curriculum in the early years. Indeed, classrooms which are resourced with different play activities and resources can appear to give children choice and autonomy. But to what extent are the choices really determined and restricted by the educators? In one nursery, all the activities were laid out at each session, and the children were not allowed to select anything else or combine materials from different areas. One display was of teacher-drawn outlines which the children had coloured with paint or filled with tissue paper. Another showed identical cut-out sheep, lambs, daffodils and ducks in a spring frieze. The degree of structure was constraining and made the children dependent on the adults for being told what to do next, what materials to use, and how. The children were well cared for, but had few opportunities for genuine participation and decision making.

In another nursery, high expectations were set for the children's achievements and independence. The children were involved in planning their own activities and selecting appropriate materials and tools. This extended to physical education when they would plan which apparatus to put out, whether they wanted the climbing apparatus high or low, and what new skills they wanted to develop. Each session ended with opportunities for the children to demonstrate new skills and achievements, how they had worked collaboratively, and what they might attempt next. Similarly the children's art work revealed their opportunities to make choices from a wide selection of media and tools. Their learning was supported by the teachers and nursery nurses who taught them the necessary skills and techniques to use these creatively and successfully. The children had to learn to negotiate, explain their ideas, share resources, and to work both independently and interdependently, drawing on adult and peer support where necessary. Their work was valued, their ideas and opinions were taken seriously, and they participated in constructing their own curriculum. Moreover, their level of confidence was such that they were less dependent on adults for approval and affection, because they used them as a source of stimulation, knowledge, support and respect.

Participation by young children needs to extend beyond the taught curriculum. The school environment can also be a fruitful area for encouraging the skills of collaboration and negotiation which are essential to citizenship. In one school, children in the reception class found it difficult to cope with playtimes with large numbers of older children in a small playground. All the children in the school were consulted about the problems and negotiated solutions. They became involved in designing improvements to the area, including large tubs for growing flowers and vegetables and a shaded seating area. The reception classes decided to have flexible playtimes. All the children were taught playground games and had the use of small equipment. Meal-time assistants and parents were involved in supporting the initiative and the positive effects on children's behaviour were immediate, because they had a shared interest in maintaining the environment and the opportunities they had created.

So how can educators foster children's active participation both within the immediate learning environment and the wider world? Fundamental to education for citizenship is an acknowledgement that this must include a global perspective. Young children are aware of the world beyond their locality through television, film, books and travel, and they are capable of going beyond first-hand experience. The following suggestions provide some guidance for translating some of these ideals into reality.

ENABLING CHILDREN TO ACQUIRE THE SKILLS FOR MAKING CHOICES AND DECISIONS

A fundamental underpinning to participation and empowerment is that children should have a voice, be listened to and taken seriously. Listening to pupils' voices should not be seen as a sentimental or romantic option but as a serious contribution to educational thinking and development (Pollard, Theissen and Filer 1997). Children need to know that their needs and abilities will be respected along with their ethnic and gender identities. Educators should encourage positive self-esteem and a sense of self-efficacy so that children feel they are seen by others as competent and worthwhile.

For example, a variety of learning resource packs published by Save the Children[1] emphasise the importance of human rights education in all early years settings. Young children may form negative beliefs and attitudes which can be evident in their play. Teasing, name-calling, bullying and excluding children from play on the basis of their gender, disability or race are all common behaviours. Such behaviours can be challenged and changed through equal opportunities policies and practices, including an anti-bias approach. It is important that such principles are stated in a policy document, but also that the taught and received curriculum does enact those principles.

A student on a teacher education course found that her class of six and seven-year-old children had already developed gender stereotypical views of their roles and future careers. In one activity they wrote about making a wish. The girls mostly wished to be fairies or princesses, whilst the boys wished for construction kits, and to be Power Rangers. Their choices of favourite stories similarly revealed gendered preferences with the boys mostly choosing adventurous roles based on powerful characters, and the girls preferring domestic, passive roles. One girl wanted to be a Power Ranger but was challenged aggressively by the boys who saw this as an exclusively male domain. The student realised that literature was exerting a strong influence over children's beliefs and she decided to use this as a basis for raising awareness of gender stereotypes and analysing traditional roles. She encouraged the children to look critically at the characters and events in stories in order to challenge existing beliefs and values. This proved to be a long process in which the children needed to learn a wide variety of skills in discussion, analysis, questioning, articulating their ideas, considering alternative perspectives, and

---

1 Save the Children Learning Resource Packs: Education Unit, Save the Children, 17 Grove Lane, London SE5 8RD.

looking at the roles of men and women in society. Thus principles of equal opportunities were embedded in the curriculum.

ENABLING CHILDREN TO CONSIDER THE IMPACT OF THOSE DECISIONS ON OTHERS

Children should be able to listen to others, including adults and peers. They are more likely to do this in a climate of trust and acceptance in which their own ideas are valued and acted upon through negotiation and co-operation. Within such a framework, the art of compromise is essential because that is part of living in democratic communities. So children have to learn to take turns, share resources, plan ahead, ask others for support, exchange ideas and use problem-solving strategies. The problems young children encounter can be of a cognitive, social, emotional or physical nature, which demand a wide repertoire of skills and strategies.

As Siraj-Blatchford (1995) argues, children need to be educated to deal confidently and fairly with one another and with others in an unjust society. Listening, understanding, participating and accepting difference are fundamental attributes. Above all, they need the confidence to try things out, to take risks, and to be prepared to adapt their decisions accordingly without fearing the consequences of failure or rejection.

PROVIDING CHILDREN WITH A LEARNING ENVIRONMENT WHICH ENABLES CHILDREN TO PRACTISE MAKING CHOICES AND DECISIONS

The skills for participation and empowerment need to be acquired and practised through the curriculum offered and the experiences designed. In a negotiated curriculum, the process of consultation helps to ensure reciprocity between teachers and learners. This does not mean that teachers abdicate their responsibility for ensuring that children have full access to the legislated curriculum, whether it is the National Curriculum (Department for Education 1995) or the Desirable Outcomes for four-year-old children (School Curriculum and Assessment Authority 1996). Educators in all settings structure and resource the learning environment in ways which both reflect and determine children's interests and choices. The critical issue is the nature and extent of the choices children are able to make, and the ability of teachers to respond to those choices.

For example, children in a reception class wanted to set up the role play area as a cafe. At first, this reflected the children's previous, but limited experiences. The teacher suggested changing the cafe every two weeks to a different nationality. As a result, the children learnt about Italian, Chinese and Indian food, lifestyles, cultures and customs. They made decisions about designing the colour schemes and menus, and were involved in cooking and tasting real food. Parents were involved as helpers and as customers and supported the children in their research at home (visiting supermarkets and libraries and finding pictures and information). The theme was so successful that it was continued during Year One with all the children and teachers collecting postcards, maps and photographs from places they visited during the holidays, either locally or further afield. In this example, the children, their parents and families and the teachers all became learning resources. Furthermore the teacher had ensured that the curriculum had a global perspective and reflected ethnic diversity.

EMPOWERING CHILDREN TO CARRY OUT THEIR CHOICES AND DECISIONS

Although children are active participants in their learning and development, they are also learning how to learn. In a disempowering educational environment, they may simply learn how to respond in order to please adults. Encouraging children to participate in decision making and to articulate their ideas and views demands that they are taught metacognitive skills and strategies. This involves teaching children conscious awareness and control of their thinking and learning, how to solve problems, how to monitor and reflect on action and events, and articulate what helps them to think and reason.

An important part of this process is using language about learning so that children come to understand what learning is all about, are able to describe their learning, and can be enabled to articulate the meaning of their activities in these terms (Wood and Attfield 1996). For example, six-year-old Hari described how he had tried to make a multi-storey car park for a model of the local shopping centre, with Kim offering some advice for improvement:

Hari: I got three big boxes, all the same size and I stuck them together. First I used too much glue so they was wet and they wouldn't stay stiff for the cars to go on. Then I made a ramp for the cars to go up and I made it with that sticky tape and I made it with stripey (corrugated) card because it's strong. The floor's still bendy, but I don't know if it will go straight when it's dry.

Kim: Why don't you try sticking some new card on the floor so it's not bendy? But don't use all that glue. Use sellotape, no, staples so it will fix better.

Fisher (1996) details how using a plan-do-review approach can encourage metacognitive skills. In this approach, the children plan which activities they want to do, either individually or collaboratively. Their plans may develop over a period of time, or just focus on one activity. They are responsible for selecting materials and resources and for carrying out their plan. The teacher's role is to support the children by modelling language, teaching problem-solving skills, encouraging questioning, thinking and reasoning, or standing back and letting the children take control. Review time is important because it allows children to reflect on what they have done or made, what they have learnt, how they might do it better, and whether they can teach other children some of the skills they have learnt. They can also learn to value each other's efforts, give praise and make suggestions for further activities.

The plan-do-review cycle can help children to develop mastery orientation to learning which includes a positive sense of self, and a 'can do' attitude. Children who develop mastery orientation are likely to be self-motivated, take on problems and challenges, use flexible approaches, have a positive view of their competence, and a positive attitude towards learning (Fisher 1995). Thus a plan-do-review approach encourages participation and empowerment through learning, and can contribute to children's overall achievements. Pupil participation in the curriculum may help to push up educational standards and achievements if educators can build on children's interests and motivations (Pollard, Theissen and Filer 1997).

TEACHING PROBLEM-SOLVING CAPABILITIES

Feinburg and Mindess (1994) argue that the ability to solve problems is a skill which children need to learn and which can be applied to cognitive problems as well as social-emotional ones. Their proposed problem-solving paradigm involves five basic steps:

1. Identifying the problem
2. Brainstorming possible solutions
3. Selecting one solution
4. Trying out that solution
5. Evaluating the results. (1994, p.261)

Such an approach encourages children to articulate their ideas, express emotional responses to difficult situations, take responsibility for their actions, and develop a range of prosocial, interpersonal skills. Again the role of educators is critical in teaching conflict resolution strategies and acting as an advocate within the classroom and in the wider educational community.

ENABLING CHILDREN TO REPRESENT THEIR ACHIEVEMENTS AS THINKERS AND LEARNERS

In the early years, spoken language is the most important tool for communication. But for all children, especially those with special educational needs and with English as a second language, different forms of representation should be encouraged. These forms include dance, drama, mime, paintings, drawings, layouts, plans, all forms of mark-making including writing, and symbolic representation in play. If educators respect children's varied means of interpreting and communicating experience, they can better understand their capacities for making sense and meaning in different cultural contexts. This understanding can then inform educators as to how they can make the curriculum responsive and culturally relevant to children.

A teacher had a Year Two class with a large proportion of newly arrived children from Pakistan. She noticed that they did not play in the home corner and attributed this to the low status of play in their culture. However, following input from an equal opportunities adviser, she included a range of materials and utensils which would typically be found in their homes. The children immediately related to the new resources and were able to represent their experience in imaginative contexts. The curriculum offered became inclusive rather than exclusive, and all the children in the class were able to communicate through shared meanings whilst their language skills developed.

RESOURCING FOR EMPOWERMENT AND PARTICIPATION

Children need access to a wide variety of learning resources such as books, information technology, different tools, media and equipment to support their creativity and thirst for knowledge. These resources should reflect cultural diversity but should also be checked for negative stereotyping so that children are not exposed to racist or sexist language and images. Children's understanding of themselves as global citizens can gradually be extended through the early years by learning about the lives of children around the world, festivals, reading traditional and modern stories and through CD Rom and other forms of information technology.

For example, a small rural school in a predominantly white community in the south-west of England set up e-mail links with a school in Canada where the population is ethnically more diverse. At first this was quite a surprise for the children in England. They knew that the dominant language in Canada is English, and assumed that everyone would be white. One boy was initially shocked to find that his new e-mail pal was Canadian but of Asian origin. The children found the differences quite challenging to their assumptions. However, this became a positive learning experience as they learnt more about each others' lifestyles and cultures, and about the concept of global citizenship.

RESPECTING AND APPRECIATING CHILDREN

Young children should not become emotionally dependent on teachers, or reliant on them for approval. However, they should be able to rely on their fairness, appreciation, respect and advocacy. Children are motivated by their own efforts and successes, by learning to have the confidence to take risks, make mistakes and deal positively with challenges. At the same time, teachers need the confidence to trust children by giving status to their ideas and self-initiated activities, including play. Respect and appreciation can be shown through displays which focus on the children's efforts and creativity. Children can be involved in monitoring their own learning through self-assessment, selecting examples of work for their portfolios and writing or talking about what they have learnt or achieved in different areas of the curriculum, including their social and emotional learning.

CONCLUSION

Children are powerful and creative learners who look to adults for collaboration, support and positive interaction to help them achieve their potential. They are motivated, positively or negatively, by the response of other significant people in their lives who play an important part in shaping their self-esteem, self-worth and self-efficacy. How they perceive themselves as learners is largely dependent on the messages they receive both at home and elsewhere.

Creating learning environments which support participation and empowerment is not an easy process, but, as Lansdown argues, it is worthwhile:

> Democratic decision-making processes are more time-consuming and can be frustrating and difficult to maintain at times but the long-term benefits will be the creation of an environment in which children have the optimum opportunity to gain in both the confidence and capacity to participate as socially responsible individuals. (Lansdown 1996, p.8)

If children are enabled to climb the ladder of participation towards greater empowerment, this can only result in positive outcomes. They need to understand the needs, rights and obligations of citizens in a democratic society, and the underpinning concepts of social justice and social cohesion which sustain democratic processes. This chapter has demonstrated that these processes should begin in early childhood, with the potential for long-lasting benefits into adulthood.

Conceptualising teaching and learning as a process of empowerment and participation results in a very different vision of what might happen in schools and classrooms. Empowerment stems from mastery of learning and from positive self-affirmation. Participation is dependent on acquiring the knowledge and skills to be involved in making choices and decisions both independently and interdependently. Both are essential to supporting children as citizens in their immediate and future lives. Inevitably such a vision is problematic, because empowering children as thinkers and learners is where true autonomy lies, which may not sit comfortably within existing social, educational and cultural norms. As part of this process, teachers need to ensure access to a broad and balanced curriculum which includes education for human rights in a culturally diverse society, and ensures equality of access and opportunity. Participation potentially has positive benefits to children and to society and may help to raise standards and achievements. Ultimately this vision is worth striving towards with children and for children.

REFERENCES

Bennett, N., Wood, L. and Rogers, S. (1997) *Teaching Through Play: Teachers' Thinking and Classroom Practice.* Buckingham: Open University Press.

Department for Education (1995) *Key Stages 1 and 2 of the National Curriculum.* London: HMSO.

Feinburg, S. and Mindess, M. (1994) *Eliciting Children's Full Potential.* California: Brooks/Cole.

Fisher, J. (1996) *Starting from the Child? Teaching and Learning from 4 to 8.* Buckingham: Open University Press.

Fisher, R. (1995) *Teaching Children To Learn.* Cheltenham: Stanley Thornes.

Hart, R. (1992) *Children's Participation: From Tokenism to Citizenship.* Innocenti Essays No 4. Florence: UNICEF/International Child Development Centre.

Lansdown, G. (1996) 'The United Nations Convention and the rights of the child – progress in the United Kingdom.' In C. Nutbrown (ed) *Respectful Educators – Capable Learners: Children's Rights and Early Education.* London: Paul Chapman.

Nutbrown, C. (ed) (1996) *Respectful Educators – Capable Learners: Children's Rights and Early Education.* London: Paul Chapman.

Osler, A. (1996) *Learning to Participate.* Birmingham: Development Education Centre.

Pollard, A., Theissen, D. and Filer, A. (1997) 'New challenges in taking children's curricular perspectives seriously.' In A. Pollard, D. Thiessen and A. Filer (eds) *Children and Their Curriculum.* London: Falmer Press.

School Curriculum and Assessment Authority (1996) *Desirable Outcomes for Children's Learning on Entering Compulsory Education.* London: DfEE/SCAA.

Siraj-Blatchford, I. (1995) 'Racial equality education: identity, curriculum and pedagogy.' In I. and J. Siraj-Blatchford (eds) *Educating the Whole Child: Cross-Curricular Skills, Themes and Dimensions.* Buckingham: Open University Press.

Times Educational Supplement (1997) 'The pupils have spoken.' 2 May.

Wood, E.A. and Attfield, J. (1996) *Play, Learning and the Early Childhood Curriculum.* London: Paul Chapman.

CHAPTER THREE

Keen at 11, Cynical at 18?
Encouraging Pupil Participation in School and Community

Cathie Holden

> We have to learn about these things, because then you might be able to stop the bad things happening. (Girl, aged 7)
>
> Some people don't want to know – they say they won't be around when it happens. (Boy, aged 14)

Young children are naturally interested in the world around them. They feel they can change things for the better, they have a strong sense of social justice and they want to be active in working for change. By the time they leave school these same pupils may be sceptical, possibly even cynical, admitting that they are unlikely to participate in democratic processes and feeling inadequately prepared for their role as active citizens. This chapter shows how teachers can address these issues by developing contexts for teaching and learning which provide opportunities for children to discuss their own values and become confident, active participants in school and community.

The first section looks at previously unpublished findings from a research study into children's attitudes to the future which is reported in Hicks and Holden (1995). This focuses on action taken by children, action their schools take and what pupils feel ought to be done. Differences of opinion and action according to age and gender are discussed and conclusions drawn. The second section debates what can be done, suggesting approaches and providing case study examples. The importance of the chapter lies in the voices of children and teachers. Rather than educationalists or policy makers saying what young people ought to do, it is children who articulate their priorities and talk about what they do and it is practising teachers who demonstrate how they try to educate for citizenship.

BACKGROUND

The 1990s has seen a growing concern that today's young people are opting out of society, that they are not being educated as responsible citizens. In the recent general election, politicians of all persuasions worried that young people were not intending to vote and appeared disillusioned with mainstream politics. A few well-publicised cases of criminal activity undertaken by young people have caused concern that we are not producing morally responsible youngsters either. There have been a variety of responses to these issues from the political 'Rock the Vote campaign' to the School Curriculum and Assessment Authority (SCAA)'s proposed Moral Code for Schools. The CSV (Community Service Volunteers) anticipates that the Labour government's commitment to 'citizens' service' projects will herald citizenship education becoming a statutory part of the national curriculum with pupils enabled to do at least 1000 hours of community service during their school years (*Guardian* 1997).

There is, then, an agreement on the part of interested adults that young people need to be more involved and more active in democratic processes and in their community. Our research contributes to this debate by providing information on what young people already do, what they are mainly concerned about and what they feel ought to be done in schools.

ACTION FOR THE FUTURE

The data was obtained by questionnaire and in-depth interviews with nearly 400 pupils from the south-west of England. Eight schools were chosen to ensure a balance of urban and rural catchment areas and different socio-economic classes. Ethnic minority children were also represented. Pupils were drawn from four age groups: 6–7, 10–11, 13–14, and 17–18, with an equal number of boys and girls. The main findings, reported in Hicks and Holden (1995), conclude that:

> British young people in the 1990s appear optimistic about their own future. They are committed to the responsibilities of adult life and wish for a good job, a good education and secure relationships with partners and children. They are less optimistic about the future for other people, both in their local community and globally. They are concerned about environmental destruction, growing crime and violence and social inequality... They feel responsible as citizens of the future for what may happen, but lack a clear vision of what their own part in this might be... Their visions thus remain fragmented and essentially conservative in a time of radical change. (p.112)

What is discussed here is previously unpublished data on action children take now and would wish to take in the future to work for change, based on their values and beliefs. As well as ascertaining pupils' hopes and fears for the future, we wished to find out whether or not children felt they could effect change. If so, what sort of action did they take which they considered to be working towards this change? And furthermore, how were they encouraged in this action by schools? Two questions, one closed and one open-ended, elicited initial responses, with subsequent interviews illuminating pupils' thinking.

Pupils were first of all asked what they could do to help make the world a better place; their responses are recorded in Figure 3.1.

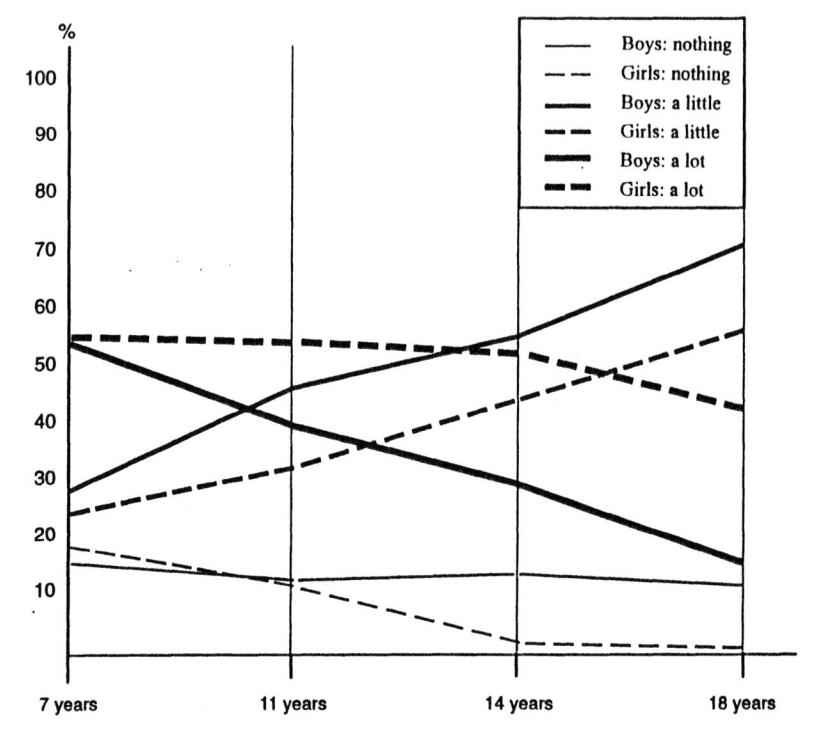

Figure 3.1 What can you do to make the world a better place? (percentage responding to each question) N=398

This figure shows that the younger children are, the more optimistic they are. The increased pessimism of the older pupils could be attributed to the onset of adolescence and a natural tendency to become more sceptical as one matures, but a closer examination of the table shows that it is mainly boys who become less optimistic. Girls appeared to be consistent in their belief that they could influence things for the better. Comments in interview indicated that boys were more likely to be cynical or unresponsive but were more likely to consider political action. Girls more often acted individually or worked for charity.

Before looking in depth at the interviews a further table indicates the kind of action pupils said they took. Pupils were asked to give examples of what they did to make the world better, following on from the above question. One third did not respond: they said they could not think of anything they did at the moment (although they had ideas for what they might do). Two thirds, however, gave examples of action they had been involved in. The majority of responses fell into six categories, as indicated in Figure 3.2.

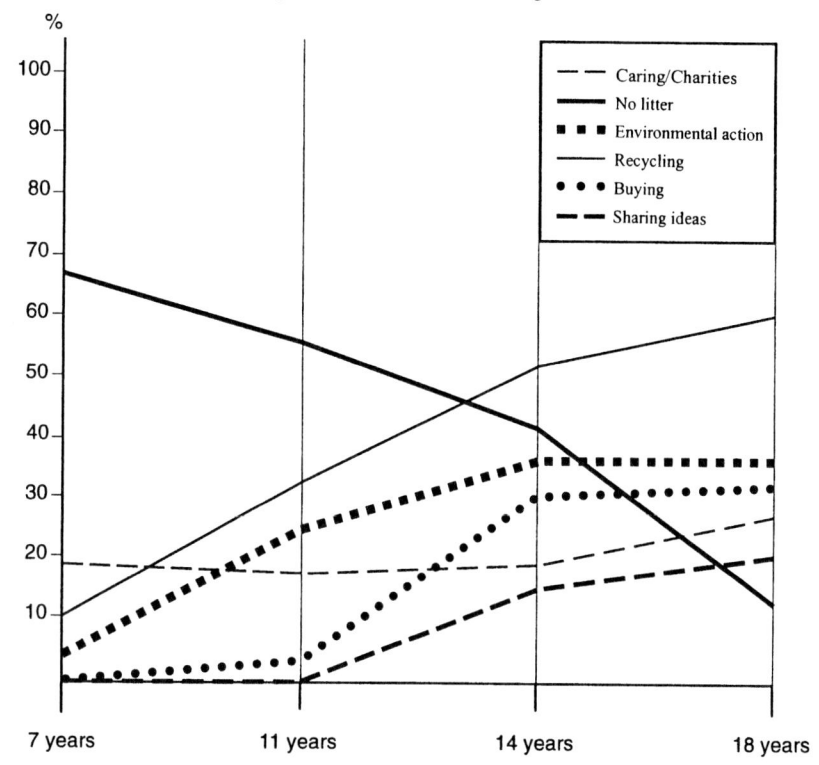

Figure 3.2 Action for change (percentage of pupils mentioning these actions) N=267

The question was open-ended and children could name any actions they wanted. (As they could name up to three actions, their responses do not total 100 per cent.) Because these were open-ended questions, rather than checklists of our devising, the findings indicate those areas which are of interest to young people and to which they are currently sufficiently committed to take action.

The first of the categories above is to do with *helping others* and *charity* work. Interestingly the data indicates that boys and girls were equally involved in this area, although it was mainly older girls who talked about charity work in interview. The next group all had an environmental basis: *recycling, not dropping litter* and *taking environmental action*. This latter category included those who cycled rather than getting their parents to use the car, had been involved in tree-planting schemes and consciously conserved energy by turning off lights.

Here boys and girls were involved equally, with the exception of environmental action where more boys than girls mentioned this. Younger pupils were much more likely to see not dropping litter as a positive contribution they made: older pupils presumably did not consider this worthy of reporting (or maybe they dropped litter...). Older pupils were more likely to be involved in recycling. The third category, *buying*, refers to children who said they bought certain products because they knew they would not harm the environment or were not tested on animals. Understandably it was only secondary school pupils who mentioned this, with many more girls taking action in this way. This has implications for children's economic education and their understanding of advertising. Certainly the ethical teenager as consumer is a phenomenon not unnoticed by the marketing world. The final category is that of *sharing ideas*. Again this was just reported by secondary pupils and was action taken mainly by girls who reported that they discussed important issues with their friends or parents and tried to influence them if they thought they were prejudiced in any way or could be persuaded to change their opinion. They felt that talking was a productive way of bringing about change and were adamant that such discussions could be classified as action.

The in-depth interviews gave more insight into what is important to today's young people. They show what children do now, what they would like to happen and the part played by schools. Responses have been separated into primary and secondary.

CHILDREN TALKING ABOUT ACTION THEY TAKE

Even the youngest children in the research, aged seven, were aware of 'good actions' and talked freely about how they contributed. For some this was to do with attitudes, as with the seven-year-old boy who stated categorically:

> I don't be silly. I help people. I help my brother to swim.

Other seven-year-olds said that they did not drop litter and were 'good' at school or at home. Others were aware of charity work at their school and mentioned 'sending coats to Bosnia' and raising money for a local hospice. Eleven-year-olds also cited work with charities as something they did, mentioning Oxfam, Blue Peter appeals and animal welfare.

When it came to environmental issues, children acted both as individuals and as a part of action taken by the school.

> I'm in both of them (WWF, Friends of the Earth)...it's for being friendly to animals and my brother's joined the RSPCA as well.

Others mentioned things they did at home such as recycling and using 'you know those light bulbs, those energy saving light bulbs'.

Secondary school pupils again mentioned recycling and a few were members of environmental organisations. Greenpeace and World Wide Fund for Nature were cited but some pupils did not feel these organisations appealed to young people. They were seen by one 14-year-old as 'having boring meetings' rather than 'doing fun things'. In some cases schools assisted their pupils to take action for the environment:

> You don't have to talk about famine and disease – you can do tree planting. We have planting projects in the school grounds – every class plants a shrub.

Secondary school pupils also gave examples of raising money for charity and two commented that their school had been very active in this area:

> Our school does a lot with SCF [Save the Children Fund]. We did a sponsor and there's leaflets in the library.

> The school does quite a lot for charity. Money from non-uniform days goes to charity.

In addition girls mentioned that they took individual action on behalf of charities. One said she 'did the 24 hour famine every year' and another was involved in writing to political prisoners through Amnesty.

As noted in Figure 3.2, secondary school pupils (especially girls) took action as individuals by buying ethically or by 'sharing ideas' to influence people's actions for the better.

Whilst the data paints a picture of children who are active and supported by their schools in particular areas (e.g. charity work) many pupils felt that much more could be done. The next section looks at what pupils felt ought to be done and why many felt frustrated and increasingly pessimistic.

CHILDREN TALKING ABOUT POTENTIAL FOR FURTHER ACTION

Younger children tended to see what might be done as something teachers needed to take on board, rather than action they could undertake as individuals. Some older pupils felt schools did as much as they could within current constraints, while others felt their schools did little and that, therefore, they had to act as individuals.

Seven-year-olds saw there being relatively easy solutions like 'planting more trees' and 'learning about these things...because you might be able to stop the bad things happening'. Many 11-year-olds thought children would be enabled to do more when the curriculum was adjusted to include more 'discussing classes' and more information about environmental issues.

> The problem is we don't learn about these things...you could recycle when you grow up. If you don't know, your children don't know.

> We don't learn anything about it [action] 'cause usually you're doing subjects like maths and stuff.

As noted above, many children of this age took action as individuals. Whilst a great many were supported in their concerns by their schools, nevertheless some felt that schools could do more.

When secondary school pupils were questioned on the role schools could or should play in helping them as young people to become active citizens, many praised their schools' efforts with charities but otherwise did not feel that they were helped to understand issues of social injustice, global or environmental problems in sufficient depth and certainly did not feel schools helped them to be actively involved in any local or global action.

Comments on the secondary curriculum by 14-year-olds indicated what they felt to be some of the limitations on what they learnt:

> In science we do mini topics on pollution and nuclear waste but most of it they don't actually teach you, you have to find out the information for yourself. If you had a lesson on it you'd learn more, instead of having to find out at home and you just write a few lines.

> We learnt the facts about what's happening but we don't learn what you can do.

> Mrs Clarke said in science there's a lot more things we could do but we're not allowed – because of the National Curriculum.

> We don't get the chance to go deeply into things.

Older pupils felt that they had covered many global and environmental issues in schools (either in science or the humanities) but pointed out that they had had no teaching of politics or controversial issues such as homosexuality. However they realised that teachers might feel constrained by government legislation and the National Curriculum:

> The problem with schools these days is they're not allowed to talk about politics. Teachers have to be neutral...

WHAT CAN SCHOOLS DO?

Many teachers will acknowledge the concerns of the children voiced above and many will be keen to prepare children for action in the future and to involve them in the here and now in bringing about change. But in the face of other curriculum demands many will say that there is no time for such issues.

This chapter argues that it is possible to incorporate such issues and perspectives, both by introducing innovative approaches within the curriculum and by involving children in school and community projects. Such approaches can be introduced in both primary and secondary schools in order to harness the enthusiasm of younger children and avoid the increasing scepticism and apathy found in older pupils.

A futures perspective

One approach which can be used by teachers to encourage children to voice their concerns and think about possible action is a futures perspective. Encouraging children to think about their own future, the future of their community and the global future will challenge them to think about the values they hold and the part they can play as adults. In thinking about their personal future, children, rather than teachers, can set the agenda for the discussion, raising issues of concern to them within the broader curriculum for personal and social education. Work on the future of the local community can involve children in discussion of what they would like to see and why. This will require them to articulate their hopes and their values and can be used by the teacher as an opportunity to provide information about the role of local democracy. Similarly, looking at possibilities for the global future can encourage debate about what is currently being done, about various groups working for change, and about the part they can play now and in the future. (Hicks (1994) provides many suggestions for practical activities to promote a futures perspective in education.)

Taking children's concerns for the future as a starting point raises moral as well as social issues. Tappin and Brown (1996) argue that for effective moral education to succeed, it must be focused on 'real problems and issues drawn from the lived experiences of the students' (p.106) and must allow a genuine exchange of ideas, not granting 'exclusive access to power, knowledge and authority to the teacher' (p.106). Introducing a futures perspective meets these criteria as if children are encouraged to discuss their concerns they set the agenda: it is their role as active citizens (now and in the future) which is under discussion.

Work on the future with young children (aged 8–10): Case Study One

As part of a humanities project on the local community, the teacher extended her work to look at the future of the local area. She asked children to think about their favourite place and to imagine what it might be like in the future. Whilst some of the resulting drawings (and writings) were positive, many were negative and showed a fear of increasing litter, pollution, deforestation, traffic and car fumes.

The children were then asked to plan the kind of world in which they would like to live in 2030. Some planned villages, some towns, and one adventurous group decided to re-plan the world. Each group had to think about the concerns the class had voiced earlier about future developments. In addition they were asked to consider the housing, energy and transport needs of the community. Finally, they had to decide how people would look after their community, the rights of the citizens and the rules which might be needed to safeguard those rights.

The children's enthusiasm reflected their interest in something they felt was of direct relevance to them. There was much discussion of what would be desirable in a new community and how one could ensure that people would look after it. While some of the suggestions may seen somewhat authoritarian, they do indicate the ability of young children to think through issues of justice, rights and morality. One group designing a town for the future drew up these rules:

- help plant trees
- keep in the speed limit
- pick up all your litter and put it in the bin
- do not smoke
- don't shop lift
- use bike tracks when you can
- you must not have people without seat belts in your car
- do not pull down old houses
- do not pollute the river.

If you do not go with the rules you will be fined 500 Euros.

Another group tried to tackle world issues. After much debate they decided that the world would be much improved if governments could get together and agree:

- no sky scrapers above eight storeys high
- talk through arguments instead of having wars
- stop all poaching and only hunt in a kind way if you really have to
- stop the fur trade and buying fur
- give some cars from the USA to poor countries, like Africa.

The role of the teacher in clarifying and extending children's thinking within such a project is important. The teacher can encourage children to look at ways of bringing about such improvements in the local community now (inviting in councillors and contacting local action groups, encouraging children to be involved in local action) and can alert children (especially older pupils) to the role they will be able to play as adults in determining the future of their local community. In this particular case, the teacher and children contacted various groups working for change, including the local Greenpeace action group, Global Action Plan and local councillors.

At another level the teacher can take the children's thinking forward, helping them to realise that solving local or global problems is a complex process. The use of a futures wheel where the child takes one proposition for a better future and looks at the possible repercussions is one such tool.

Futures Wheel

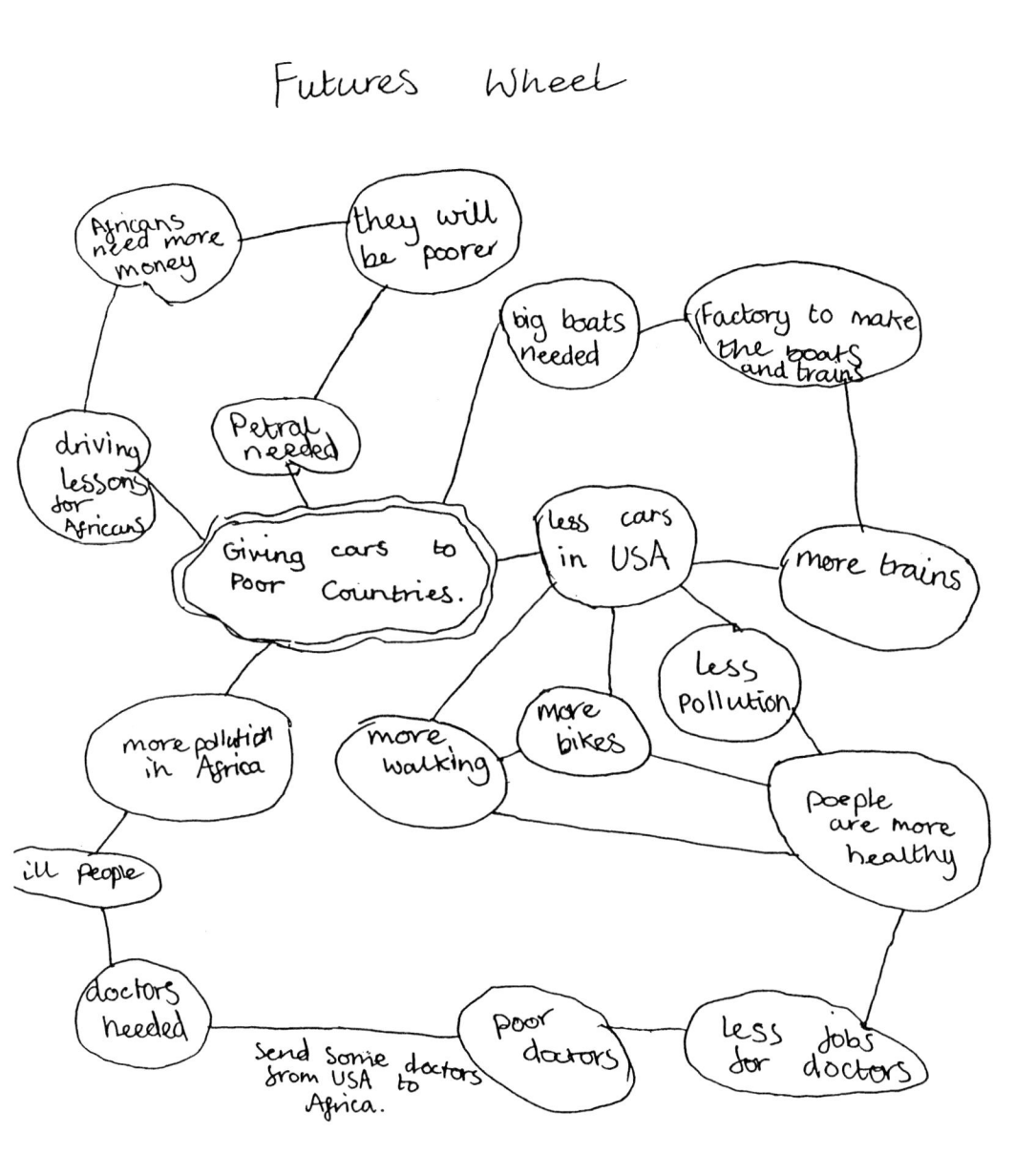

- Africans need more money
- they will be poorer
- big boats needed
- Factory to make the boats and trains
- driving lessons for Africans
- Petrol needed
- Giving cars to Poor Countries.
- less cars in USA
- more trains
- more pollution in Africa
- more walking
- more bikes
- less Pollution
- ill People
- poeple are more healthy
- doctors needed
- Send some doctors from USA to Africa.
- poor doctors
- less jobs for doctors

Figure 3.1 Jodie's futures wheel

Figure 3.1 shows eight-year-old Jodie's futures wheel. She had been working on plans for 'a better world' and took the statement 'give some cars from the USA to poor countries like Africa' as her focus. Doing a futures wheel challenged her assumptions and brought her to realise that any action is complex and has repercussions. At the end of the exercise she said:

> Well, giving cars to Africa could be a good idea because in one way you'd have less doctors and they could go to Africa. So in one way it's good. But then there's a bad thing – it would still be the same pollution. In the end I think it's good in some ways and bad in others. It's better to walk by foot. Doing a futures wheel shows you the rights and wrongs. It shows you if things will work or not.

School councils

It is often maintained that schools are mini-societies that reflect the world at large and that part of children's education is to learn to live in the school community, a process which will prepare them for adult life. On this premise many schools have established school councils, where one or two children represent each class and are part of a large council of pupils, teachers and others involved in the running of the school. The rationale is that such involvement will educate children in the processes of democracy and model for them the role of the active citizen.

Whilst some of these councils undoubtedly do work (see Chapter Five in this volume), many have failed to involve pupils beyond the level of what Hart (1992) would refer to as tokenism. In such cases pupils are invited to participate and represent the views of their peers, but often only certain issues are acted upon such as toilets, school dinners and uniform. These are areas that school management teams feel are safe for pupils to debate, whilst wider issues such as teacher–pupil relationships, curriculum content and delivery or issues of sexual or racial harassment are rarely discussed. Rudduck maintains that councils work best if they are part of school-wide democratic practice. She points to the danger of the council becoming 'a way of formalising and channelling students' criticisms – an exercise in damage limitation rather than an opportunity for constructive consultation' (Rudduck, Wallace and Day 1997). Real involvement, says Fielding, would go 'beyond student comment on aspects of their lives which are seen as safe or without significant impact on the work of adults with the school' and would be 'embedded at classroom level…at institutional level…and at the interface between local, national and international communities' (Fielding 1996, p.19).

Thus, if a school council is to contribute to education for citizenship, pupils must be involved in the decision-making process, in exercising rights and responsibilities and in participating and contributing to the school community.

The Council of Europe's recommendation on the teaching and learning of human rights in schools endorses this:

> Democracy is best learned in a democratic setting where participation is encouraged, where views can be expressed openly and discussed, where there is freedom of expression for pupils and teachers, and where there is fairness and justice. (Council of Europe 1985)

The case study which follows shows how school councils can be established where children participate both in setting the agenda and in bringing about the required action. This example has been chosen because of the involvement of even the youngest of children.

Establishing a schools council in a small primary school: Case Study Two

The school was a rural primary school of just over a hundred children. The deputy head, new to the school, wanted to establish a school council. In this sense the project was adult-initiated but he was insistent that the children were fully involved in the decisions. He said he believed 'children should be encouraged to speak their own minds' and that it was 'their school as well so they should be encouraged to take responsibility'. He continued:

> When children ask for something adults always look for reasons why they can't do it. I wanted to change that. With my own class we always solve things, so it was a consistent approach... We have to give children the ability to say what they want to say... It gives you more work initially but it's of benefit to the school in the end.

Each of the seven classes (from age four to 11) was asked to elect two representatives, a boy and a girl. Meetings were held twice in each half term in the lunch hour. As well as the deputy head, a meal-time assistant (MTA) attended. In the first term the council was used by the children to request:

- mirrors in the toilets
- five-a-side football posts
- more picnic benches
- a choice of school dinners
- a tuck shop
- lunch hour clubs
- signs to tell people to turn off taps in the toilet area (recent flooding).

These requests could easily have resulted in the deputy head finding himself with a great deal of work. However he made it clear to the children that it was their council and that all were to find solutions together. So great was the enthusiasm to seeking solutions that the problem became not who was to do the work, but equality of opportunity for the younger children to be involved.

The 10 and 11-year-olds offered to run the tuck shop: 'we can do it – we did the bring and buy sale' – and agreed that there would need to be both 'healthy' food and sweets. Emma (aged 11) wrote to the governors asking that they provide the money for mirrors. The nine-year-olds agreed to put up a sign about the sinks flooding and an eight-year-old girl arranged for her father to make football posts. The MTA said she would ask the county's school dinner supplier about a choice of meals. Daniel (aged ten) had a solution to the lunch time clubs:

> We thought the big boys could teach the little ones how to play football and the big girls could teach the little girls how to do stickers – like junk modelling. We could have a test to see if we're OK to do it.

The deputy agreed to this idea – 'it sounds great' – but then a six-year-old girl stopped him, saying 'I don't see why six-year-olds can't do netball'. This was in many ways the test of the council: would the deputy intervene or would the children be able to resolve this among themselves? The older boys argued that the older pupils were 'really good' and that two clubs might be needed, whilst the older girls said it could perhaps be a sports club rather than a football club. Here the deputy did intervene to suggest that the council members find out just how many younger children would like to play which games, so that a fair decision could be reached at the next meeting.

The fact that the six-year-old had queried the decision of the older children gave another six-year-old the confidence to speak out. Just before this particular meeting ended, he asked:

> Can people in Year One and Two help with something, because we haven't really got anything to do?

The older children agreed that these five and six-year-olds would be too young to handle the money for the tuck shop, but that they could give out the fruit. It was also agreed that they could help with the signs for the toilet area.

Whilst these requests and decisions are relatively uncontroversial, the principles on which the council operated stand as an example to other schools. The fact that the youngest pupils were involved and had the confidence to speak out belies the opinion of many teachers that school councils cannot operate effectively until secondary school. The enthusiasm of the children to act also indicates that whilst a teacher must provide some initial input and guidance, there is sufficient interest and ability amongst pupils themselves to find solutions and work for effective change.

In another primary school (*Guardian* 1996), pupils discussed in circle time[1] the issues they wanted their representatives to take to the school council.

> We talk about messages, problems and successes and freedoms and responsibilities. The representatives can take something to the school council and they sort it out. (Girl, aged 10)

As well as a school council, democratic processes extended to pupils interviewing prospective teachers and classroom assistants, mediating in playground disputes and discussing the school's development with the headteacher.

It is interesting to note that such examples come from primary rather than secondary schools. Pupils in a local secondary school were asked about their school council and were much less enthusiastic. One council member explained the process.

> We think of things we want and things we could do. We discuss how we might do it and then we ask for it to be 'put forward' on a piece of paper, then it goes to Mrs X [headteacher]. If she was actually there and took note it would be better. Some things got done last year like some planting and the toilets got painted, but this year we've put through lots of ideas and nothing's been done. We wanted more bins and more drinking fountains and mirrors in the boys' toilets, but it hasn't been done. (Girl, aged 13)

It is interesting that many of these requests relate to basic rights in terms of health and hygiene and yet they are still not met. Another pupil in the same school commented:

> The council works: the headteacher doesn't. She only says 'yes' to boring stuff that doesn't actually cost anything – she's so old-fashioned. (Girl, aged 14)

Perhaps understandably, a request for a 'smoking room' was turned down. However, had the request been turned back to the pupils to solve (as in the primary schools) this would have been a good opportunity for real decision making about a controversial issue. Pupils could have canvassed other pupils on their views, found out about the LEA's policy on smoking in educational establishments and interviewed parents. In this way the school could have allowed adolescents to take responsibility for decisions which were of importance to them.

---

1 Circle time involves children sitting in a circle, taking turns to share feelings or opinions, in an atmosphere of mutual respect.

Community involvement: Case Study Three

Both Hart (1992) and Higgins-D'Alessandro (1996) maintain that real education for citizenship must involve participation in community action. The work of Groundwork Plymouth Trust[2] provides excellent examples of what can be done, when there is financial commitment from the local city council or other partners and where schools are prepared to be involved.

In one secondary school, pupils were asked to evaluate the area around the local ferry, which was used by many tourists and was a first point of call in Cornwall. The pupils surveyed the area and were helped by their maths, English and science tutors to put together a presentation. As a result money was spent redesigning and refurbishing the area, but most importantly the adults were so impressed by the ability of the young people to present practical but creative ideas for improvement, that two of the pupils were invited to sit on the Torpoint 2000 Committee, a group planning improvements to the local area. Pupils have since been asked to look at the local high street with a view to improving it.

Groundwork Plymouth was asked in another instance to assist with an initiative which focused on the local landscape and local issues and needs. In one primary school this involved a group of 10 and 11-year-olds seeing how safety outside the school could be improved. The children worked with a school governor in the lunch hour and after school. They studied interview techniques through role play and drama and then interviewed parents, children and villagers to ascertain their views of what should be done. They used drama to explain the issues to the younger children in the school and surveyed all children to see how they got to school. Videos were made of the problem and solutions were suggested. The children then presented their case to the local council. Whilst the children were not able to get their preferred solution (double yellow lines), they did get parents to consider the safety aspects of where they parked and to realise that they themselves contributed to the problem. The children suggested walking to school, car sharing and using the school bus as solutions. In addition they persuaded the bus company to move the bus stop. The school now has a new problem: it has expanded and wants to take over the village hall for much of the school week. Rather than argue this case herself, the headteacher has given this job to the children who are now able to articulate their views, present a case clearly and sit through lengthy public meetings. Not only have these children demonstrated to adults that their views are worth listening to, they have learnt much about democratic processes and the skills needed to make one's voice heard.

A much more ambitious plan has been that of the Stonehouse area of Plymouth. Four hundred pupils from five schools in Stonehouse were consulted

---

2 More information on Groundwork Plymouth Trust can be obtained from 1, The Crescent, Plymouth, PL1 3AB.

and their ideas have been recorded for the Stonehouse Area Plan. Whilst plans for this area are still being discussed, already it appears that two of the children's requests, traffic calming and the creation of new play parks, have been given high priority.

CONCLUSION

At the beginning of this chapter, young people indicated that they were interested in working for change and many cited their involvement in action, either as individuals or as part of an organisation. But the majority of pupils felt that more could be done in schools to educate them about current social, moral and global issues, both in terms of discussion of such issues and encouraging active participation. The case studies described above indicate how it is possible within school and community to involve young people in debate about values and subsequent action. None of the examples cited involved charity work or collecting litter, two of the actions most frequently mentioned earlier. Whilst giving money to charity may be laudable, it does not necessarily ensure an understanding of the issues or foster a wider involvement with the community. What is notable about the above case studies is that they all required children to think about issues of importance to them and to articulate their responses. In the examples focusing on school councils and community work, the children had to learn the skills of arguing persuasively and presenting their ideas to a critical audience. An atmosphere of mutual respect was evident when adults and children worked together to solve problems in authentic contexts.

Education for citizenship is thus best exemplified where children's views are taken into account and where children are invited to articulate and act upon these views. In so doing young people can learn about democratic processes and be made aware of the power of their voices now and in the future. Whilst it may not be possible for every child to be involved in community action, certainly all children can be informed of the issues and involved in debate. Global issues can also be debated, if not acted on, as was seen in the case study of the futures wheel. Such an approach will require time in the curriculum, and will thus require teachers who are open-minded, prepared to take risks and to move beyond the basic curriculum. However, if the end result is young people who understand local and global issues, who value democratic processes and who feel confident that they can work towards effective change, then surely such time and effort is justified.

REFERENCES

Council of Europe (1985) 'Recommendation No. R(85)7 of the Committee of Ministers to Member States on Teaching and Learning about Human Rights in Schools.' Strasbourg: Council Of Europe. In H. Starkey (1991) *The Challenge of Human Rights Education*. London: Cassell.

Fielding, M. (1996) 'Beyond school effectiveness and school improvement: lighting the slow fuse of possibility.' *The Curriculum Journal 8*, 1, 7–27.

Guardian, The (1996) 'School learns pupil power.' 1 April.

Guardian, The (1997) 'A level in decency.' 13 May.

Hart, R. (1992) *Children's Participation: From Tokenism to Citizenship*. Innocenti Essays No. 4. Florence: UNICEF International Child Development Centre.

Hicks, D. (1994) *Educating for the Future: A Practical Classroom Guide*. Godalming, Surrey: WWF.

Hicks, D. and Holden, C. (1995) *Visions of the Future: Why We Need to Teach for Tomorrow*. Stoke-on-Trent: Trentham.

Higgins-D'Alessandro, A. (1996) 'Moral education as an historical/political/social science.' *Journal of Moral Education 25*, 1, 57–66.

Rudduck, J., Wallace, G. and Day, J. (1997) 'Student voices: what can they tell us as "partners in change"?' In K. Stott and V.N. Trafford (eds) *Partners in Change: Shaping the Future*. London: Middlesex University.

Tappin, M. and Brown, L. (1996) 'Envisioning a postmodern moral pedagogy.' *Journal of Moral Education 25*, 1, 101–109.

CHAPTER FOUR

Emerging from the Tunnel
Some Dilemmas in Environmental Education

Nick Clough

INSIDE AND OUTSIDE THE CLASSROOM

On a recent visit to a classroom I was immediately impressed with what appeared to be a brightly decorated tree in one corner. When I looked at the tree closely I noticed that the red, amber and green papers which were hanging from the branches each had messages on them. It was then that the teacher explained that the tree had a function. Each child had been asked to identify an environmental problem which needed addressing (stopping). They had described the problem on a piece of red paper and had hung it on the tree. They had then thought of some relevant action that they could take. One 'environmental citizen' had noticed that the area around a local supermarket was littered with plastic bags – non-biodegradable material – and had described the dangers of this on a red piece of paper and had attached it to the tree. He had planned some action to persuade his parents to buy a large re-usable shopping bag so that they would not need to use smaller plastic ones. He had written down this intention on an amber piece of paper and had attached it to the tree. He was only allowed to use a green piece of paper when the shopping bag had actually been bought and used – outside the classroom.

There were a number of such actions in the environment which were recorded by the children in this way on the tree. The children called the tree 'the millennium tree'[1] because its purpose was to make them work towards a more sustainable world in the new millennium when they themselves would act out their adult lives. There is potential here for a wide range of activity and learning, developing children's knowledge base, for example about the properties of

---

1 The 'millennium tree' idea came from Martin Ashley, a teacher at Selwood Middle School.

plastics, encouraging children to reflect on the consequences of their own values and behaviours and stimulating their intention to take action.

As a model, however, it does pose some serious questions about the purpose and scope of children's participation in environmental issues. The particular focus in this example – the problem of non-biodegradable bags littering the space outside a supermarket – did not raise controversies in the way that other examples might. If the focus had been the use of cars in the local neighbourhood, a different and more challenging set of issues might have emerged for both the children and the teachers. What, for example, if one child had signalled her/his intention to join the protest group 'Reclaim the Streets' whose campaigns include the closure of some urban thoroughfares by illegal barricading?

The discussion in this chapter focuses on dilemmas which can arise within an environmental education programme, taking cars as an example. This involves consideration of the training needs of teachers, in particular in relation to handling the controversial issues which arise. The analysis will raise questions about the relationship between schooling and the state, in particular the function of opening up such discussion with young learners who will have to face the risks and responsibilities of the environment in their future lives.

Case study material draws on children's experience of a curriculum project about a controversial road construction in the locality of the school and also the experience of student teachers working on a programme about education for citizenship.

CHILDREN, CARS AND THE FUTURE

> Risk belongs to progress as much as a bow-wave belongs to a speeding ship. Risk is no invention of modern times. It is tolerated in many areas of social life. The deaths from traffic accidents, for instance. Every year a middle sized city in Germany disappears without trace, so to speak. People have got used to that. (Beck 1992, p.46)

Within the UK there is considerable concern and protest over a transport policy which prioritises the use of the car over other forms of transport. In 1989 the Department of Transport forecasted that road traffic would increase by between 83 per cent and 142 per cent by 2025. To provide for this increase the government announced a £12 billion road improvement scheme in spite of public knowledge about the environmental depletion this will cause (Doherty and Hoedeman 1995). This has stimulated different forms of direct action by citizens including those to prevent the construction of by-passes that cut through rural areas in the UK. At the same time some communities in urban areas have campaigned to have heavy traffic passing through their housing estates diverted elsewhere.

SCHOOL ONE

During the academic year of 1996–97 children in a small primary school in a Devon village found that they had a new community living on their doorstep – a community of protestors against the building of a new highroad through 'Fair Mile' to provide relief for the overstretched A30 route between Honiton and Exeter. A teacher in the school commented.

> It was fascinating to see the first tree houses go up. As you know in the end Swampy was the last one to be dug out of the tunnels. I met some of the protestors when they were thumbing a lift back to 'the fort'. This is what they called their tree houses and they were on their way to do 'night duty patrol'. They seemed to be about 16–17 years old. I felt that they were all in it together. They had a real sense of purpose, a real sense of community.

When the staff of the school met to make decisions about their locality work and drama production for the year, they chose to focus on these local events which were already receiving attention from the national press. The issues were clear but complex. The same teacher, herself a local resident, summarised the case:

> The impact of traffic on the road had worsened in the past few years. The pressure was felt throughout the year, not just in the summer months. There had been bad accidents and people had been killed. At the same time it was a beautiful location. Nearly all the local people wanted a new road but not through or near their village. Farmers were anxious about their land. There was a fear that the new road would attract more traffic. The protest was not violent. There was no damage to property. Locals were impressed that the protestors were prepared to put their lives on the line. But they were seen as outsiders.

What was even more complex for the school was finding a way for children to investigate this issue in a fair and interesting way. The teacher commented:

> We were very conscious that we should not be seen to be taking sides. We knew we would be criticised if the children had left home to become protestors. We wanted the children to have enough information so that they could make up their own minds on the issue. We thought a local issue like this was a good way to start.

The key question arising in this case study was how teachers can ensure that the children are well informed about all aspects of a local issue.

SCHOOL TWO

Elsewhere in a primary school in Bristol a group of student teachers found another starting point for some environmental work. They asked a class of children aged 9–10 years about what they thought might happen to the environment by the time they were 50 years old. The responses from the children were typical for their age and experience. The children's expectations were summarised by the students:

> more cars, the depletion of the ozone layer, animals being hunted to extinction, pollution, incurable diseases, acid rain, litter, increasing asthma, disappearing forests/countryside, harvests failing through lack of rain, more drugs, more homeless people, changing climates, poverty...

The students reported that after the discussion the children wanted to take action immediately, including making collections of money and old clothes and starting an anti-rubbish campaign. They wanted to send messages, through the Internet and through posters designed by themselves to encourage people 'to make a cleaner world with less cars'. One child declared that he would stand at the end of the road outside his house and draw everyone's attention to the poster. One of the students admitted to being a little overwhelmed by the strength of the children's responses and sought advice about how best to manage their enthusiasm for action. Education for participation had not been a focus in her training up to that point!

It is not surprising that one of the expressed concerns of these children was the problems of traffic. They were living in a busy urban area where they faced dangers from cars every day. In fact the high use of private cars in the city is causing concern. Staff in the City of Bristol Planning Department estimate that 40 per cent of the 100,000 workforce who make their way every day into the centre of Bristol, do so in a car of which they are the sole occupant. The management and control of this problem, which contributes to high levels of pollution and is cited as a cause of asthmatic attacks in the Bristol area, is now part of the action plan for this department. The Health and Environment Services have also published a report indicating the need to reduce further the levels of roadside and background nitrogen dioxide levels (Bristol City Council 1996, pp.7–8). This will be a process of gradual change stimulated by the introduction of cars with catalytic converters and other economic incentives for the public to leave cars at the perimeter of the city.

The key question arising from this experience was how teachers can best harness children's enthusiasm for action and provide information about traffic in their locality.

SCHOOL THREE

Elsewhere in a small rural primary school near Haslev in Denmark, children were identifying their hopes for the future. They were differentiating between probable and preferable futures and were beginning to consider what action would be necessary for their preferable futures to be realised. The class teacher was anxious that the activity might have the negative effect of making the children feel powerless in face of the concerns which they raised. As it happened the children were able to imagine a positive future world in which there were:

> no bad drugs, cures for diseases like Aids and cancer, cars that can fly and are environmentally friendly, clean energy from solar panels, less pollution, less crime, no divorces, less smoking, less people without money, peace on earth, more boats powered by sails, longer lives for everyone (100 years)...

Even in this rural school the problem of cars was a focus for discussion by the children and they were most intrigued by a suggestion by one of their peers, Svante (ten years), that someone should invent a flying car, that was powered by vaporised water which would be non-polluting and would not need roads! He pointed out that the alternative fuel would have to be introduced gradually as many people depended for their incomes on the oil production industry. There was some discussion about what Denmark would look like with only small roads for emergency services and bicycles. The key question arising in this case study was how teachers can support children in developing a positive view of the future and their involvement in it.

Each lesson described above provides an example of a different starting point for some participatory environmental work, in each case about traffic and the use of cars. The first has the potential to involve children in the development of a land use issue in their local community. The second concerns developing children's skills in taking action in the school/community. The third might be a starting point for some shared work on envisioning a preferable future and for considering what factors would allow/prevent the achievement of a better world. All of these activities require teachers to listen carefully to and understand the views expressed by children in response to environmental concerns.

DIFFERENT RESPONSES TO THE ENVIRONMENT: PERSPECTIVES AND VALUES

The process of taking children's expressed opinions seriously through active environmental education involves engagement with a range of complex controversies. At a basic level there is likely to be disagreement about aims and approaches as these depend on cultural, moral, social and political perspectives. Hicks (1991, p.101) has identified four different views of the future in an attempt to outline a typology of responses, as shown in Table 4.1.

The technocentric view expressing confidence in the potential of science and technology to solve the challenges facing us is contrasted with the view of sustainable development which anticipates major changes in the way people think about the planet and each other, drawing inspiration from deep ecological perspectives based on ideas of social justice. The two other outlooks derive from different levels of optimism and pessimism. A view that things will continue as they are without much need for change (business as usual) is sharply differentiated from a view of the present time as 'the edge of disaster' and of a future that offers a worsening situation for all forms of life. These four perspectives underline how decisions we make depend in part on our view of the choices before us and our understanding of them (Hicks 1994, p.53).

Table 4.1 Four different views of the future

Technological Growth

This view is held by those who believe that the answer to most problems lies in the accelerated growth of science and technology. Various applications of technology are seen as offering dramatic rewards, especially for business.

Sustainable Growth

This view is held by those who believe that the future must involve a major change of direction away from a mechanistic and fragmented view of the world to a more holistic and ecological one in which sustainable development is a possibility.

Business as Usual

This view is held by those who argue that the future will be very much like today. In other words there will be the usual alarms and excursions, but nothing that cannot be effectively dealt with.

Edge of Disaster

This view is held by those who believe that we are on the verge of one or more major catastrophes, the signs of which are already cleary evident. Life as we know it is nearing breakdown and when various elements collapse it will never be the same again.

Source: Hicks (1991, p.101)

Such differences in outlook are highlighted by the problems of traffic in urban areas. For example, the developing 'National Cycling Strategy' relying on the technical advances of bicycle and street design does little to reassure members of the 'Reclaim the Streets' group who argue for more radical changes in transport policy that require a significant shift in public opinions over the environment and political process. Even if the National Cycling Strategy meets its own targets and the number of trips by bicycle in the UK (currently 2 per cent of all trips) quadruples over the next 16 years, our record would still fall short of current practice in Sweden which is 10 per cent of all trips. It has been noted in the Bristol area that the increase in the number of cyclists over the last four years has been modest, in spite of advances in bicycle design and improved routes for cyclists. The users are predominantly those already living in the city centre so this very slight change makes no difference to the number of cars entering the city every day (Bristol City Council 1996, p.5).

As spokesperson for the 'Reclaim the Streets' group, Roger Geffen described his frustration with the actions of politicians to the *Guardian* newspaper:

> If we are to move to a more responsible society, people have to do things themselves. If you see something you believe wrong, then it is no use leaving it to politicians. You have to take responsibility yourself. (Vidal 1995)

Vidal outlines different kinds of direct action which groups have recently been taking to accelerate the pace of change and to raise consciousness about the increasing pollution levels resulting from the use of cars belonging to two thirds of households in the UK. These include:

- individuals making personal decisions to use cars less often and to rely where possible on public transport
- pedestrians writing rude messages about car users on advertising hoardings advertising cars
- cyclists painting lanes on busy roads for use by cyclists only
- large groups of cyclists jamming busy city roads while ringing their bells
- pedestrians reclaiming the streets and creating temporary car-free zones
- old age pensioners working in groups together to physically remove cars parked on pavements
- groups of citizens obstructing (with their own bodies) the paths of bulldozers which are clearing land for newly planned roads. (Vidal 1995)

We could now add to this list the well-known strategy adopted by Swampy and others of digging networks of tunnels under the proposed route of the new road and occupying these to hinder the progress of the engineers.

Some of these actions represent a problematic stance for citizens in a democracy. At one level they may be undemocratic and therefore a threat to the existing political/social framework. In some cases they are technically illegal. At another level they may all be considered a committed response to environmental/social problems. They need not endanger lives and have the potential to raise the awareness of citizens who have not involved themselves previously in such environmental issues.

What is apparent is that these actions involve prioritising of ecological values over other values such as social welfare and democratic/legal processes. Through disrupting traffic the actions of the 'Reclaim the Streets' group put at risk the rights of individuals to earn their living. Through trespassing onto land designated for road building, tunnel constructors also disrupt the ongoing discussion and development through the existing democratic decision-making process.

However, at the same time these kind of actions raise valid points about the democratic framework in the UK. They serve to highlight issues about the rights of individual citizens on the land (given the historical backcloth of enclosure and the concentration of land ownership into the hands of a small minority) and about the flexibility and responsiveness of government and its independence from other significant vested interests. They raise a question for those involved in education as well as politics: what will generate the shift in consciousness and pace of change that is necessary to prevent continuing ecological degradation?

It is perhaps helpful to take an example from recent history in which the achievement of rapid social/political changes had been judged to be necessary. Prior to the Equal Franchise Act of 1928, some members of the suffragette movement chose to accelerate the pace of change by adopting strategies which although unaccept- able to many at the time are perhaps judged to be acceptable in hindsight in the late twentieth century. It is difficult to know how a future generation will judge our responses to pressing road traffic problems in the 1990s.

Roger Geffen's statement about 'having to do things for ourselves' raises pertinent questions about whether inaction or non-participation is acceptable (Vidal 1995). Hicks and Holden (1995) point to the tendency of some citizens in modern society to be disorientated by rapid changes and developments around them and to deny themselves involvement in environmental and social questions raised in their day-to-day lives:

> The value of such denial is that it saves us from having to face the problems or thinking what needs to be done. (Hicks and Holden 1995, p.6)

Is it justifiable socially, economically, politically or morally to ignore these issues? So many of our own behaviours in our everyday lives (e.g. driving a car with no other passengers over walkable distances or alternatively not joining a Reclaim the Streets Party) are themselves statements of a kind in that they preserve the status quo.

CLARIFYING VALUES WITH STUDENT TEACHERS

This discussion relates environmental education to social, moral and cultural dimensions of the curriculum. Consideration of one of our everyday behaviours (car transport) and of action taken by individuals and groups over some environmental issues that result from this behaviour has shown how complex preparation for adult life in a democracy can be. The content of teacher training programmes should develop the knowledge and skills which are necessary for teachers to be able to support children in making sense of these issues in the classroom. An example of a student teacher feeling ill-prepared for coping with children's enthusiasm for taking action has already been noted.

A small-scale survey conducted with a group of 33 undergraduate student teachers about their attitudes to the environment revealed that their own outlook was based more on pessimistic than optimistic forecasts. The questionnaire and a summary of the students' responses are presented in Table 4.2 at the end of this chapter. It was conducted in an interactive mode which allowed for some discussion and clarification of the questions. The main findings can be summarised as follows:

- In their view the rate of environmental degradation is very serious and needs to be reversed.
- The students had a high value and respect for the natural environment.
- The students' own expressed values prioritised the environment above economic activity.
- They demonstrated a scepticism about the effectiveness of democratic systems to address environmental issues. (In discussion the same group of students rejected the suggestion that an alternative to democratically achieved environmental changes might be a form of eco-fascism.)
- The students expressed an expectation that some environmental problems might be resolved through technological means but that a change in political will and commitment would be necessary.
- Eighty-two per cent of the students believed that 'citizens are right to take direct action to prevent environmental damage'. Seventy per cent thought that 'in some cases citizens are right to break the law to protect the environment'. Twenty-seven per cent agreed strongly with this statement, though they were at pains to point out that law breaking that involved injury to persons was not acceptable. These students cited as an example that it was not acceptable to shoot rhino hunters but that climbing trees and digging tunnels to prevent by-pass construction was acceptable.

The main finding which suggests a relatively low value held by this group for democratic and even legal processes in face of the need to protect the environment was surprising and perhaps demonstrates the power of such social movements as have been described in this chapter to influence attitudes. It is noticeable that the new curriculum for Initial Teacher Training and the standards for judging the quality of the professional work undertaken by students do not include any reference to the handling of such controversial issues with children (DfEE 1997). Teachers may find useful a short list of professional competences related to democratic process and handling controversial issues for use with student teachers (Clough and Holden 1996, pp.42–3). In the meantime the process of training teachers should provide opportunities for them to discuss the reality of the tensions identified here. Whilst student teachers should develop their ecological insights through a study of such writers as David Orr (1994) and Theodore Roszak (1995) they should at the same time recognise the significance of the Statement of Values recently prepared by the National Forum for Values in Education and the Community. Established by SCAA (School Curriculum and Assessment Authority) this forum has consulted widely developed statements of ideals that we should try to live up to related to 'The Self', 'Relationships', 'Society' and 'The Environment'. The document includes two references relevant to the discussion here:

> We should accept our responsibility to maintain a sustainable environment for future generations.
>
> We should respect the rule of law and encourage others to do so.
>
> (Talbot and Tate 1997, pp.13, 14)

The moral conflict identified by these students is best explored through case studies taken from the real world, for example the one cited in 'School One' above which developed a project about the road construction scheme on the A30.

HELPING CHILDREN TO APPRECIATE DIFFERENT POINTS OF VIEW

Discussion with the headteacher in School One indicated that the children had also been impressed by the actions of the protestors. He said:

> What I noticed with the media attention at the time of the evictions and the clearance of protestors from the tunnels was that the majority of the children were for the protestors.

A main aim of the resulting curriculum project was to allow children to look at the issues from all sides. The children prepared a questionnaire which was issued to parents. The questions included:

- Do you drive a car?
- Are you for the road improvement?
- Do you think people should have more say about the building of the new road?
- What do you think of the protestors?

- Did the police handle the situation properly?
- What should the police do with the protestors?
- Would you protest if you had to?

The responses from 52 parents communicated a wide range of value positions and illustrated that events surrounding the building of the road were indeed controversial. While seven advocated severe punishments for the protestors, 14 offered supportive comments about their activities. There were differences too in the responses to the question about the police handling of the situation.

The teacher also arranged for some of those closely concerned to visit the school to answer questions put by the children. These included a representative from the Sheriff's Office who was able to explain the significance of trespassing and also a representative from the construction engineer company who gave his perspective on the events. The teacher had hoped that some of the protestors would also be able to visit the school but unfortunately after the evictions many of them moved on to other sites at Yeovil and Manchester. It was also not possible for the local MP to visit the school to talk about the long-term strategy for road building. The headteacher's expressed intention was that these kind of interactions would give opportunity for the children:

> to make up their own minds and to realise that what they hear on the radio or see on the TV is not the whole story and that they need to take time to consider what their own response might be.

However, the headteacher's account demonstrated that there was some difficulty in representing a balance of the views.

At the end of the project a play about the local event was performed in a local theatre. A large audience was guaranteed as each child in the school had a part to play. As the teacher explained, it gave an account of the story from the perspective of those who are not always heard, 'the animals who inhabit the wood at Fair Mile'. There were many strengths in this approach to extending the curriculum through the performing arts. In particular it allowed time for discussion of the issues to continue and importantly ensured that parents were able to see that the school was trying to be fair in the way that the controversy was handled. Everybody heard arguments from different sides including:

Extract 1

Owl: I tell you things are going to change around here (*waves a wing*). All this woody peacefulness and plenty will become a new Human Run, a roady thing through our homes.

Extract 2

Councillor: Just mark your preference for the route. Now's your chance to have a say. It's no use sitting back and doing

> nothing and then thinking you can complain. Then it will be too late!

Interviews with the 9, 10 and 11-year-olds at the end of the project showed that they had developed their thinking about the issues since the early stages when the headteacher had thought that many supported and identified with the protestors. Some sample responses are presented below.

> More roads may mean that there will be more cars. The protestors did not have the right to trespass but I do think that they have the right to protest.

> I have learnt you can protest in different ways, for example by writing a letter. Protesting can be very civilised, through talking and negotiating. You don't have to use force to stop something.

> Before building the road they should put up a hut with charts about the road. People should be able to write their ideas on the chart.

> The protestors don't need to worry about the animals. Environmental experts have looked after the animals. They will put wolves eyes along the main road so that deer won't cross. The light will be reflected in their eyes.

> Sooner or later the whole world may be covered in concrete – but the road should be built because more people will be killed.

> Roads themselves are all right. They are not the real problem. It's the form of transport that we use, the way we power is seriously wrong. The world will get seriously damaged unless we find some new way of powering cars, buses and taxis.

> We learnt that votes are important and so is the countryside. Before I wasn't really interested in the road.

> I've learnt that people will go to extreme levels to stop another person doing something they don't want to happen. The protestors could have killed themselves. The tunnels were not supported properly.

Their apparent confidence in the fairness of democratic processes was reflected in their responses when they were asked about their views on the statement: 'In some cases people are right to break the law to try to protect the environment'. Unlike the student teachers all the children strongly disagreed with this statement.

There were a number of strengths in this project which provide an appropriate summary to this chapter. It is clear that the children involved were able to reconsider their original positions on this issue. Through being involved in the arguments and counter-arguments they began to develop social and structural insights and to express an understanding about values and action. Arguably their comments did not reflect a developing understanding of ecological perspectives or of sustainability and it is clear that they have confidence in technological solutions. However, their concern for the environment was matched by a corresponding concern for democratic processes. It helped them to begin to understand the significance of intentions and motives to behaviour and action. They were also able to do this as a collective group and not just as individuals. This was possible because it was a local community event in which they all were already involved.

This kind of experience is fundamental to developing competence for participation. There was opportunity for the children to make up their own minds and there was no expectation from the school that there was one correct way to understand this controversy. This constitutes what Jensen and Schnack have referred to as good liberal education in which:

> being critical does not mean to be in opposition or negative but on the contrary to have an interest in analysing underlying structures, conditions and preconditions for the appearance of phenomena. (Jensen and Schnack 1994, p.8)

The result, perhaps sadly, was that the new road was built regardless. 'Fair Mile' could not be saved. The children and school could not have achieved this and anyway its fate was probably already sealed even before Swampy and others emerged from the tunnel. The achievement was that a process of critical thinking had been encouraged by teachers in spite of the sensitive issues involved. This is as important for society as for the children themselves. A democratic system needs to be reflexive and responsive and to take account of all the challenges that it faces. It needs to be self-critical and to encourage rigorous debate about such issues within its own formal structures – and these include its schools.

The implication of this for the developing argument in this book is that learning to participate involves preparation of a fundamental kind – involvement by children in ongoing critical debate about events in the wider world and about the moral, social and cultural conflicts which arise. The resulting development of children's thinking can not only empower a new generation as active citizens but can also strengthen democratic responses to the environmental challenges which we face. The significance of this needs to be recognised by those responsible for the training of teachers so that they themselves are able to manage open, critical and balanced discussions around a millennium tree – for the good of children and of society.

Table 4.2 Survey: the citizen and the environment: findings (N=33)

A Human beings have the right to use the natural environment for economic purposes.
    Agree   12 per cent
    Disagree   88 per cent (3 per cent strongly)

B The processes of democracy protect the environment from damage by economic activity.
    Agree   3 per cent
    Disagree   97 per cent (12 per cent strongly)

C Trees are as important as human beings.
    Agree   82 per cent
    Disagree   18 per cent

D Humans will develop technological solutions to environmental problems.
    Agree   12 per cent
    Disagree   88 per cent

E Human self respect is linked to respect for nature.
    Agree   48 per cent
    Disagree   52 per cent

F Safeguarding employment is more important than protecting the environment.
    Agree   9 per cent
    Disagree   91 per cent

G No one can stop the process of environmental depletion.
    Agree   18 per cent
    Disagree   82 per cent

H Humans should prioritise the protection of the natural environment.
    Agree   100 per cent

I Citizens are right to take direct action to prevent environmental damage.
    Agree   82 per cent
    Disagree   18 per cent

J Democratically elected governments develop effective policies to protect the environment.
    Agree   3 per cent
    Disagree   97 per cent

K In a democracy citizens have access to information about real threats to the environment.
    Agree   9 per cent
    Disagree   91 per cent

L Everything can continue as it is. There is no need to worry about the environment.
    Agree   0 per cent
    Disagree   100 per cent

M In some cases citizens are right to break the law to protect the environment.
    Agree   70 per cent (27 per cent strongly)
    Disagree   30 per cent

REFERENCES

Beck, U. (1992) *Risk Society: Towards a New Modernity*. London: Sage Publications.

Bristol City Council (1996) *Sustainability Update: Supplement to the State of the Local Environment Report: Consultative Draft*. Bristol: City of Bristol.

Clough, N. and Holden, C. (1996) 'Global citizenship, professional competence and the chocolate cake.' In M. Steiner (1996) *Developing the Global Teacher: From Theory to Practice*. Stoke-on-Trent: Trentham.

DfEE (Department for Education and Employment) (1997) *Circular, October: Teaching: High Status, High Standards: Requirements for Courses of Initial Teacher Training*. London: DfEE.

Doherty, A. and Hoedeman, O. (1995) 'High speed ambition.' *Guardian*, 5 April.

Hicks, D. (1991) *Exploring Alternative Futures: A Teacher's Interim Guide*. London: Global Futures Project.

Hicks, D. (1994) *Educating for the Future*. Goldaming: WWF.

Hicks, D. and Holden, C. (1995) *Visions of the Future: Why We Need to Teach for Tomorrow*. Stoke-on-Trent: Trentham.

Jensen, B. and Schnack, R. (eds) (1994) 'Action competence as an educational challenge.' *Didaktiske Studier: Studies in Educational Theory and Curriculum 12*, 5–18. Royal Danish School: Copenhagen.

Orr, D. (1994) *Earth in Mind: On Education, Environment and Human Prospect*. Washington: Island Press.

Roszak, T. (1995) 'Where psyche meets Gaia.' In T. Roszak *et al.* (eds) *Ecopsychology: Restoring the Earth, Healing the Mind*. San Fransisco: Sierra Club Books.

Talbot, M. and Tate, N. (1997) 'Shared values in a pluralist society?' In R. Smith and P. Standish (eds) *Teaching Right and Wrong: Moral Education in the Balance*. Stoke-on-Trent: Trentham.

Vidal, J. (1995) 'On the road to Carmageddon.' In *Guardian*, 22 July.

PART THREE

Secondary Pupils
Values and Action

CHAPTER FIVE

The Voices of Young People with Disability

Rhiannon Prys Owen and Jane Tarr

INTRODUCTION

This chapter describes a process which took place in a special school over a period of five years. Those involved were attempting to develop a climate in which all young people felt valued and safe to express their own views and opinions and could begin to feel confident that changes could occur within their school as a result of their actions. Schools, including special schools, communicate the way they value children and young people in many ways: for example through their expectations of each pupil's achievement; through their statements on children's entitlement to aspects of the curriculum; through their expectations of pupil behaviour; through their provision and allocation of resources; through the attitudes of staff towards pupils and through day-to-day decisions about teaching and learning styles. In this case study the teachers and pupils worked together on a continuing programme which included the following stages:

- responding to concerns expressed about the physical environment
- consideration of social relationships in the school and the establishment of a school council
- responding to concerns expressed about aspects of challenging behaviour
- the launch of a local disability equality project within the school and the wider community.

The case study raises many pertinent questions about education for participation and its application for young people with disability. It also provides a useful context for exploring key ideas in policy development.

THE BROADER CONTEXT: PROVISION FOR YOUNG PEOPLE WITH DISABILITY

The last decade has seen a developing understanding of the legitimacy of human rights in relation to children and young people. Gradually, judicial, legal and social systems are starting to acknowledge that children should be heard and their opinions taken seriously in matters that involve them.

The Fish Report *Educational Opportunities for All?* (Inner London Education Authority 1985) included disability as a fourth dimension alongside race, gender and class in developing a non-discriminatory education system (Potts 1986). This emphasis on the rights of pupils with disability to equitable opportunities has fuelled the debate concerned with social justice. An inclusive philosophy continues to gain ground as it:

> chimes with the philosophy of a liberal political system and a pluralist culture; one that celebrates diversity and promotes fraternity and equality of opportunity. (Thomas 1997, p.106)

The Children Act 1989 encouraged the practice of placing the views of young people as central in decision making about their own future. In the field of social services the child's perspective was thus given due weight and consideration. This has important implications for young people with disability as their care often extends from education into the social services. This was endorsed by Part 3 of the Education Act, the Code of Practice for the Identification and Assessment of Special Educational Needs (1994), which states that a reason for involving the child is that:

> children have the right to be heard...[and] should be encouraged to participate in decision-making about provision to meet their special educational needs. (Education Act 1994)

Educational legislation has been slower to involve children with disability in decision-making processes, but there are some examples of consultation with pupils who have particular educational needs. Wade and Moore (1993) address the variety of forms of consultation between professionals and pupils with a range of special needs, Cooper (1993) explores the voice of pupils with emotional and behavioural difficulties and Lewis (1995) pupils with severe learning difficulties.

Despite such examples, the recent legislation has not made sufficient changes to the experience of disabled young people. The Education Act 1993, and Children Act 1989, whilst empowering and providing children with opportunities and entitlements nevertheless label children with any form of disability as being 'in need' which implies that they are weak and incapable of independence.

Young people and indeed adults with disability have a very difficult experience because society continues to carry negative and deficit models which result in the devaluation of them and the experience for them of a high level of social oppression. These young people and adults can face personal and institutional discrimination from many aspects of British society that denies them the same opportunities as the general population. Many state that as they have grown up they have internalised society's view of themselves as dependent, second-class citizens who frequently experience discrimination, violence and harassment towards their person.

There is still a lack of recognition or understanding of disability as a civil rights issue and as an element within policies for equality of opportunity. The inclusion of all pupils in truly comprehensive schools will require the development of a new understanding of the nature of schooling, of the relationship between school and local community, of the roles and relationships that develop between young people, and of the duties, rights and responsibilities of being citizens together. These four broad areas are crucial to preparing young people with disability to participate more fully in society. Participation refers to many types of involvement: economic, social, political and cultural, both within the community at large and in educational terms (Organisation for Economic Co-operation and Development 1997). In order to ensure such participation, the voice of the young person needs to be listened and responded to.

Such participation is endorsed by Article 12 of the UN Convention 1989 for the Rights of the Child which states that the child has:

> the right to express his or her own views freely in all matters affecting them. (United Nations 1989)

Furthermore, Article 2 states that all the rights safeguarded by the convention are to be applied without discrimination on the grounds of disability. Article 23 sets out specific rights for children who have disabilities and learning difficulties. It states that children should:

> enjoy a full and decent life, in conditions which ensure dignity, promote self-reliance and facilitate the child's active participation in the community... and that the child achieves the fullest possible social integration and individual development. (United Nations 1989, Article 23)

Despite the move towards integration initiated by the Warnock Report in 1978, many children with disability continue to be educated in special schools. The percentage of pupils attending such schools in England varies between none in the Isles of Scilly and 2.4 per cent in some areas of London (DfEE 1997). Thus, developing participatory skills with young people with disability is made more difficult because many opportunities for social integration are denied when these children are educated in special schools separate from their peers. Special schools and the staff working in them consequently have a particularly complex task to ensure that they engender self-confidence in young people with disability in order that they feel valued and able to have their voice heard.

DEVELOPING PARTICIPATORY SKILLS

Young people with a disability are young people first and the same rights bestowed upon all children should be available to them. Knowledge and understanding of human rights in school is all the more important for the young person with disability as they will enter a world where they will have to struggle to be heard and to ensure that they gain equal access to environments and conditions suitable to their needs.

The Council of Europe Recommendation on Teaching and Learning about Human Rights in Schools (1985) identifies the skills that are associated with understanding and supporting human rights. For the purposes of this chapter the following skill recommendations are highlighted:

Intellectual skills

- associated with written and oral expression including the ability to listen and discuss, and to defend one's opinions
- skills involving judgement such as the collection and examination of material from various sources, including the mass media, and the ability to analyse it and to arrive at fair and balanced conclusions
- the identification of bias, prejudice, stereotypes and discrimination.

Social skills

- recognising and accepting differences
- establishing positive and non-oppressive personal relationships resolving conflict in a non-violent way
- taking responsibility
- participating in decisions
- understanding the mechanisms for the protection of human rights at local, regional European and world levels

(Starkey 1991, p.258)

These intellectual and social skills are essential elements in the education of pupils with disability and the case study below describes how they can be developed within the special school environment. The Council of Europe document also identifies the importance of the climate of the school and writes that:

> democracy is best learned in a democratic setting where participation is encouraged, where views can be expressed openly and discussed, where there is freedom of expression for pupils and teachers and where there is fairness and justice. An appropriate climate is therefore an essential complement to effective learning about human rights. (Starkey 1991)

Young people at present educated within segregated provision must be empowered to develop a strong voice if the level of social oppression they currently experience in the community and in later life is to be significantly diminished and even eradicated. Awareness of issues concerning their human rights will facilitate this process.

CASE STUDY: THE SCHOOL CONTEXT

The school is a co-educational, all-age special school for two hundred young people with a diverse range of disabilities that include learning, emotional and physical disabilities and serves a large district of a major city. The main catchment area contains numerous families whose members have experienced long-term unemployment, poor service provision and some extreme levels of deprivation. The school at one time had the highest percentage of children in the county requiring some level of social services involvement. A significant aspect is the unfortunate frequent victimisation of young people attending the school within the neighbourhood. The following incidents were reported in 1996.

> Jimmy, a 12-year-old boy with learning and physical disabilities, was walking across a zebra crossing in his neighbourhood. A group of youths pushed him to the ground and kicked him. One youth stamped on his arm until he broke it. Jimmy needed major surgery to repair the physical damage.
>
> Barbara, a young adult with learning difficulties, walks to work every day and when it rains, local youths throw bags of flour over her. She also experiences constant sexual harassment.
>
> Lisa has cerebral palsy and a learning disability. Her twin sister is able-bodied. Lisa would like to attend the local youth club with her sister, but there is no access for wheelchair users and some local youths take delight in pushing Lisa off the pavement into the road. Lisa has become too afraid and disheartened. Each week her sister takes home a can of Coke for her from the youth club.

Similar experiences have also been highlighted in the Norah Fry Research Centre report, *Crime against People with Learning Difficulties* (1993) which states:

> the types of victimisation experienced…include harassment, verbal abuse, theft, simple assault, abduction, arson, indecent assault and rape. (Williams 1993, p.11)

The school was reorganised by the LEA during the time covered by this case study; a process which was challenging to all concerned. The school had been designated as a special school for children with moderate learning difficulties, and had in addition a high percentage of pupils with significant emotional and behavioural difficulties. The school buildings and grounds had suffered years of vandalism and neglect and there was a need for quality resourcing that would enhance the learning experience and self-esteem of the young people. As more pupils were referred to the school the LEA recommended that the secondary-aged students be transferred in 1993 to an adjacent building previously functioning as a school for secondary-aged pupils with physical difficulties. Twenty of these physically impaired students still remained, however, as their needs were judged to be too extreme for them to be moved to mainstream schools with the rest of their peers. Thus these 20 physically impaired students joined with the secondary-aged pupils with moderate learning, emotional and behavioural difficulties to create a new department. Movement between the two sites was fluid, however, which meant facilities in the original school building had to be adapted for the physically disabled students as is outlined below. The work described in this chapter was initiated in the original school but was continued and developed by some of the same students in what was a new and challenging context.

INITIAL STAGES

In 1992 some young people with learning difficulties and some concerned teachers from the school initiated a project that has led to significant changes in the attitudes, behaviour and environment within their school community and more recently also within their local community. The project was founded on the principles of equal opportunities for the young people and their right to be actively involved in decision making through democratic processes, consultation and ownership.

At that time the school was involved in the process of formulating an equal opportunities policy. It was recognised that effective implementation of the policy was only possible if all members of the school community had a clear understanding of, and a commitment to, its principles. Relevant in-service training sessions were organised for the staff.

Responding to the curriculum

As a result many aspects of the curriculum were developed to create a context for awareness raising and implementation with the pupils. For example within the English curriculum for Key Stage Four (ages 14–16) there was a focus on equality of opportunity. Pupils studied such texts as *The Diary of Anne Frank, A Kestrel for a Knave, The Poetry of War 1914–1918, Dr Jekyll and Mr Hyde.* All of these texts evoked discussions around acts of racism, sexism, segregation, victimisation and bullying. A key vocabulary emerged which became commonly understood and used when addressing equal opportunities issues including such words as: fairness; rights; safety; feelings; respect; environment; sharing; differences; the same.

Through science, the pupils considered such environmental issues as litter, recycling, materials and their use. Health and safety issues were addressed in a mini-enterprise scheme focusing on protective clothing and conditions of work. Personal and Social Education tackled issues around relationships, respect and rights for the individual.

Responding to the physical environment of the school

The school community and its buildings experienced a high level of vandalism, graffiti and harassment generated by its own members and by members of the local community. Within the school, the physical environment was in an extremely poor state of repair. This became clearer to the pupils when they were able to visit some of the local schools as part of their English curriculum work. They began to note that their own school did not compare favourably in terms of the environment and the learning resources. One pupil commented:

> The showers are in a disgusting state. They are not cleaned properly, there are no locks on the doors, no soap is provided and the paint is peeling off the walls. (Sarah, aged 14 years)

The classrooms were small, poorly furnished, with inadequate physical and learning resources. There was an underlying feeling of isolation, anger and frustration that manifested itself in frequent incidents of verbal and physical abuse by pupils directed at peers and staff. This often resulted in disrupted lessons and low expectations of behaviour and achievements.

The 14 and 15-year-old pupils initiated a media project entitled 'The Video Box' which involved conducting a survey of the school environment. Their work included a broad range of methods and resources according to the nature of the concerns expressed and the learning disabilities experienced by the particular pupils. They produced questionnaires for staff and pupils, took still photographs and used a video camera to film areas of the school buildings and the playgrounds. The outcome of the survey was of no surprise to them. On a scale of one to five (one being very poor), not one area of the school scored above two. Photographs were displayed; pupils across the age phases were interviewed and expressed their dissatisfaction at the condition of the school, suggesting that this could possibly adversely affect pupil behaviour and attitudes. There was also a feeling of resignation, that 'nothing would change, no one takes any notice of what we say anyway'. Having collated the evidence, they wanted to know how they could effect the changes they wanted. They felt that the voices of those most concerned had a right to be heard.

It seemed that the equal opportunities policy statement was not reflected in practice and was in danger of becoming pure rhetoric. There needed to be a democratically elected, representative body of pupils that was formally recognised and involved in the consultative and decision-making processes. With the help of a group of concerned teachers, a school council was proposed and established, with two members democratically elected by secret ballot from the primary phase and two from each of the secondary year groups. A teacher, school governor and learning support assistant were invited to assist and support the council. In mainstream school councils, pupil autonomy is of primary importance with adults attending only when specifically invited. In the context of a special school for young people with learning disabilities, some support from staff was needed to develop levels of personal autonomy.

Once elected the council agreed a constitution that laid down its purpose, aims and structure, with clear guidelines on the code of conduct and procedures for meetings. Minutes were issued to the year representatives who would then feed back to their tutor groups. Involving all the pupils in the processes of council work and procedures encouraged a continuing interest in, and concern for, the issues raised. The governor representative was to ensure that information reached the full governing body.

The council considered the findings of 'The Video Box' survey and proposed that the school environment and challenging pupil behaviour would be the main issues to target. It was seen that the two were in fact interrelated and one could not be considered without the other, but further evidence needed to be gathered. This work was undertaken by the pupils who presented evidence for their case. This helped them to identify some key issues to be addressed.

A report and photographs were submitted to the governing body illustrating and describing the poor state of repair in the classrooms and main entrance, the inadequate showering and toilet facilities, the graffiti covering the walls and the amount of litter and broken glass that were found both in the school and outside in the surrounding play areas. The school council invited a member of the Governers' buildings sub-committee to join the next council meeting, the outcomes of which were:

- an agreed budget allocation for the renovation of the showers and toilet areas
- an agreement that the caretaker would be asked to inspect the playgrounds and clear any broken glass before the children arrived
- an agreement that litter bins would be purchased and placed around the school.

In turn the school council agreed to:

- initiate a litter campaign by designing posters and spot-checking areas
- through presentations and discussions, raise the issue of pupils' responsibility for the conditions and care of the repainted areas (no graffiti or silly behaviour in the toilets or showers)
- invite pupils to submit their preferred colour schemes and specifications for the new fitments.

The pupils returned after the holidays to find the playground cleared of glass and the improvements completed. This was the first major achievement that gave credibility to the democratic processes the pupils had been involved in, and allowed management to recognise that pupils were capable of making valid contributions that enhanced their learning experiences and environment.

RESPONDING TO CONCERNS ABOUT THE SOCIAL RELATIONSHIPS IN THE SCHOOL

The pupils themselves continued to take pride in and care of the newly refurbished environment. The school council moved on to address the issue of unacceptable behaviour. The pupils had identified bullying, in a variety of forms, as a major concern. Incidents described included name-calling, sexual harassment, verbal and physical abuse, exclusion from the group and damage to personal property.

The following are examples of pupils' comments:

> People are always teasing people about their lives and making fun of their families. (Mary, aged 10)

> People are threatening to each other and they steal my things. (John, aged 12)

> I hate it when people gossip about people in school. (Peter, aged 12)

The school council launched the project by producing and distributing large posters that drew attention to acts of bullying and encouraged victims to report incidents to council members or a trusted adult. A core of interested pupils established a monitoring system that supported both the victim and the perpetrator. It was recognised that many perpetrators were themselves victims of abusive acts within their homes or community. Through long discussions, pupils, staff and parents worked together to produce a behaviour policy with agreed systems of sanctions and rewards. It was also agreed that a clear message had to be given that persistent and serious acts of violence and bullying were obvious child protection issues and would be referred to the appropriate agencies. Fighting in the playground was also raised as an issue. Council members filmed several lunch-time sessions to monitor the frequency and severity of incidents and interviewed pupils of different ages. One pupil commented:

> We should have a room where children can go when they felt angry or aggressive, hitting punchbags would be better than hitting each other. Could we convert one of the classrooms? (Simon, aged 13)

Many complained of:
- being bored
- having nothing to do
- not having equipment to play with so we get into trouble
- not having lunch-time clubs.

In response the school council initiated 'The Playground Games Project'. Pupils entered a competition to design a playground game that could be painted onto the playground walls or floor. Members of the local probation service were involved in selecting the winning entries and themselves undertook to realise the designs. Once completed, 'The Playground Games Project' was incorporated into PE lessons, where the pupils learnt how to play the games. The school council then approached the Governors' Finance Committee and requested a budget allocation to purchase playground apparatus and equipment. This was agreed and pupils took responsibility for the supervision of the equipment. A council member suggested that:

> School council members will run the music club for the younger children. We will provide the tapes and organise the room. We would have to have a teacher to help us but we will organise it. (Susan, aged 15)

With staff support, lunch-time clubs were established and well supported by pupils. Over a period of time, evidence was gathered and staff and pupils agreed that the levels of difficult behaviour at break-times had been significantly reduced.

In 1994 the LEA reviewed provision in the school and reported as follows on the work of the school council:

> The School Council, is a valuable initiative. There is evidence of responsibility and strong pupil involvement in decisions and actions in relation to the school environment. Such activity helps children to learn about living in society.

The school council was now firmly established and valued as a forum for the pupils. It was beginning to effect change within the school community.

THE AMALGAMATION: RAISING AWARENESS ABOUT PHYSICAL DISABILITY

As described above, the secondary school pupils were amalgamated with another school for pupils with learning and physical disabilities which resulted in pupils sharing both sites for particular activities. The school council was fully consulted in the assessment of the institutional needs of the new school, as concern had been expressed regarding the physical environment and modifications that would be required for wheelchairs.

Additional members were elected who were wheelchair users and the council made several recommendations that were accepted by the Governors' sub-committee for building improvements and adaptations to furniture. Comments from pupils included:

- we would have to provide ramps for the wheelchairs
- we would need special toilets around the school

- what will we do if they have an epileptic fit?
- some of the playground games are very rough. We would have to be more careful. We might hurt them.

A further 'Playground Games Project' was initiated and new designs submitted for adventure playground equipment that would be fully accessible to all physically disabled pupils. The actual production of the apparatus was to be carried out by inmates of the local prison, thus developing links from previous projects. The school council also requested an assessment of the playground areas by the occupational therapist to ensure that existing surfaces met with safety standards. Disability awareness training had also been an issue for staff and pupils. Many learning experiences arose naturally in a variety of contexts and the principles of the equal opportunities policy statements applied to the new members of the community. Changes in the pupils' language use occurred and derogatory terms such as 'spastic', 'cripple' and 'divvy' were frowned upon and discouraged by the pupils. Secondary pupils established disability awareness workshops for the primary pupils in preparation for working alongside pupils with learning and physical disabilities in the secondary phase.

The following comments illustrate the developing level of awareness that had emerged through the process of amalgamation in relation to the young people with physical disabilities:

> Their handicap hasn't spoilt their brain in some cases, so they are cleverer than us. This would be good for the school and our pupils. It would help us to improve. (Peter, aged 14)

> We are able bodied and can help them physically. They can talk to us about their lives. We can talk to them. They can help us with our work. (Teresa, aged 10)

> If they join us in PE it would make us more caring and more thoughtful. (Tom, aged 12)

> Being together would be teaching the people who are making fun of handicapped people how they feel and we could teach people how to help handicapped people. (Hannah, aged 16)

An OFSTED inspector observed one of the weekly disability workshops. James, a young person with cerebral palsy, and his able-bodied friend Alan, who has a learning disability, demonstrated to a group of 11-year-olds how utensils and plates were modified to assist James at the dining table. Supported by his friend, James answered the numerous questions that were asked about his physical impairment and offered them the use of his manual wheelchair, an offer that was eagerly accepted by the able-bodied youngsters. After the session, the inspector commented on the good quality of the learning experience and the empathy shared amongst the pupils. He reported that he had not experienced disability workshops in schools before and that they could be valuable in developing mutual respect for others.

Further sessions gave pupils the opportunity to discuss learning and behavioural difficulties, hearing impairment and epilepsy. Staff and pupils shared the disability awareness training.

The school council had steered a variety of significant initiatives that gave the pupils a sense of ownership and shared responsibility for the quality of their learning experiences. OFSTED summarised the situation in their report:

> Pupils are listened to with respect and they learn to listen to and respect the views of others. They discuss with growing maturity issues of citizenship, personal rights and responsibilities. The older pupils show sensitivity to the rights of the disadvantaged. There is an active school council in the secondary area of the school and this encourages the pupils to express their opinions and helps them to see that their ideas are valued. (OFSTED 1997)

FUTURE DIRECTIONS: THE DISABILITY EQUALITY PROJECT

It is encouraging that the work of the school council can now be extended through its involvement in a new initiative – the Youth Start Disability Equality Project. This project, which is supported by the LEA, aims to ensure that policy developments in the direction of inclusive education are complemented by appropriate activities to challenge the discrimination, negative stereotyping and harassment of young people with disabilities of the kind described earlier in this chapter. The work will involve young disabled people through supporting the development of positive self-image and the confidence and ability to challenge discrimination when it occurs. These same young people will also be involved in working with non-disabled young people to facilitate their understanding of disability as an equal opportunities issue. Resources from the LEA (some of which are derived from the Regeneration Fund) include the funding of a full-time disabled project worker who will be based in the school. The students on the school council will be able to liaise and develop their own initiatives on behalf of all the children in the school with ongoing support from this paid worker.

CONCLUSION

The process described above reveals how important it is for young people and particularly young people with disabilities to feel valued and to be able to express their thoughts and feelings about the experiences they have in school and in the community. The case study provides an example of a way forward which embodies the principles of inclusion and attempts to enhance the experiences of young people within a segregated setting. The organisation of the school council allowed for the views of young people with disability to be heard and valued. Through people actively listening and responding to pupils' perceptions of the effectiveness of the education provision, major changes ensued. The enhancement of the environment, the curriculum and the pastoral system within the school came about in consultation with pupils. Through the process of involvement the young people have grown in self-confidence and are in a better position to meet the challenges of the wider community from which they have been removed. They have become increasingly more aware of their entitlement to be educated with their mainstream peers, recognised and valued as members of their communities.

Educationalists working in the field of special education have a complex task ahead of them as the desegregationalist and anti-discriminatory political environment develops and grows in strength. One of the major issues is that of funding as pupils in special schools receive a much higher level of funding than those in mainstream comprehensives. There are other dilemmas, summarised by Porter (1995, p.302) in Table 5.1. His table clarifies the conceptual dilemmas which local authorities, schools and individual teachers are struggling with in order to ensure that young people with disabilities achieve their entitlement to inclusive education. He contrasts the traditional and the inclusionary approaches to the organisation of educational provision.

Table 5.1 Traditional and inclusionary approaches

Traditional approach	Inclusionary approach
Focus on student	Focus on classroom
Assessment of student by specialist	Examine teaching/learning factors
Diagnostic/prescriptive outcomes	Collaborative problem-solving
Student programme	Strategies for teachers
Placement in appropriate programme	Adaptive and supportive classroom environment

Source: Porter (1995, p.302)

Walker (1995) provides a clear distinction between the terms used stating that segregation tends to emphasise categorisation of the disabled person, integration emphasises changing the disabled person, whilst inclusion moves us towards changing schools and organisations.

This level of change will require considerable strength and forbearance from young people with disabilities, supported by teachers and other professionals with a clear vision of inclusive education systems. They will need to have the self-knowledge and self-confidence to be able to voice their thoughts and feelings and to be able to challenge society for its discrimination against them as disabled people. They will need to move from the relative security and safety of their school into the local community and beyond to speak out with confidence about their experience of life and within the framework of a democratic process bring about further awareness and understanding for themselves as disabled young people. Let's hope that their voice will be heard.

REFERENCES

Cooper, P. (1993) *Effective Schools for Disaffected Students: Integration and Segregation*. London: Routledge.

DfEE (Department for Education and Employment) (1994) *Code of Practice on the Identification and Assessment of Special Educational Needs*. London: HMSO.

DfEE (Department for Education and Employment) (1997) *Statistical Bulletin: SENs in England*. January 1996. Issue No.12.

DES (Department for Education and Science) (1978) *Special Educational Needs*. (Warnock Report). London: HMSO.

Department of Health (1989) *The Children Act*. London: HMSO.

Frank, A. (1989) *The Diary of Anne Frank*. London: Pan Books.

Fuller, S. (1990) *The Poetry of War 1914–1918*. London: BBC; Longman.

Hines, B. (1968) *A Kestrel for a Knave*. London: Joseph.

Inner London Education Authority (ILEA) (1985) *Educational Opportunities for All?* (The Fish Report). London: ILEA.

Lewis, A. (1995) *Children's Understanding of Disability*. London: Routledge.

OFSTED (1997) *Reports on Schools: July 1997*. Internet: http://www.ofsted.gov.uk/ofsted.htm

Organisation for Economic Co-operation and Development (OECD) (1997) *Education and Equity in OECD Countries*. Paris: OECD.

Porter, J. (1995) 'Organisation of schooling: achieving access and quality through inclusion.' *Prospects 25*, 2, 299–309.

Potts, P. (1986) 'Equal opportunities: the fourth dimension.' *Forum 29*, 1, 13–15.

Stevenson, R.L. (1925) *Dr Jekyll and Mr Hyde*. London: Dent.

Starkey, H. (1991) *The Challenge of Human Rights Education*. London: Cassell.

Thomas, G. (1997) 'Inclusive schools for an inclusive society.' *British Journal of Special Education 24*, 3, 103–7.

United Nations (1989) Convention on the Rights of the Child.

Wade, B. and Moore, M. (1993) *Experiencing Special Education*. Buckingham: Open University Press.

Walker, D. (1995) *Postmodernity, Inclusion and Partnership*. Unpublished M.Ed dissertation: Exeter University.

Williams, C. (1993) *Crime Against People With Learning Disabilities*. Bristol: Norah Fry Research Unit.

CHAPTER SIX

Education after Auschwitz
A Task for Human Rights Education[1]

Hanns-Fred Rathenow and Norbert H. Weber

INTRODUCTION

More than 50 years after the end of World War II, it is remarkable to see how the film *Schindler's List* — like the TV mini-series *Holocaust* — has led to a broad discussion in Germany's media and schools. Despite this discussion, it is still questionable whether our collective consciousness has responded to Adorno who writes '...that Auschwitz should not happen again' (Adorno 1967, p.111). Our observations of education both inside and outside schools indicate that real learning about this issue will only take place through active experience and participation.

Due to the increasing passage of time since the era of National Socialism and genocide, this subject is seen by students and even by teachers simply as distant history. This creates a challenge for those developing appropriate curriculum and teaching/learning styles, in other words a pedagogy which responds to these historical and political issues. Such a pedagogy should increase the students' awareness of this era and help them come to grips with the issue at both a cognitive and an emotional level. Only then is there a chance that young people will accept the era of National Socialism as a part of their own history. It is with this thought in mind that Germany's former president, Richard von Weizsaecker (1985) pointed out that 'Youths... are not responsible for what occurred then, but they are responsible for what is derived from this history'.

Such a pedagogy requires a variety of teaching methods. For example, youths might research the history of National Socialism in their region or town (searching for evidence), study biographies of people persecuted by the Nazi

---

1   We thank Marco Parizek of the Institut fuer Fachdidaktiken at the Technical University of Berlin for many of his thoughts incorporated into the section on methodology.

regime, visit concentration camp memorials, or interview contemporary witnesses about everyday life during the Third Reich. Whilst the memories of such witnesses are subject to the vagaries of time, nonetheless they should not be ignored. In the words of Christa Wolf, 'The past is not dead; it is not even gone. We separate ourselves from it, and pretend not to know...' (Wolf 1979, p.9).

The goal of this chapter is therefore to encourage forms of participatory learning and to emphasise the significance of historical and political pedagogy as part of human rights education.

THE GOALS OF HOLOCAUST EDUCATION

Looking at the guidelines for teaching history and social studies in the states of Germany, one can see an emphasis on the cognitive elements in teaching history. However if we wish to promote democratic behaviour through teaching we need to engage with the emotional aspects of learning because

> Auschwitz is not a subject which can be understood and discussed within the normal constraints of a school structure. Auschwitz can not be taught within the curriculum in the same way as any other subject, such as quadratic equations or hexameters. (Dudek 1989, p.114)

The type of experience which one has when visiting a memorial site can provide the key to a different (subjective) reality of Auschwitz. This insight cannot be gained or worked out only in the classroom situation. At a memorial site the students can learn through experience, by for example participating in conservation of the site. This is an active form of coming to grips with history, which makes the experience easier to handle. This pedagogical approach attempts to overcome the separation of school and life, theory and practice, by encouraging projects and activities within active learning approaches. These might include role playing, sketches, field trips and workshops, which can enrich children's cognitive and emotional learning.

The willingness to defend human dignity, wherever it might be violated, is a demand voiced in the American Declaration of Independence and in Abraham Lincoln's Gettysburg Address. It is also a principle of western European, particularly French, British and, since World War II, German, political pedagogy. Text books and lectures on their own are not sufficient to ensure that this principle is understood. What is required is that students and teachers identify and examine the technical, social and political developments which led to Auschwitz. At the same time they need to recognise those aspects of the contemporary world which might lead again to totalitarianism – or even to a new Auschwitz.

It must be recognised that the Holocaust was the logical product of a rigid rationalism, and therefore could occur again today at a different place and under different political-economic, social and ideological conditions. It should be remembered that Auschwitz was the result of a trend in the history of German thought within the European enlightenment, whereby the separation of subject and object led to the transformation of an entire people into objects. The ultimate expression of this can be seen in the book-keeping performed at the concentration camps and death camps. In this sense, one must agree with Adorno (1967) who expresses the fear that civilisation can create and intensify uncivilised behaviour.

METHODOLOGY

If teachers have the responsibility of not just analysing contemporary political events, but also of changing students' understanding and attitudes, then this encompasses – much more than previously practised – coming to grips with our collective consciousness. Such an approach to historical and political education, based on the principles of human rights, requires time and patience. Only if the school provides this time, can it meet these aims. It should be remembered that the original Greek definition of school included time for leisure, peace, and pause in work. Today's schools, by contrast, are often factories of learning, where tailored knowledge is conveyed.

Those involved in Holocaust Education frequently face the dilemma that such education must encourage communication and discussion which can conflict with traditional teaching methods. Today's classrooms are often characterised by 'great uniformity and teacher domination of the classroom in all types of schools and subject areas' (Hage 1985, p.147). Indeed the 'chalk and talk' or lecturing approach is used disproportionally more often in the social sciences, compared to other subjects. This shows how difficult it is to achieve more student participation and involvement with democratic processes. We present below some methods for the teaching of historical and political subject matter which in our opinion are particularly suited for handling controversial issues including the rise of National Socialism and its subsequent outcomes.

CREATIVE APPROACHES TO CONTROVERSIAL ISSUES WITHIN THE SUBJECTS OF HISTORY AND POLITICS

Historical and political pedagogy in its traditional form involves conveying historical information through a variety of sources. These may include pictures, photos, particular texts such as legal documents, treaties, letters and reports by witnesses. Modern history textbooks present a great variety of such material, and attempt to keep their own commentary to a minimum. Few texts encourage students to question, discuss and come to their own understanding of events. Our examples aim to do this.

Brainstorming the ideas of the group

This method can be used at the beginning of a project. Take as an example 'The Persecution of Jews under National Socialism'. Ask each student to complete the following sentences on a card or small piece of paper:

- 'The Holocaust' interests me because...
- I would like to learn more about...
- Something I haven't understood about 'The Holocaust' is...
- I am not at all interested in...

The answers, which can be collected on the blackboard, give the teacher an overview of the students' interests, the gaps in their knowledge, and an insight into misinformation or prejudices in the class. For example: 'I always wanted to know why Jews are so rich'. This can provide a basis for a class project which relates the historical realities to the interests of the students. Participatory learning can then be encouraged through:

- co-operative planning
- reference to the historical realities
- activity-based learning
- interdisciplinary learning
- product orientation
- group and process-oriented realisation.

Acrostic

Acrostic (Haas 1997) offers an entertaining and creative means of coming to grips with emotionally charged historical terminology. The task involves taking terms such as 'National Socialism', 'Third Reich', 'Persecution of Jews', or 'Holocaust' and arranging the letters vertically. Students must then attach words they associate with the term, horizontally. This then becomes a different method for brainstorming collaboratively. Figure 6.1 illustrates the use of such an approach by student teachers at the Technical University of Berlin.

HELL

H**O**PELESSNESS

KI**L**LING

B**O**NES

BOX **C**ARS

ARREST

DO **U**BT

GA **S**CHAMBER

RESIS**T**ANCE

Figure 6.1 Acrostic

Poetry

After World War II Adorno remarked that it would be barbaric to write a poem after Auschwitz. Later a reading of Celan's 'Dirge' (Celan 1952) motivated Adorno to retract this, reasoning that 'The burning anguish has just as much right to be expressed as martyrs have to scream; for this reason it would be wrong not to write poetry in the aftermath of Auschwitz' (Zych and Mueller-Ott 1993, p.10).

Poetry is one way for teachers to enable students to express their confusion about Auschwitz. In this exercise students sit in a circle (without desks) and are asked to write a poem about the issue under discussion. Each student writes just one word which she associates with the subject on a piece of paper and passes the paper to the student on her left. Each student then writes two words below the first, which if possible should relate to what the student to her right wrote on the line above. The papers keep moving to the left until three words on the third line, four on the fourth, five on the fifth and six words have been written on the sixth line of the papers. The seventh student writes only five words in the seventh line, and the number of words declines with each successive student until the eleventh student writes only one word in the eleventh line. Finally, all the poems, which may have been composed simultaneously, are read out loud to the class. For example:

> Horror
> Has a
> Name – Adolf Hitler.
> He murdered his critics,
> But he had his supporters
> Including – finally – all the German people.
> Remember, Hitlers are found everywhere.
> So be wary. Please!
> Act! Don't hide.
> Not war!
> Peace.

The aim is to allow students to express themselves subjectively and emotionally, thus eliciting what the students know, their prejudices, misinformation, and questions.

Visit to a memorial site

Memorial sites, particularly former concentration camps, are convincingly authentic because they physically represent the past. Students are presented with a learning environment with genuine artefacts rather than the secondary source they meet in a classroom. They are confronted with 'silent witnesses', which can give them the feeling of being more than spectators. Such an experience can motivate students to investigate the terminology and political and historical contexts. Although very often memorial sites are graveyards, they are also places of learning.

However, the teacher needs to exercise caution. There is a danger of students assuming that the reconstruction represents the totality of the whole event and the victims' experiences. In fact visitors far too often ignore the elements of National Socialism which are not on display at the site and so fail to understand the historical context.

The tables provided at the end of this chapter are intended to help address this problem.

When planning a Holocaust study programme, it is important to keep in mind the organisational questions, and also the personal effect of the visit on both the students and teachers. It is particularly important for the students to know something about National Socialism before they visit the memorial. A checklist of questions for the teacher might be:

- What knowledge and opinions do the students have of the Holocaust?
- What are the special interests of the students?
- What do they already know about National Socialism? Have they visited other memorial sites?
- Are there any personal histories relating to the period of National Socialism within their families or peer groups?
- Have the students been prepared to take a critical look and come to grips with their own history?
- What pedagogical and psychological problems could occur among the students during the visit to the memorial site?

Interviewing witnesses

Ido H. B. Abram once said it is a mistake to assume that horror will not repeat itself if it is described extensively and in detail. If extreme violence is given too much attention, this can make 'lesser' horrors seem not so bad after all (Abram and Heyl 1996). Our experience shows that the best way forward is by working with biographies, in particular the lives of ordinary people. For example, it can be very helpful to examine the abuse Jewish students were forced to accept in German school classes during the late 1930s. This means that 'Education after Auschwitz' needs to include education about events leading up to Auschwitz, and needs to avoid discussion only of the extreme acts of violence. One of the most fruitful forms of historical and political study is 'grass-roots history' – looking at everyday life. This may encompass interviewing former victims who survived, or ordinary people who went along with the system as observers participating at the time. This can also include discussions with perpetrators who share the guilt of the National Socialist era. These discussions can help reconstruct the time period from the perspective of the people who were repressed, arrested, or forced to submit. Young people are increasingly interested in talking to people who actually experienced these events. Contemporary witnesses can particularly enrich a discussion with members of their grandchildren's and great-grandchildren's generation because they are able to recall the names and tell the stories of some of the unnamed millions of Holocaust victims. Along with the 'silent witnesses' we encounter in concentration camp memorial sites and in the history books available, interviews with contemporary witnesses can provide a view of the Holocaust which is based on both the historical detail and individual experience and impressions.

Dramatic sketches

Dramatic sketches offer an original means for students to communicate a subject matter amongst themselves and with an audience. The goal is not verbal communication, but an attempt to find new means of communication including body language such as gestures and mime, rhythm and the use of scenery, colours, costumes and props.

First the students need to be familiar with the source materials available (pictures, poems, key words, caricatures, stories, source materials, colours, objects, music, etc.). Then they need to develop an approach and decide how they want to use these materials, and plan as a group how best to present their own interpretation of the subject matter using as many means of communication as possible.

The goal is to awaken in the members of the audience an interest in the subject. The students should express their own interpretation of the subject matter using their artistic and acting abilities. The teacher takes a subordinate role in this process. She starts the project, provides support when needed, and helps the students stay on track by ensuring that the different scenes fit together (Rogers 1983).

Taking on a role

The students first examine a famous picture, for example of Jews in Vienna sweeping a sidewalk, under the watchful eyes of secret police, Hitler Youths and passers-by. The students are then asked to assume the roles of different people in the picture by taking on a chosen character's perspective. Based on the recognisable gestures and body language and their own knowledge of the participants, students try to find the character's perspective and to understand and empathise with their character's thoughts and behaviour (Breit 1991). The object is to express the emotions depicted in the picture such as pleasure, pain, grief, or fear, and to develop a small sketch which uses a minimum of verbal communication. The characters should freeze as in the photo at a particular point in the sketch. Students can work in parallel groups on the same picture or on different pictures. During the final presentation, the parallel groups assume the roles of audience and critics. The review should take these questions into consideration:

- What did I see?
- How did it affect me?
- What did I not understand?

- What should be improved?

In a second step, the students write role biographies for the different characters, which discuss the person's past, present and future life. This allows students to combine their knowledge of the historical and political situation with their own subjective impression of the characters. Some questions follow which may be useful when writing role biographies.

- What function does this person/do I have in the scene?
- How does the person/do I feel in the scene?
- Who are my friends in this scene? Why? How do I treat them?
- Who are my enemies in this scene? Why? How do I treat them?
- What processes of change are taking place in the scene? Why?

Understanding status

The goal of this activity (Johnstone 1993) is to make the students aware of the need to reflect on their actions or behaviour in dealing with other people. Power and status can adversely influence our actions. Below we present an exercise which examines the roles of dominant and submissive people such as a supervisor and an employee assigned to her.

The students form pairs. One student assumes the role of king, the other is his servant. The servant has to fulfil all the king's wishes. The teacher must make it clear that no 'mean' or painful wishes can be made. After a brief period of play, the roles are switched. Afterwards while sharing their reflections on the experience, each participant is asked to say which role they preferred. It would be wrong to assume the students would feel most comfortable in the role of king and dislike their forced submission in the servant role. On the contrary, the servants are often pleased to fulfil their king's wishes because this allows them to feel they are important to somebody. The kings often have trouble in determining what they want. At a metacognitive level, the students need to consider how satisfying it can be to simply follow orders and feel they are needed. Only later should this concept be transferred to the context of people from the National Socialist era.

Sculpturing a statue

Once the students have acquired a differentiated knowledge of National Socialism, they can be asked to create a statue (Boal 1979) on the topic of 'National Socialism', 'Persecution of the Jews', or 'The Holocaust'.

The aim is to allow students to experience historical events as if they themselves were there. They should draw on their own creativity to try to answer the question 'What would happen if...?'. This creative response is more important than the process of displaying their statues. The sculptured statues represent a frozen point in time at a key point in a course of events. For example students might choose to portray the behaviour of a Berlin janitor in 1944. How would he have reacted if he opened the door to his attic and discovered a group of Jews hiding from their oppressors?

The students form pairs as they did for the status improvisation and decide which of the partners will be the statue and who will be the sculptor. Neither of the partners is allowed to speak during the creative process. The partners should take their time. Traditional sculpture is a slow contemplative process. The sculptor is not permitted to touch certain parts of the statue's body which should be specified in advance. The sculptor's responsibility is to situate the statue in the scene as a whole so that any outsider immediately knows:

- who the statue is depicting
- what the statue is trying to express
- what function the statue serves within the depicted event.

The sculptor demonstrates the desired facial expression which the statue should try to imitate. The sculptor is not permitted to touch the statue's face because this is an intimate space. The sculptor can place the statue in a room by itself or in a group of other statues. The different sculptors are not permitted to talk to each other. Once all the sculptors have finished, they take a new look at their results. They can discuss their overall impression, conjecture about the individual statues and what they are trying to express through them. Some sculptors may want to make a few corrections.

Later the sculptors might try to create an 'anti-picture'. They can change the gestures, facial expressions and the locations of the individual statues to create a new event. These scenes should be viewed as historical or political utopias rather than as viable alternatives for people at the time.

Staging and performing texts as a sketch

The staging and performance of texts allows students to reflect on and communicate about an historical event. Subsequently they can create a new story-line relating to a time and place in the future. They can even move from the past to the present to the future (Schulz-Hageleit 1982). The negative roles (such as a concentration camp guard) present a special challenge. However, students are regularly confronted with violence in the media and even in their own personal lives, so they can be asked to accept these roles in a suitably modified form.

The students are divided into small working groups and receive texts to work with such as a poem, historical document, a headline, excerpt from an essay, etc. After several readings of the text, the students mark the most important words, expressions or sentences. Finally, each small group develops a short sketch in which each performer takes a role. This role could be taken from the text or it could be fictional. However, the sketch dialogue should only be taken from the given text. The students compensate for the lack of verbal expression by using different tones of voice, gestures, mime, props, costumes, etc. The aim is for the performances to convey their impression of the text to the audience.

When developing the sketches, students should bear in mind the following:

- It should be clear who you are
- The location depicted in the scene should be clear to the audience
- The audience should understand what is going on in the scene.

In the discussion following the sketch, the members of the audience describe their impressions; they say what they saw, understood, and felt. They also mention what they think was good, and what did not work, along with the questions they think still need to be answered.

Finally the performers answer the questions and explain how the sketch was developed. Then as a large group, comparisons are made between the initial texts and the project results. Subjective, emotional impressions are mingled with historical facts and rational argument. The teacher may need to intervene during this stage.

Reflection phase

It is absolutely essential that this method of teaching be accompanied by a period of reflection about the work and the outcomes. Misinformation needs to be corrected, prejudices need to be recognised and discussed. However, such an approach which confronts the emotional responses to the subject of National Socialism and genocide is not sufficient on its own. Learning about historical/political events requires an interplay of both the emotional and the cognitive learning processes.

PROJECT EXAMPLES

Example One: Work at the Jewish Cemetery in Breslau/Wroclaw

Jewish cemeteries can be found around the world in places where there is or was a Jewish community. The Jewish culture was put to an abrupt end wherever it came in contact with the National Socialist policy of genocide. The cemeteries in Germany and particularly in the former Eastern Bloc, Poland, the former Soviet Union and the Baltic states give silent testimony to this fact. The Jewish Cemetery in Breslau/Wroclaw offers an interesting point of focus for looking at the Jewish tradition in Europe. Many of the people buried there played an important role in the history of German and European thought. Ferdinand Lassalle was one of the founders of the German Social Democratic Party. Siegfried and Auguste Stein were the parents of the German philosopher and poet Edith Stein. She converted to Catholicism and served as an assistant to the philosopher Edmund Husserl before she died in Auschwitz in 1942. The Catholic Church has proclaimed Edith Stein to be a saint. The cemetery is also interesting because it was the scene of fighting near the end of World War II when Breslau served as a fortress. Later the cemetery decayed during the Communist era.

Since 1993, students from the Thomas-Mann-Oberschule, a comprehensive school in the Berlin district of Reinickendorf, have helped assume responsibility for the conservation of the four-hectare Jewish Cemetery grounds in Wroclaw. Their aim is to maintain awareness of the cemetery and help with the conservation work. Each year a group of 16 to 20-year-old students spend a week clearing weeds from the graves, repairing paths, and doing preparation work for stone masons. In so doing, the students are confronted with the fate of the Jewish population in Nazi Germany. Since 1995, students at a Polish high school in Wroclaw have joined the effort. As they share the physical labour, there is a chance for some of the Polish students to talk about the fate of their parents and grandparents during the Nazi occupation. German students can be shocked to learn that almost every Polish family suffered during the Nazi dictatorship. Many family members died in the war or in the Warsaw Uprising: many Poles were conscripted to perform forced labour in German industrial plants. Others were arrested as political prisoners and deported to concentration camps. The discussion of the problems in German–Polish relations has led to a number of friendships between German and Polish students.

The students have received numerous positive reactions to their work: newspapers, radio and television have reported on this German-Polish project. An official photo exhibit in both cities documents the project. Wroclaw's tiny Jewish community has demonstrated its thanks by inviting the German students to attend Shabbat.

Example Two: 'Windows for Mauthausen'

For more than 15 years the Berlin Berufsschule fuer Bau und Holzgewerbe (Trade School for Construction and Carpentry Trades) has conducted regular visits to the former concentration camp and death camp at Mauthausen (Austria). The memorial site, which is located near Linz, was liberated by American troops in 1945. Because it has still been kept in its original state, it is one of the few concentration camp memorials which has lost little of its authenticity. This applies not only to the prison barracks and the gas chambers but also to the well-preserved stone quarry where visitors can see for themselves the inhuman conditions under which the prisoners were forced to labour.

The annual field trips to the memorial site were the initiative of a teacher who wanted to do more than simply discuss the theory of National Socialism. The first visit was dedicated to the project 'Windows for Mauthausen'. This was a response to a plea from the Austrian Ministry of the Interior for help in restoring the window frames in the former prisoner barracks. The apprentices at the trade school decided to help during the period of a 14-day excursion. Since then the apprentices have performed a variety of restoration projects depending upon what has needed to be done. Over the years they have performed:

- carpentry on the doors, windows, floors and roof timbers
- electrical and sanitary work
- simple masonry or pouring of concrete.

The students usually prepare for the trip by taking part in intensive classroom discussion. The understandable psychological stress can be difficult. The apprentices show their scepticism and worries when they ask questions such as: 'Where will we sleep? Not in the former SS barracks?' or, 'Do we really have to restore a gas chamber?'. The students are afraid of nightmares or sleepless nights. They also worry that the experience at Mauthausen will put an end to their laughter, their normality, their youth. What first had seemed like an attractive class trip, now seems terrifying because they will have to sleep in the memorial grounds, in a former concentration camp. Some youths even consider staying at a youth hostel or in a tent outside the grounds. In short, contradictory feelings, disquiet and reluctance dominate the initial discussion.

Responding to the students' questions requires time which is frequently not available due to curricular demands. One way to find the time is to schedule a seminar outside the regular school setting in a place where students can articulate their thoughts and misgivings about visiting a memorial site (Fransecky 1995). Sometimes an outsider leading the sessions can make it easier for the students to reach an objective decision on whether or not to attend the field trip. By being conscious of and accepting any negative feelings, the students can help avoid suppressing their emotions or being locked in stereotypes. This is important because of the resistance many students feel toward 'anti-fascism on command'.

Experience with these field trip preparation seminars shows that the discussion can effectively alleviate the accumulated tensions and help the students feel positive about such a visit. Exploring their emotions before the visit is an important first phase. The students are not lectured or provoked into paying lip service to feelings of shock which improves the chances of reaching the students at a personal level. The final decision on whether to attend is not made until after the 'clarification phase'. In the words of one student, 'This day helped reduce my fears in respect to the trip'. Another student said after the trip:

> The emotional preparation was very important to me. Otherwise I would not have been able to stand the psychological stress.

At the end of their visit, the students were very pleased with the results of their six hours of physical labour. During their 14-day visit to the memorial site they made a visible contribution to the maintenance of the historical structure. After all, the pedagogical aim of a visit to a memorial site is not only to enhance students' factual knowledge of National Socialism, but also to allow them to find their own way of understanding and coming to terms with German history.

CONCLUSION

More than 50 years after the Holocaust, education about this event and its consequences faces radical change. The generation of the perpetrators, the victims and the bystanders will not be able to give testimony of their experience and involvement for very much longer. And yet we observe a continuous interest and search for authentic experiences by the young generation of today, which challenges traditional methods of instruction about history and politics. It is intended that the experimental teaching methods suggested in this chapter will go some way towards replicating the experiences provided by authentic witnesses, thus still making it possible to reach the emotions and sensibilities of students. This is essential as knowledge and understanding of this chapter of German/European and human history remains an indispensable prerequisite for the understanding of present society and politics.

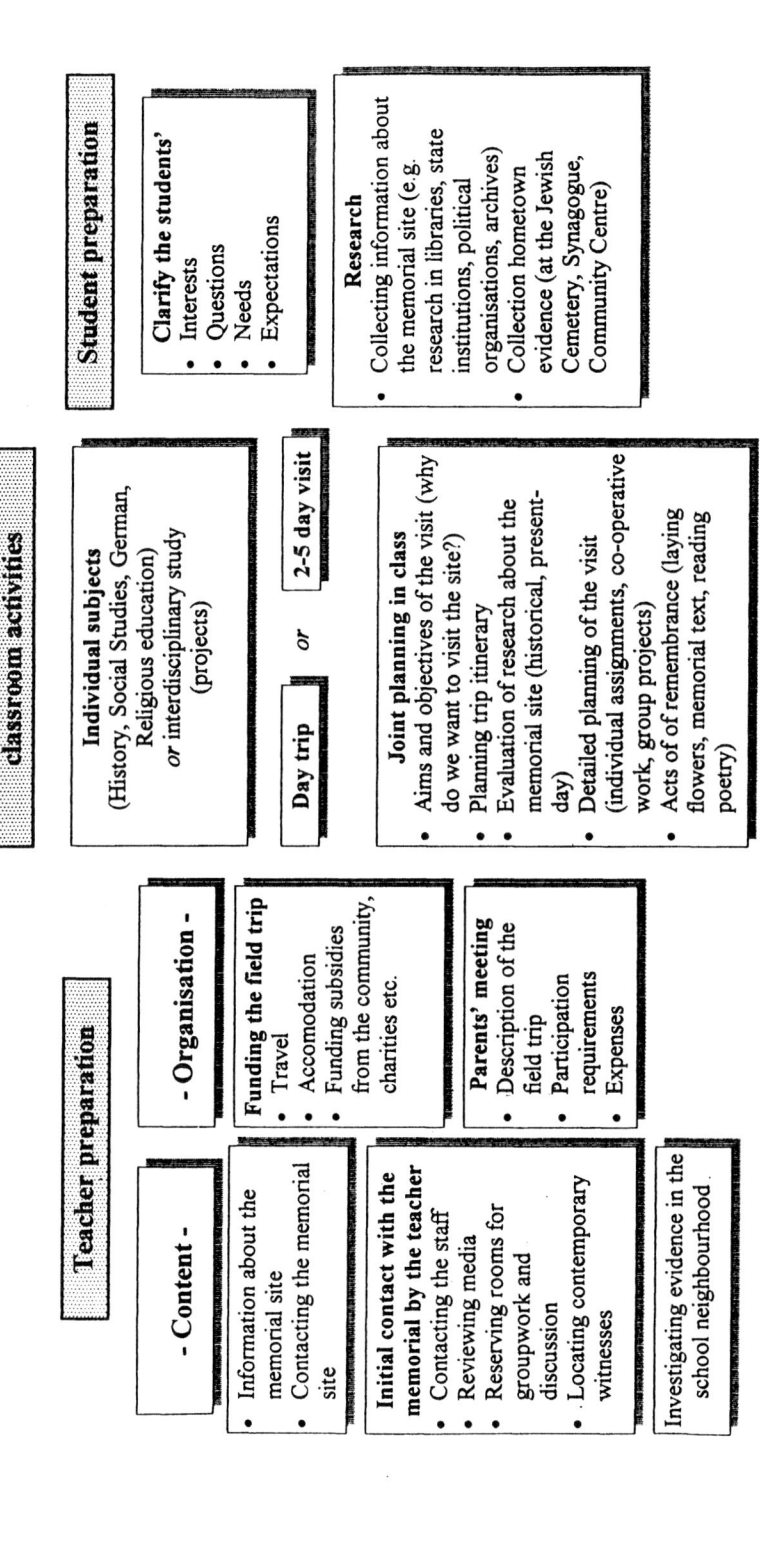

EDUCATION AFTER AUSCHWITZ 109

Student preparation

Clarify the students'
- Interests
- Questions
- Needs
- Expectations

Research
- Collecting information about the memorial site (e.g. research in libraries, state institutions, political organisations, archives)
- Collection hometown evidence (at the Jewish Cemetery, Synagogue, Community Centre)

Integration of the field trip in classroom activities

Individual subjects
(History, Social Studies, German, Religious education)
or interdisciplinary study (projects)

Day trip *or* 2-5 day visit

Joint planning in class
- Aims and objectives of the visit (why do we want to visit the site?)
- Planning trip itinerary
- Evaluation of research about the memorial site (historical, present-day)
- Detailed planning of the visit (individual assignments, co-operative work, group projects)
- Acts of remembrance (laying flowers, memorial text, reading poetry)

Teacher preparation

- Organisation -

Funding the field trip
- Travel
- Accomodation
- Funding subsidies from the community, charities etc.

Parents' meeting
- Description of the field trip
- Participation requirements
- Expenses

- Content -

- Information about the memorial site
- Contacting the memorial site

Initial contact with the memorial by the teacher
- Contacting the staff
- Reviewing media
- Reserving rooms for groupwork and discussion
- Locating contemporary witnesses

- Investigating evidence in the school neighbourhood

Figure 6.2 A visit to a concentration camp memorial. Part 1: Preparation

Source: Rathenow and Weber (1995)

CHILDREN AS CITIZENS

Entering the memorial grounds
(e. g. through the main gate, following the route used by inmates)

First tour of the memorial grounds
(getting to know the site - maps...)

Visiting the on-site exhibit
Exploring, investigating special questions; children in the concentration camp, 'extermination' through labour, resistance in the camp, etc.

Films

Discussion with Holocaust-survivors

Work in the archives

Preservation work on-site

Initial discussion of the (emotional) impression caused by the memorial visit (not structured by the teacher)

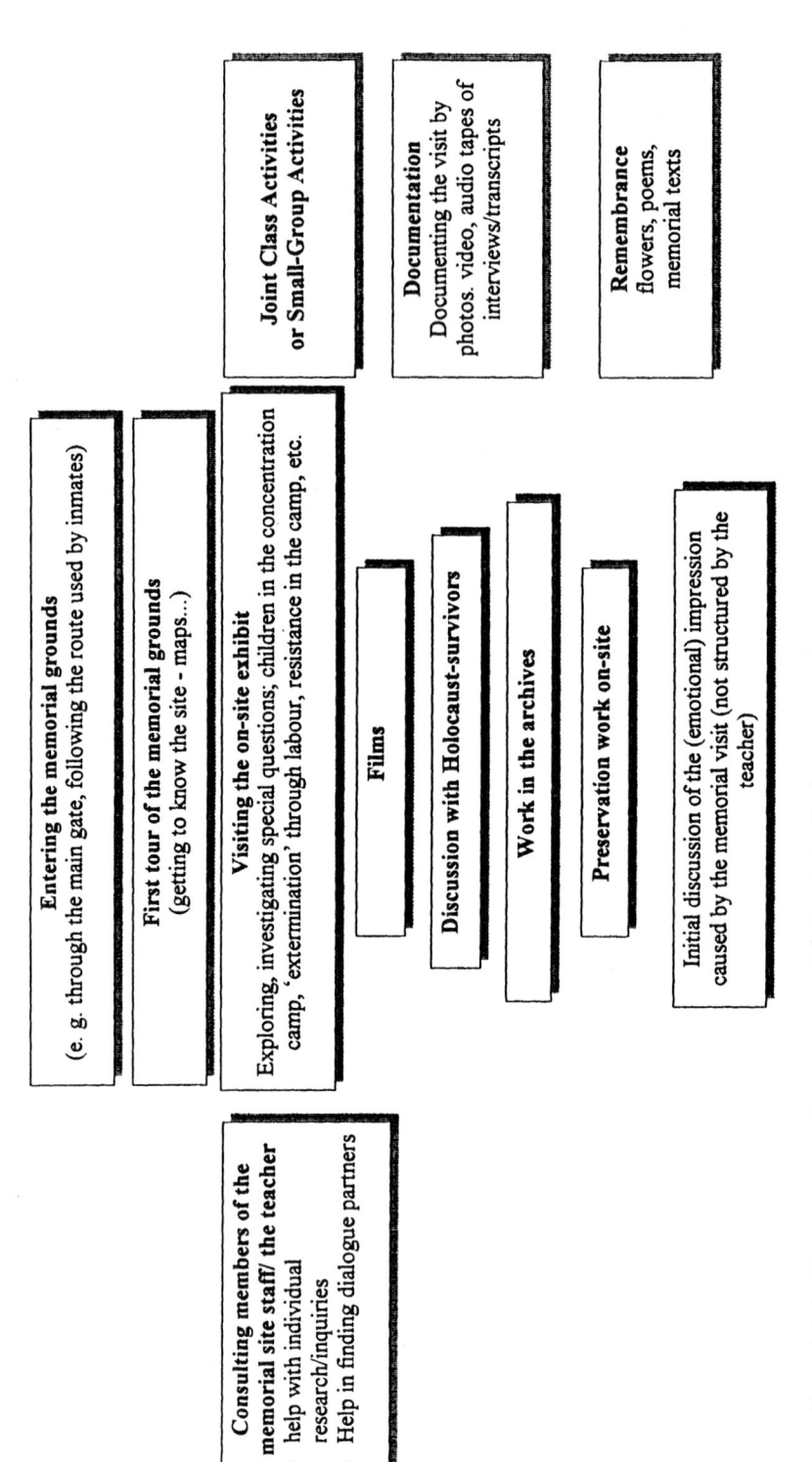

Joint Class Activities or Small-Group Activities

Documentation
Documenting the visit by photos. video, audio tapes of interviews/transcripts

Remembrance
flowers, poems, memorial texts

Consulting members of the memorial site staff/ the teacher
- help with individual research/inquiries
- Help in finding dialogue partners

Figure 6.3 A visit to a concentration camp memorial. Part 2: Realisation
Source: Rathenow and Weber (1995)

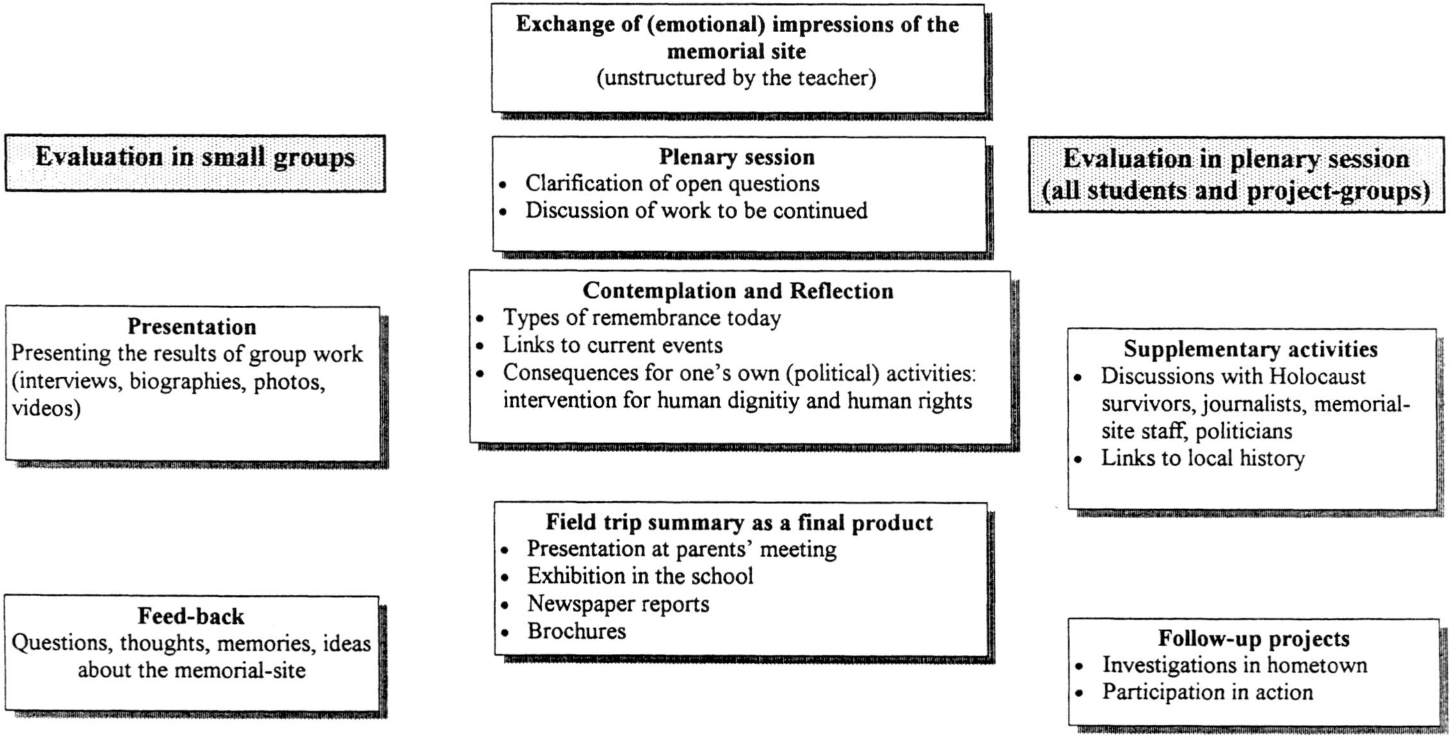

EDUCATION AFTER AUSCHWITZ

Evaluation in plenary session (all students and project-groups)

Exchange of (emotional) impressions of the memorial site
(unstructured by the teacher)

Plenary session
- Clarification of open questions
- Discussion of work to be continued

Contemplation and Reflection
- Types of remembrance today
- Links to current events
- Consequences for one's own (political) activities: intervention for human dignity and human rights

Supplementary activities
- Discussions with Holocaust survivors, journalists, memorial-site staff, politicians
- Links to local history

Field trip summary as a final product
- Presentation at parents' meeting
- Exhibition in the school
- Newspaper reports
- Brochures

Follow-up projects
- Investigations in hometown
- Participation in action

Evaluation in small groups

Presentation
Presenting the results of group work (interviews, biographies, photos, videos)

Feed-back
Questions, thoughts, memories, ideas about the memorial-site

Figure 6.4 A visit to a concentration camp memorial. Part 3: Evaluation
Source: Rathenow and Weber (1995)

REFERENCES

Abram, I. and Heyl, M. (1996) *Thema: Holocaust. Ein Buch fuer die Schule*. Reinbeck: Rowohlt.

Adorno, T. (1967) 'Erziehung nach Auschwitz.' In H.-J. Heydorn *et al.* (eds) *Zum Bildungsbegriff der Gegenwart*. Frankfurt: Diesterweg.

Boal, A. (1979) *Theater der Unterdrueckten*. Frankfurt: Suhrkamp.

Breit, G. (1991) *Mit den Augen des Anderen Sehen; eine Neue Methode zur Fallanalyse*. Schwalbach/Taunus: Wochenschau-Verlag.

Celan, P. (1952) *Mohn und Gedächtnis*. Stuttgart: Europäische Verlagsanstalt.

Dudek, P. (1989) '"Aufarbeitung der Vergangenheit" im schulischen Unterricht?' In H.F. Rathenow and N.H. Weber (eds) *Erziehung nach Auschwitz*. Pfaffenweiler: Centaurus.

Fransecky, M. von (1995) 'Fenster fuer Mauthausen.' In A. Ehmann *et al.* (eds) *Praxis der Gedenkstaettenpaedagogik*. Opladen: Leske and Budrich.

Ginott, H. (1972) *Teacher and Child*. New York: Macmillan.

Haas, G. (1997) *Handlungs– und Produktionsorientierter Literaturunterricht*. Seelze: Kallmeyer.

Hage, K. *et al.* (1985) *Das Methodenrepertoire von Lehrern*. Opladen: Leske und Budrich.

Johnstone, K. (1993) *Improvisation und Theater*. Berlin: Alexander-Verlag.

Rathenow, H.F. and Weber, N. (1995) 'Gedenkstaettenbesuche im historish-politischen Unterricht.' In A. Ehmann *et al.* (eds) *Praxis der Gedenkstaettempaedagogik*. Opladen: Leske and Budrich.

Rogers, C.R. (1983) *Freedom to Learn for the 80s*. Columbus, Ohio: Charles E. Merrill.

Schulz-Hageleit, P. (1982) *Geschichte: Erfahren, Gespielt, Begriffen*. Brauschweig: Westermann.

Weizäcker, R. (1985) Speech to German Parliament. Bohn: Federal Institution of Political Education.

Wolf, C. (1979) *Kindheitsmuster*. Neuwied: Luchterhand.

Zych, A. and Mueller-Ott, D. (eds) (1993) *Auschwitz*. Gedichte Oswiecim: Verlag Staatliches Museum in Auschwitz.

CHAPTER SEVEN

Conflicts, Controversy and Caring
Young People's Attitudes towards Children's Rights[1]

Audrey Osler

INTRODUCTION

Legal measures such as the UN Convention on the Rights of the Child and, in the UK, the Children Act (1989), go a considerable way towards protecting the rights of children and young people and encouraging their participation in society as citizens. Legal measures alone are however not enough. Equally important is the degree of commitment within the wider community to put the law into practice. The successful implementation of the UN Convention on the Rights of the Child and the securing of human rights more broadly are likely to depend on the attitudes of today's youth to the rights specified within the Convention and within other international human rights instruments. Yet we know relatively little about young people's attitudes to children's rights or human rights generally, with most studies focusing on the perceptions of adults. This chapter reports on a small-scale research project designed to assess attitudes towards children's rights among young people aged 16 to 18. Rather than merely assess their commitment to abstract principles it explores their response when rights are set within specific contexts.

The project developed out of the 'Human Rights and Equality in Education' programme of study at the University of Birmingham. The participants on this course, an international group of experienced teachers and professionals working in related fields, had been introduced to a variety of international human rights instruments, including the Universal Declaration of Human Rights (UDHR) and the UN Convention on the Rights of the Child (CRC). Through a series of workshops, group and individual assignments they had had an oppor-

---

1 I would like to thank Kay Fuller for administering the questionnaire.

tunity to apply international human rights texts to their various professional contexts. All acknowledged that human rights principles were universal in application and asserted that they were in agreement with Articles 1 and 2 of UDHR, namely that:

> All human beings are born free and equal in dignity and rights...
>
> Everyone is entitled to all the rights and freedoms set forth in this Declaration, without distinction of any kind, such as race, colour, sex, language, religion, political or other opinion, national or social origin, property, birth or other status.

Yet informal conversations revealed that some of these educators accepted that particular groups of people, for example, those with criminal records, or gays and lesbians, should not expect equality of rights. In other words, they assumed that when human rights principles were applied to specific contexts, or when rights appeared to be in conflict, various individuals and groups should not necessarily expect their rights to be maintained or protected by others within the community. The principle of universality of rights which everyone claimed to accept was thus, in practice, subject to specific restrictions; some individuals appeared to accept a hierarchy of entitlement. Yet these conflicts of opinion were not surfacing in groupwork and were not therefore subject to open debate or examination.

In order to stimulate such debate, and for members of the group to consider the application of rights within their various cultural contexts, I devised an activity in which participants are presented with a series of rights statements, based on international human rights legislation and particularly on the CRC, but adapted in such a way that the rights are not expressed as abstract principles but are subject to various qualifying clauses. These qualifiers acknowledge contexts in which the implementation or protection of rights may require resource allocation or may not be recognised by certain sections of the community, for example:

> The right of minorities to multicultural programmes to preserve their own cultures, despite financial costs.
>
> The right of gays and lesbians to equal opportunity and treatment, even if this is upsetting to others.

Individuals were asked whether they agreed or disagreed with each of the various statements. The exercise brought differences of opinion into the open and encouraged a more thoughtful debate about the application of human rights within different cultural contexts, and particularly the meaning of the phrase from UDHR: 'Everyone is entitled to all the rights and freedoms set forth in this Declaration, *without distinction of any kind*'. Individuals were encouraged to consider the implications of defending and protecting or ignoring the rights of oppressed groups within specific cultural contexts. It became clear that the protection of rights is not necessarily secured by legal means but requires the explicit commitment of the community. This in turn implies explicit teaching and learning about human rights. It was for this reason that we decided to investigate young people's commitment to these rights.

CHILDREN'S RIGHTS AND THE PRINCIPLE OF PARTICIPATION

The UN Convention on the Rights of the Child not only reaffirms Article 26 of the Universal Declaration, the right to education, but it specifies that the promotion of human rights and fundamental freedoms should be a central aim of such education (Article 29) and that governments which are signatories to the Convention have a duty to make the rights in the Convention 'widely known, by appropriate and active means, to adults and children alike' (Article 42). Clearly one of the most effective means of achieving this is through schooling. The young people in our research sample were students aged 16 to 18 years, who had recently completed their compulsory schooling. An understanding of their knowledge and levels of commitment to human rights might enable us to make an assessment of the effectiveness of existing educational programmes in education for human rights and to make recommendations for the development of future programmes.

The UN Convention on the Rights of the Child marks an important step forward in recognising that children and young people under the age of 18 are not only entitled to specific provisions and protection but that they also have *participation* rights (Cantwell 1992; Osler 1994; Osler and Starkey 1996). At an international level the Council of Europe has promoted the concept of children's participatory rights through the development of the European Convention on the Exercise of Children's Rights which was opened for signature by member states in January 1996. The Convention is based on the understanding that children should be assigned greater autonomy in judicial proceedings and it therefore focuses on the exercise of children's procedural rights. The Parliamentary Assembly of the Council of Europe has developed a strategy for children – *The Child as Citizen* (Jeleff 1996) – which recognises that the implementation of children's rights depends not only on their protection but on the recognition that children have citizenship rights and a responsibility to themselves, their families and society. Children's participation is seen as critical to future democratic development.

Research and policy agendas are now beginning to recognise that an important first step in securing children's participation rights is to listen to them. For example, in a review of the extent to which law, policy and practice in the UK comply with the CRC, the consultation process was designed to give particular attention to the views and experiences of children themselves (Lansdown and Newell 1994). The well-established British Social Attitudes Survey, which provides valuable data on adult citizens, is now complemented by a survey into the social attitudes of young people aged 12–19 years (Roberts and Sachdev 1996). There is thus a growing awareness within social policy research of the importance of children's 'voice'.

THE RESEARCH CONTEXT AND METHOD

I adapted a series of rights statements developed by Canadian researchers Katherine Covell and Brian Howe (1995) which were devised to examine support for children's rights among Canadian youth. A questionnaire containing the rights statements was administered in Spring 1996 to a group of 34 students (24 males and 10 females) aged 16–18 years. The students were all following GCE Advanced Level courses which are the traditional route to university. They were attending an 11–18 mixed comprehensive school of some 1100 pupils in Birmingham. The school is situated in a suburban area with housing of mixed age, predominantly owner-occupied, but with a significant number of pupils coming from homes rented from housing associations or the city council. Overall, the level of deprivation is below that of the city as a whole, with one or two localised pockets of poverty. The school population is predominately white, with just 9 per cent of pupils from ethnic minority backgrounds. Given the relatively small size of the sample we did not ask students a question about their ethnic identity, as it seemed unlikely that the data generated would reveal significant trends according to ethnic background.

It is worth noting that a number of the young people in this sample already have the right to vote or will shortly be able to claim it; of those surveyed more than two thirds became eligible to vote in the 1997 general election. Their levels of political understanding and degree of commitment to children's rights and to human rights in general are thus of some significance. Students were asked to indicate their support for each of the statements on a five-point scale. The full list of statements is shown in Figure 7.1. Each statement includes a qualifier, similar to those given to the teachers following the university course in human rights education, designed to place the right within a political context, rather than present it as an abstract principle. The intention is to assess the students' levels of commitment or support for human rights in contexts where there may be conflicting interests rather than their belief in abstract principles. The intention is also to invite responses which reflect individuals' political or practical judgements when competing interests are introduced, rather than their ideals or desirability. Most of the statements may be seen to have a direct link with children's rights, although some which refer to adults, such as the provision of safe women's refuges (statement 7) are also likely to have an impact on children's protection rights. A few, such as the right to vote (statement 4) or the right of women to equal employment rights (statement 15), refer particularly to adults but are of particular relevance to those about to attain adult status.

1. The right of all individuals, including children, to express their views in public as long as these do not restrict the rights of others, and even to express opinions which may offend some people.
2. The right of all members of ethnic minorities to equal opportunity and treatment, despite what people think about them.
3. The right of all persons with past criminal records to equal opportunity and treatment, even those convicted of horrible crimes.
4. The right of all adults to vote, even those without much education.
5. The right of all women and girls to equal opportunity and treatment, even those who are undeserving.
6. The right of people in Wales to a bilingual education, despite financial costs to all taxpayers.
7. The right of women who have suffered abuse to safe women's refuges, despite financial costs to government and taxpayers.
8. The right of religious minorities to their own special religious education classes in schools, despite financial costs.
9. The right of mentally disabled persons to equal opportunity and treatment, despite the concerns of others.
10. The right of minorities to multicultural programmes to preserve their own cultures, despite financial costs.
11. The right of gays and lesbians to equal opportunity and treatment, even if this is upsetting to others.
12. The right of children (up to age 18) to have their own lawyer in legal proceedings which affect them, despite what their parents say.
13. The rights of persons with physical disabilities to equal opportunity and treatment, despite the concerns of others.
14. The right of gay and lesbian couples to the same pension and insurance benefits as others, even though some may consider this immoral.
15. The right of women to be employed in traditionally male occupations, even although other workers may not wish to work alongside them.
16. The right of all persons in economic need to social welfare or social assistance, despite financial costs to taxpayers.
17. The right of children (up to 18) to be free from homelessness, despite financial costs to taxpayers.

Figure 7.1 Rights statements

> 18. The rights of all persons to good quality health care when they need it, despite financial costs to taxpayers.
> 19. The right of disabled persons to equal employment on the basis of their qualifications, even when this involves additional costs to employers.
> 20. The right of children to good quality day care and after-school care when their parents work, despite financial costs to taxpayers.
> 21. The right of prisoners to study for university degrees while in prison, despite the crimes they were convicted of.
> 22. The right of ethnic minorities to be employed on an equal basis in all jobs and in all areas, even where employers might prefer a white employee.
> 23. The right of all persons to a clean and healthy environment, despite financial costs to taxpayers.
> 24. The right of children (up to 18) never to receive physical punishment at home or in school, no matter what they do.
> 25. The right of all persons to high quality education, despite financial costs to taxpayers.
> 26. The right of children (up to 18) to protection from involvement in the production of pornography, despite that some teenagers might want to be involved.
> 27. The right of children (up to age 18) in trouble with the law to be sentenced differently from adults, despite calls for the same treatment as adults.
> 28. The right of minority linguistic communities to bilingual services, despite financial costs to taxpayers.
> 29. The right of children (up to 18) to an adequate standard of living, even if this means government financial assistance to parents who cannot meet this responsibility.
>
> *Figure 7.1 Rights statements (continued)*

The introduction to the questionnaire also asked the young people about their hopes and expectations for their personal futures, including their expectations of further study and employment. We might expect those respondents who are most optimistic about their own personal futures to be more supportive of the rights of others. In terms of their educational futures, four fifths of the girls and just over half the boys expected to gain the exam grades that would allow them to continue their education. Half the students were confident of obtaining a place at a university of their choice. Regardless of their assessment of their immediate educational opportunities, the students in the sample were optimistic about their longer-term employment prospects. All the female students and nearly nine out of ten among their male counterparts had high expectations of obtaining a 'good job'.

The data was analysed by identifying four broad categories of rights: social and economic rights, legal rights, political or participatory rights and children's protection rights. The categories selected are to some extent arbitrary; rights are in reality interdependent. Nevertheless the intention was to assess respondents' levels of commitment to specific areas of human rights so that, where appropriate, these might be addressed through the development of educational programmes. Individual's scores within each of these areas were added and averaged. It was also anticipated that respondents might vary in their levels of commitment to the human rights of specific groups. The data was similarly analysed to assess the extent to which respondents recognised the equal rights of women, ethnic minorities, gays and lesbians and people with disabilities.

GENDER AND LEVELS OF COMMITMENT TO HUMAN RIGHTS

An overall analysis of students' responses reveals an overall higher level of commitment to rights among females than males, one which is statistically significant. However, when specific categories of rights are considered both females and males show similar and encouragingly high levels of commitment to social and economic and participatory rights. The mean scores to the four broad categories of rights, by sex of respondent, are shown in Figure 7.2. The data suggests that respondents of both sexes have lower levels of commitment to legal and child protection rights. Females score highest on economic and social rights whereas males score highest on political and participatory rights. Gilligan (1993) argues that as a result of differential socialisation and consequent psychological development girls and boys adopt different moral perspectives, with girls tending to show greater consideration for questions of care, and boys for abstract justice. These results neither support or refute her theories, since within this sample there are relatively small differences in levels of commitment between the sexes to either legal or social and economic rights.

It is when we consider the levels of commitment to the equality of rights of specific groups – ethnic minorities, gays and lesbians, people with disabilities and women – that females' greater commitment to rights becomes apparent. The young women in the sample indicate higher levels of commitment to equality of rights for all four groups. The maximum score for each statement is five, with participants invited to assess their level of agreement or disagreement on a five-point scale. Average scores for females and males for statements in each of the four groups are presented in Figure 7.3. Young women are consistent in their support for the rights of gays and lesbians (4.5), people with disabilities (4.3), and women (4.3). They show their lowest average level of commitment to the rights of ethnic minorities (3.8). The young men demonstrate higher levels

120 CHILDREN AS CITIZENS

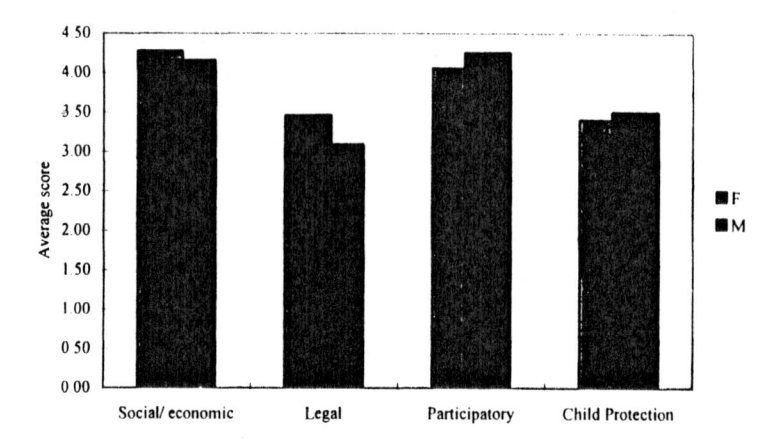

Figure 7.2 Levels of commitment to four broad categories of human rights
  Note: maximum score = 5

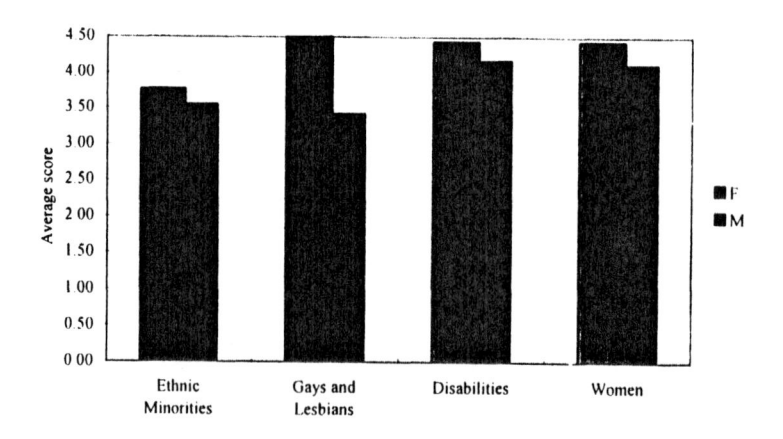

Figure 7.3 Levels of commitment to equality of rights for specific groups
  Note: maximum score = 5

of support for the rights of people with disabilities (4.2) and women (4.1) than they do for ethnic minority rights (3.5) or gay rights (3.4). Female socialisation patterns typically emphasise interdependence and caring for others, and this may encourage a more sympathetic attitude towards equality of rights for specific groups, particularly those which historically have been disadvantaged. These findings suggest that one factor which might enable the more effective promotion of human rights is the development of a greater emphasis on caring and interdependence in the socialisation of males.

EQUALITY OF RIGHTS

Overall the young people within the sample show encouragingly high levels of support for the rights of women and people with disabilities. There is less support from both males and females for minority rights and a relative lack of support among males for gay and lesbian rights.

Currently young people may have few opportunities to discuss or learn about different expressions of sexuality. The Education Act 1993 restricts the right of secondary-age students to sex education, apart from basic information about human development and reproduction provided in national curriculum science. The school's governing body is responsible for ensuring that their school offers a programme of additional sex education but parents have the right to withdraw their children from any such provision. The Local Government Act 1988, section 28, prohibited the intentional promotion of homosexuality through publishing or teaching by local authorities. This legislation's explicit denial of the validity of homosexual relationships and the (largely unfounded but real) concerns of teachers that if they teach about sexuality they may be infringing the law, may mean that many children and young people do not have the opportunity to discuss homosexuality or explore their own attitudes and beliefs.

Whereas the young women in this sample show high levels of commitment to gay and lesbian rights, the average score among young men reflects a wide range of opinion, with some supporting gay rights, others unclear about their position on this issue and a significant minority showing hostility to gays and lesbians. A recent survey found that 53 per cent of young people surveyed believed that sex education should be compulsory for those aged 11–16 years and only 9 per cent felt it should be the parents' choice (Newman 1996). It is not clear from the data why there should be such a disparity between the attitudes of the male and female respondents towards gay and lesbian rights but it would seem important that if young men are to develop tolerance, as a first step towards guaranteeing gay and lesbian rights, then opportunities to understand and learn about their own sexuality are critical.

Respondents' attitudes towards the rights of ethnic minorities are more difficult to interpret. For example, statement 2, which affirms the right of minorities to 'equal opportunity and treatment' encouraged an overall positive response, yet this statement is relatively abstract. Statement 22, which affirms the right of ethnic minorities to employment on an equal basis 'even where employers might prefer a white employee', gained a more mixed response, suggesting that although individual students had a broad commitment to racial equality they were willing to condone discrimination by employers. There is evidence of continuing racial discrimination in employment within Britain (Jones 1993) particularly within the youth labour market (Drew 1995). Moreover, young white people recognise that black and ethnic minority people may experience such discrimination (Sachdev 1996). The evidence from this sample would suggest that while most do not display hostile attitudes towards black and ethnic minority communities a number are willing to overlook prejudice by others which may result in infringements of rights.

Although Article 29 of the UN Convention on the Rights of the Child confirms it is the duty of the government to ensure that education encourages respect for a child's 'own cultural identity, language and values' and Article 30 states that children from ethnic, linguistic or religious minorities shall not be denied the right 'to enjoy his or her own culture, to profess his or her own religion, or to use his or her own language', many were not in agreement that resources should be made available to guarantee such rights. The data also suggests that there was less tolerance for religious rights than for linguistic rights within the sample.

LEGAL RIGHTS AND EDUCATION

One explanation for the apparent lower levels of interest in legal rights may be respondents' limited knowledge and experience of this area. Many English schools have a well-established tradition of teaching about social and economic rights through their programmes of Personal and Social Education (PSE), and social and economic issues are also taught through such subjects as history and geography. Students' formal legal education is however likely to be somewhat more limited. There is no obvious place within the framework of the statutory national curriculum where students are likely to study legal rights in any depth. Schools generally have less experience of teaching about legal issues. Unless individuals have direct personal experience of the legal system, for example in child custody disputes or as defendants, it is unlikely that they will have much understanding of the particular legal rights of children. Those that find themselves in such a position may be ill-informed and ill-equipped to claim their rights.

Respondents showed themselves to be least sympathetic to the legal rights of children. Although the statements about children's legal rights covered more than just the treatment of juvenile defendants, it is possible that the respondents have been influenced by public debate about juvenile justice following the highly publicised James Bulger murder trial. Media representations of the two child defendants as 'monsters' and the subsequent discussion of child sentencing presented 'choices' between child welfare or justice. Prime Minister John Major spoke of the need for 'more condemnation' and 'less understanding' (King 1995). A number of respondents made additional comments concerning the rights of convicted criminals which suggest that they were not able to conceive of legal rights within either a welfare-with-justice or justice-with-welfare perspective. Respondents showed a lack of sympathy for the rights of juvenile offenders and this is in keeping with findings relating to Canadian youth (Covell and Howe 1995). The Canadian researchers suggest that the young people in their sample wished to be tough on juvenile offenders since they believed that a juvenile justice system which sought to give particular rights and protection to adolescent offenders had led to a climate of opinion where all adolescents were treated with suspicion by adults, particularly those in authority over them.

English law remains ambivalent about young people's moral responsibility and their ability to understand right and wrong (McNeish 1996). In the last 15 years or so there have been numerous changes in the law affecting the treatment of young people who offend, and a media-engendered 'moral panic' concerning the behaviour of young people. In such a climate it is perhaps unsurprising that some young people are themselves ambivalent about the rights of children to legal support and to the principle that recourse to judicial proceedings and institutional placements should be avoided wherever possible and appropriate, as stated in the UN Convention on the Rights of the Child, Article 40.

CHILDREN'S RIGHTS: AN UNFAMILIAR NOTION?

These results also raise questions about the relatively low level of support for children's protection rights within this sample. Close examination of the data reveals that a number of female respondents were ambivalent about the right of the child to be free from physical punishment at home and at school. A number of girls questioned this right but qualified their response by explaining that they were against the use of excessive force or any instrument against children. These young women nevertheless argued that a smack from parents was sometimes important to achieve discipline. Their replies also indicate that they have had practical experience of caring for young children and have faced the challenge of difficult behaviour. It seems likely that in a climate where many people accept that light smacking by parents is acceptable, the replies of these young women may reflect an ability to empathise with carers more easily than their male counterparts.

To our knowledge the young people in this sample had received no teaching which sought to provide them with basic knowledge about children's rights and, at the time when the questionnaire was administered, were unfamiliar with any of the international human rights instruments. Many of the issues raised in the rights statements were ones with which we might have expected them to be familiar since they have featured in television and radio broadcasts. Nevertheless, they had not had the opportunity to examine such issues within the framework of international legislation. At the time of writing the issue of moral values and how they should be taught in schools remains high on the political and media agenda. In particular the question is asked about whose moral values should be taught in a society which is both multifaith and secular. These are issues which are discussed in detail elsewhere (Osler and Starkey 1996), where it is argued that human rights values provide us with a set of basic minimum standards which do not deny or undermine the cultural or political expression of minorities. It would seem that one reason why these young people appear to find children's rights, and in particular children's protection rights, an area of potential controversy is that they have not had an opportunity to study these rights, their underlying principles or the implications for policy and practice.

CONCLUSIONS

This study has in some respects produced encouraging results. Given the small-scale nature of the investigation these results are necessarily tentative. The young people surveyed seem well disposed to human rights and have a broad general commitment to the rights of others and to equality of rights within the community. Nevertheless, they are ambivalent about certain categories of rights, particularly legal rights. Females are generally more supportive of human rights than males, and this difference is most striking when we consider the rights of gays and lesbians. Close examination of the data suggests that while many may support the principle of equality for ethnic minorities, in practice they may be less willing to defend their rights. Those categories of rights about which they are best informed, such as economic rights, attract most support. I have argued that the implementation of rights requires the commitment of the community; the evidence presented here suggests that while the young people surveyed tend to support human rights principles, such as justice and equality, educational programmes also need to address directly international legislation such as the Convention on the Rights of the Child, if such legislation is to be successfully implemented. The research would seem to suggest that there may be a particular need to develop students' understanding of legal frameworks and their contribution to the protection of human rights.

The Universal Declaration of Human Rights (Article 26) does not simply identify the right to education but states its aims: 'Education shall be directed to the full development of the human personality and to the strengthening of human rights and fundamental freedoms'. The right to an education designed to promote respect for human rights is again confirmed in the Convention on the Rights of the Child (Article 29). Most schools include a statement supporting the full development of the child's personality within their general aims. An important step forward would be for schools also to stress the importance of strengthening human rights and fundamental freedoms within their general aims. This implies direct teaching about human rights and familiarity with key human rights texts within programmes of study and an opportunity for all pupils to understand their rights and duties in protecting the rights of others. It also implies an examination of various forms of injustice, inequality and discrimination together with knowledge of people, movements and key events in the ongoing struggle for human rights. Curriculum programmes need to address key human rights concepts such as equality, dignity, security, and participation. Students need to explore the meaning of the universality of human rights and to recognise that the protection of the rights of all will depend on their expression of solidarity and on the principle of reciprocity.

If such teaching is to be effective students will also need opportunities to develop skills to enable them to exercise their rights and responsibilities in school. Such opportunities can, of course, begin at an early age and are not dependent on students first grasping human rights concepts. Nevertheless, if there is to be genuine education for participation and democracy, schools will need to develop structures to enable young people to develop such skills, for example, through the development of school councils or other decision-making bodies.

REFERENCES

Cantwell, N. (1992) 'The origins, development and significance of the United Nations Convention on the Rights of the Child.' In S. Detrick (ed) *The United Nations Convention on the Rights of the Child: A Guide to the 'Travaux Preparatoires'*. Dordrecht: Martinus Nijhoff.

Covell, K. and Howe, R.B. (1995) 'Variation in support for children's rights among Canadian youth.' *International Journal of Children's Rights* 3, 2, 189–96.

Drew, D. (1995) *'Race', Education and Work: The Statistics of Inequality*. Aldershot: Avebury.

Gilligan, C. (1993) *In a Different Voice: Psychological Theory and Women's Development*. Cambridge, MA: Harvard University Press.

Jeleff, S. (1996) *The Child as Citizen*. Strasbourg: Council of Europe.

Jones, T. (1993) *Britain's Ethnic Minorities: An Analysis of the Labour Force Survey*. London: Policy Studies Institute.

King, M. (1995) 'The James Bulger murder trial: moral dilemmas and social solutions.' *International Journal of Children's Rights* 3, 167–187.

Lansdown, G. and Newell, P. (1994) *UK Agenda for Children*. London: Children's Rights Development Unit.

McNeish, D. (1996) 'Young people, crime, justice and punishment.' In H. Roberts and D. Sachdev (eds) *Young People's Social Attitudes*. Ilford: Barnardos.

Newman, T. (1996) 'Rights, rites and responsibilities: the age of transition to the adult world.' In H. Roberts and D. Sachdev (eds) *Young People's Social Attitudes*. Ilford: Barnardos.

Osler, A. (1994) 'The UN Convention on the Rights of the Child: some implications for teacher education.' *Educational Review* 46, 2, 141–150.

Osler, A. and Starkey, H. (1996) *Teacher Education and Human Rights*. London: David Fulton.

Roberts, H. and Sachdev, D. (eds) (1996) *Young People's Social Attitudes*. Ilford: Barnardos.

Sachdev, D. (1996) 'Racial prejudice and racial discrimination: whither British youth?' In H. Roberts and D. Sachdev (eds) *Young People's Social Attitudes*. Ilford: Barnardos.

CHAPTER EIGHT

Citizenship Education through Literature

Chris Spurgeon

THE PERSONAL CONTEXT

As a novice teacher in the late 1980s, I was keen to teach about political issues including such themes as human rights, the effects of racism and alternative views of society. I wanted to explore the reality of citizenship education in the classroom. In my early years of teaching I quickly encountered some difficult issues which arise where a teacher is trying to extend students' political knowledge and their ability to participate in political processes. This chapter describes lessons from an action research project exploring the experience of my attempts to infuse some political learning into a mainstream academic subject.

THE RESEARCH CONTEXT

The literature of secondary English teaching reveals that while English teachers are exhorted to address controversial issues, there are few studies which evaluate learning outcomes. Great claims have been made for English as a medium for moral and political education and literary texts in particular have often been thought to offer valuable insights to students (Mathieson 1975). Drawing on evidence from research into political education I decided that well-chosen active learning strategies alongside the provision of factual information would be a sensible way to proceed (Lister 1991). I wanted to evaluate how elements of education for citizenship could be infused into English schemes of work meeting the requirements of the National Curriculum (National Curriculum Council 1990) and the GCSE examination boards (NEAB 1992).

The study took place within a practitioner research tradition (Stenhouse 1973, Elliott 1981). It represents four years of work with several hundred students in two schools. In these four years a substantial proportion of my English teaching was devoted to the delivery of citizenship education through literature. An outline of my rationale for the selection of texts is presented in Table 8.1.

Table 8.1 Rationale for the selection of texts

1. The text should have demonstrated literary merit/interest. This includes texts which may be within or outside the major literary canons.

2. The texts should correspond to applicable GCSE criteria and/or National Curriculum statutory requirements.

3. The text should relate to a citizenship issue directly or indirectly. The citizenship issues should arise naturally when the text is studied rather than as a bolt-on extra (i.e. a citizenship issue should not be imposed upon a text).

4. The text should not be so didactic/prescriptive that it alienates students from its message.

5. The text should offer possibilities for imaginative, analytical and language work.

6. Ideally, aspects of the text should facilitate active learning which could contribute to the development and refinement or oral skills.

In both schools the students were made explicitly aware of my research and their consent for the reproduction of their views was obtained. The great majority of the students with whom I have worked over the period have been interested and often supportive. They enjoyed the fact that a teacher was interested in their views and I made a point of showing students when their work appeared in print. They appreciated the extra careful scrutiny of their written work in particular. This, to me, is one very good reason for the encouragement of such studies by practitioners.

THE TWO SCHOOLS

My knowledge of the students, some of whom I had taught for three years, developed from the study of both their written and oral work and from the myriad social interactions of school life. The opportunity for comparisons and contrasts provided by my move after one year to the Midland Industrial Fringe School was welcome as the initial work took place in a more prosperous context. It gave me the chance to see if certain reactions to texts were context-specific or more generalisable. Table 8.2 illustrates some of the main contextual differences between the schools.

Table 8.2 The research context

Middle England School
- Mixed 11–16 comprehensive
- Purpose-built comprehensive (1976)
- Local authority school
- Approximately 5% of students entitled to free school meals
- Approximately 57% of students achieving 5 GCSEs (A–C)
- English taught in all-ability groups throughout the school

Midland Industrial Fringe-School
- Mixed 12–16 comprehensive
- Originally designed as 1950s secondary modern
- Grant maintained since 1992
- The catchment area consists of a large council estate and mixed public/private housing on outskirts of an industrial town (circa 90,000)
- Approximately 16% of students entitled to free school meals
- Approximately 35% of students achieving 5 GCSEs (A–C)
- English taught in all-ability groups in Years 8 and 9 and then broad sets in Years 10 and 11

THE CITIZENSHIP FOCI

My starting point was that some key citizenship issues could be studied through literary texts. While political philosophers and indeed politicians may debate the nature of citizenship protractedly, I decided to identify some key foci and then to explore the subsequent learning as presented in Table 8.3.

I was keen to see if there were commonalities in terms of students' responses to texts. Concerns such as racism and social justice need to be addressed by teachers, and if documents such as Citizenship Guidance Eight (National Curriculum Council 1990) and the OFSTED inspection framework (OFSTED 1994) offer opportunities for such work, I believe that they should be taken. In this chapter I shall outline the issues which arose from the different citizenship foci. They are all relevant to the process of educating students for participation in life at school and the wider community.

Table 8.3 Texts used to explore issues in citizenship

Racism	*Roll of Thunder, Hear My Cry*, M.D. Taylor
	Underground to Canada, B. Smucker
	Come to Mecca, F. Dhondy
Alternative Visions of Society	*Animal Farm*, G. Orwell
	Brother in the Land, R. Swindells
Insiders, Outsiders and Society	*The Outsiders*, S.E. Hinton
	The Outsider, A. Camus

Citizenship Focus One: racism

Racism among students was evident in both of the very different schools in which the research took place. In line with research such as that of Troyna and Hatcher (1992), racism appears to be a persistent problem in mainly-white schools among a certain section of the school population. As suggested by Naidoo (1992), it seems particularly prevalent among white working-class boys. This said, the research in the Middle England School based on Mildred D. Taylor's *Roll of Thunder, Hear My Cry* identified racism in more middle-class milieux too.

A significant number – not just the odd one or two – admitted to having made racist remarks in the Middle England School. A greater number had stood by and done nothing when others had made such remarks. The quotations below are taken from students' essays prepared during their work on the text *Roll of Thunder*.

> I would object to racist comments in most cases, but not if the person had done something to me. (Chris)

> I do not react very strongly to racism but I am slightly racist. I don't like the idea of killing people for their colour as I think it is bad. I wouldn't object if one of my friends made a racist remark as it is their own view that they are expressing. (Paul)

> I would not respond to a racial comment so long as the person that the remark was against wasn't within earshot, but I know it is wrong. (Peter)

It was encouraging though in the Middle England School that a number of students said that reading *Roll of Thunder* had changed their outlook through presenting them with racism as experienced by black children:

> I think that I do now have a better understanding of racial problems, because before I read the book, I did not really know how some whites treated blacks or how the blacks felt. (Rowen)
>
> Even blacks who do nothing wrong except for being black get burnt e.g. the Berry family. The blacks respond by helping the families of persons who are the victims as if to say 'We may be down, but we are not out'. (Alistair)
>
> This book has helped me to understand racism better and to see it from the point of view of the oppressed rather than the oppressors. (Peter)

What was striking was their general ignorance of non-white societies past and present despite the fact that many of them lived near the boundaries or within the boundaries of a large multi-ethnic city.

This ignorance was all the more apparent in the Midland Industrial Fringe School where the students lived further from multi-racial areas. Approximately one quarter of the Key Stage Four (14–16) students admitted to being racist. Also notable was the fact that over 80 per cent of the students were not aware of ever having previously studied any literature featuring black characters. In terms of attitudes, a number of students again explained why the reading of the novel had helped to reduce or eliminate racist views which they had previously held. It was also encouraging that 60 per cent of them thought that more such books should be studied. So overall, it was pleasing that some students admitted to altered views, but there remained a hard core who stayed resolutely and unashamedly racist. Awareness of racism as a phenomenon was high, with two thirds of students suggesting that racism was still a significant problem in the American South. A willingness amongst self-declared racist students to try to change their views and the views of some of their fellow students was less pronounced.

Students' attitudes to black resistance to racism are also worth considering. In the case of *Roll of Thunder*, three quarters of the respondents to the questionnaire believed that the blacks in the novel did not stand up for themselves enough. Yet when an Asian takes matters into his own hands and stabs his white attacker in Farrukh Dhondy's *Come to Mecca*, only half of the students felt that he was justified. The majority of respondents commenting on *Come to Mecca* did not feel that the story would improve relationships between ethnic groups. There thus seems to be something of a tension here. On the one hand there is a sense that the oppressed should stand up for themselves; on the other some anxiety about the possible consequences for the white perpetrators of racism.

The moral rightness of black resistance was also acknowledged by 11 to 13-year-old children during the study of Barbara Smucker's *Underground to Canada*. With only one exception, the Year 8 students said that they too would have tried to escape and that they believed that all people should be treated equally. In spite of this, neither the Year 8 nor the Year 9 students showed unanimous admiration for the work of the Quaker Abolitionist, Alexander Ross. Again this implied some tensions and elements of an apparent refusal to acknowledge a clear moral case. Around 10 per cent of the children in both year groups were unwilling to acknowledge the bravery of the escaped slaves. Both year groups also felt strongly that words like 'nigger' should not be allowed in books. So an interesting variety of attitudes was seen to emerge, reflecting complex reactions to generally acknowledged racial injustice. While racism seemed to be abhorred by many students, others seemed to be afraid that peer pressure or other factors might lead them or some of their peers to be racist.

With all these reservations, it would be wrong to underestimate some of the progress made. In both schools there were a number of heartening positive testimonies reflecting changes in attitude. Obviously the impact of one literary text or a series of texts is not going to eliminate racism. But the use of appropriate texts with carefully thought-out teaching strategies has been shown to offer some positive outcomes. An awareness of the milieu in which one happens to be teaching has also been shown to be particularly important. Having established students' starting points and prejudices, one can re-teach a novel with the benefit of some insights. For example, I have completely reviewed my approach to *Come to Mecca* and included far more background material in an attempt to contextualise students' discussions of the issue. Students are now taught the stories in the context of apparently growing racism in Britain, Europe and the United States so they can view the events described by Dhondy in a wider context.

Citizenship Focus Two: alternative visions of society

The second focus involved alternative visions of society based upon readings of George Orwell's *Animal Farm* and Robert Swindells' *Brother in the Land*. Some interesting responses relevant to education for citizenship emerged during the study of these texts. The idealism and enthusiasm of the animals in the earlier chapters of Orwell's novel served to interest many Middle England students in the idea of a socialist society. Virtually without exception, they believed that the animals were right to rebel and had some good ideas for developing a society of their own. However, once they saw the undermining of the community by Napoleon and the humans, students began to doubt whether the animals' great plans were in keeping with human/animal nature. As the story progressed they increasingly expressed doubts about whether people were sufficiently selfless to work together for equal reward. So while acknowledging in most cases the apparent attractiveness of a socialist society, they did take a message from the novel that this could be corrupted and that good could be betrayed by evil. This said, there were significant numbers of Middle England students who contended that Orwell was being unduly pessimistic. Many students wrote thoughtfully about equality of opportunity and equality of outcome. Some showed that they could argue cases such as why the revolution failed or why students need a political education. Many Middle England students expressed a belief that the novel had made them think more carefully about the words of politicians:

> We can protect ourselves from the likes of Napoleon and Squealer by educating ourselves politically – exercising our rights and voting for those who will genuinely help us...so we aren't fooled by long fancy words which twist the truth of selfishness into something which we believe helps ourselves. (Helen)

Some expressed disappointment at the unflattering view of human nature to emerge from the fable's latter stages. In the Midland Industrial Fringe School, some of the lower ability students saw the creative tasks as an excuse to complain about their own position in the social order. They aired their grievances about teachers and other agents of authority. What to others had seemed to be pessimism about human nature, seemed to be realism to many of these marginalised, mainly male students. The attitudes they wished to express largely involved frustration with the status quo and little faith in human nature. Many of the boys in particular showed little sympathy for any concept of good citizenship. The pupil-school scenarios which they developed generally featured student-run schools quickly declining and ultimately self-destructing. It appears that certain variables such as class, gender and academic ability seem to influence students' attitudes towards citizenship. Texts, as we saw in the racism section, have different meanings for different readers.

In the case of *Brother in the Land*, where individuals' attitudes to different models of citizenship are explored most students believed strongly that it was vital to safeguard democracy when faced with human greed and selfishness. Democracy as a pragmatic response to the potential misuse of arbitrary or unjust authority was a key notion which arose from both the questionnaire responses and the written assignments. Having read Swindells' novel, most students disapproved of the appointment of unelected individuals to control society following a nuclear war, believing that they would be tempted to abuse the power and influence. The new feudalism operated by Kershaw Farm repelled the students who warmed to the alternative, all-welcoming society known as MASADA. While recognising the temptations to exploit one's fellows, the great majority of the students expressed a preference for the co-operative run by Branwell. Some of the most perceptive students noted that Swindells, in portraying a possible future, was drawing upon historical experience of feudalism, fascism, slavery and oppression:

> Swindells has based his novel on human history, and I feel here he supports the theory that history repeats itself... I think that this sort of dictatorship would occur because of man's natural passion for power. His vision of a local authority turning power crazed and fascist is one I could see happening. (Rachael)

> [The regime run from] Kershaw Farm demonstrates grave misuse of power and they try to form a concentration camp instead of a democracy. (Jeremy)

The gravity of the situation portrayed in *Brother in the Land* seemed to make students think seriously about society. The lack of an artistically neat ending such as that which occurs in *Animal Farm*, where the pigs end up looking like the very humans whom they had originally overthrown, left the students with more decisions to make for themselves about likely outcomes and about which group they might belong to. Most of the students felt that Swindells had not been unduly pessimistic and some felt that he could have been more graphic in showing the damage which nuclear bombs cause. So overall, these higher ability students at the Midland Industrial Fringe School displayed an understanding of the power of the majority within a democracy. At the same time they strongly disapproved of all those who would abuse power and deny others food, clothing or shelter.

Citizenship Focus Three: insiders, outsiders and society

The third citizenship focus was 'Insiders, Outsiders and Society'. S.E. Hinton's (1967) novel, *The Outsiders*, when first taught in the Middle England School produced clear evidence of young people's attitudes to those on society's margins drawn from their own, largely secure 'middle-class' position. While admiring some aspects of the outsiders' rebelliousness, the students' general feeling was that in the final analysis, the gang of marginalised youths should smarten up, conform and join the 'middle classes'.

This was most strongly felt by those students who considered that they themselves came from less advantaged homes. They appreciated the good qualities of the outsiders such as their sociability, their loyalty to their group and their rescue of schoolchildren from a blazing church but saw these as benchmarks of that type of behaviour to which all should aspire. To these Middle England students, disadvantage was no excuse for deviancy. So, interestingly, despite the apparent attractiveness of elements of the outsiders' lifestyle there was a clear feeling that they should conform without necessarily sacrificing their individuality. The more privileged and able students in the Middle England School concurred with these sentiments:

> It is easy to become a Greaser. All you have to do is act illegally, violently and abusively. (Ben)

> The Greasers stand for a right scumbag that goes around breaking the law and disturbing the peace. They stand against 'Goody goodies' e.g. Socs, the Law and shopkeepers etc. (Sandra)

Less academically able students were more attracted to the defiance of social convention. Many of the boys in particular did not feel that the outsiders should make an effort to conform. Interestingly, many of these students observed that the outsiders deserved their bad reputation and did not view them as victims. They saw their acts of law-breaking as more acceptable than had their Middle England peers. So in the case of this particular citizenship text we saw variables of class, academic ability and gender affecting the attitudes the students brought to the text and took from the text. This experience counters the simplistic view that some commentators on education periodically express, that the teaching of certain texts automatically leads to the promotion of certain values be they anti-racist, anti-sexist, left-wing or right-wing.

I was only able to teach Camus' (1949) *The Outsider* in the Middle England School. Again some interesting attitudes related to citizenship emerged. The students discussed the issue that outsiderness may not be limited to ethnic, class or gender groups.

> A typical outsider is somebody who does not fit in with society's physical ideal, someone without money, friends or a stable home. His friends, daily acquaintances and people from work talk to him although most do not seem to be aware of his candid nature. Meursault's daily activities, although sometimes tactless, are kept within the boundaries of order until he is involved in the murder of the Arab. (Shee-Fun)

They gained valuable insights into the world of adult morality where the boundary between right and wrong may be blurred and where there is often no one to help you to make the right decision. While understanding Meursault, most of them did not sympathise with aspects of his attitudes and actions. Just as in the case of *The Outsiders*, they saw considerable room for improvement and believed that with more sensitivity he would have survived. Many of the students' views were informed by thorough reflection on what it means to be a citizen in a particular context. Many appreciated that Meursault's preparedness to let his friends engage in some cruel and degrading activities showed his unwillingness to consider the needs and rights of other citizens. For all the apparent attractiveness of his pleasure-loving existence, the Middle England students felt that his behaviour had to meet certain minimum standards. The students were prepared to tolerate difference but not a complete disregard for laws and conventions which did not fit in with Mersault's instincts and intuitions.

> Although conforming with some standards, he does not comply with them by any means. He murdered an Arab, treated the death of his mother lightly, both his friends are social outcasts and he broke the law by lying to the police on Raymond's behalf. Conformity involves more than the law, it is your behaviour, views and attitudes... (Fiona)

I would hope that the challenge of such an existentialist novel helped students in the development of their own personal moral codes. The geographically and culturally distant setting may have helped students to be objective in their outlook.

RECOMMENDATIONS

Recommendations emerging from the research can be divided into various categories. I shall first address that relating to an individual teacher contemplating the teaching of a text with the hope of engendering some political learning. An awareness of the age, gender, race, academic background and social class of one's students is a prerequisite which is too easily ignored. This research has shown significant differences in response between students in the same school and students in different schools. Students bring their own cultural background and values to texts which may or may not be modified or reinforced by the teaching strategy employed. The reactions of, for example, the white, less academic boys, indicate that whilst they engaged with the issues their own values influenced their responses in ways which the teacher may find difficult to resolve. For this reason, work on such sensitive themes needs to be addressed in other curricular areas and in particular in Personal, Moral and Social Education.

An awareness of students' initial level of political ignorance or knowledge is also important as is repeated checking of the absorption of knowledge and of key terms. Monitoring their enjoyment of the work must not be forgotten. Encouraging active learning has been seen to contribute to both student enjoyment and to their acquisition of knowledge. For example, producing a propaganda sheet oneself takes more thought than recognising the lies and exaggerations in someone else's text. Similarly, recording a radio programme with basic equipment in a short time encourages students to experience strategies of resistance to a corrupt authority, by working on tasks based on the pirate radio station which existed in Santiago, Chile.

The issues described above extend beyond the confines of the English curriculum and involve pupils' values. Because of this the work needs to be done within the framework of a whole-school policy. Coverage of citizenship issues within English needs to be co-ordinated with work by other colleagues in both pastoral and academic roles. However, subject-teaching departments, including English, are able in many cases to ensure a certain degree of continuity through the delivery of structured yet flexible curricula. For all the debate about National Curriculum English over the years of this research, teachers are able to teach virtually the same texts as before the National Curriculum legislation appeared, if they so wish. There is still a great deal of flexibility and even the reduction in the permitted amount of coursework can be used profitably for the discussion of issues and the reading of more texts. So all is not bleak. The would-be teacher of citizenship has myriad possibilities and also has the backing of powerful support in the shape of the OFSTED inspection criteria and, to a lesser extent, Curriculum Guidance Eight when viewed as a document of permission.

I suggest that education for modern citizenship is a central element of English teaching and that the subject-teaching community should explicitly promote it. This could be part of a positive redefinition of the subject. In such a process, the consideration of research outcomes is vital. As Mathieson (1975) suggested, for too long the ideologues of English have delighted in their rhetorical calls for action often with scant regard for what was happening in classrooms. Ultimately, only the close study of actual practice will inform the development of such fine ideals and targets. There will always be generations of prospective citizens keen to learn about their rights and responsibilities in a complex and challenging world. While media, technology and texts change, key issues of citizenship including rights, duties, racism and inclusion and exclusion from society will be as current as they were in the Athens of Aristotle.

REFERENCES

Camus, A. (1949) *The Outsider*. Harmondsworth: Penguin.

Dhondy, F. (1978) *Come to Mecca*. London: Collins.

Elliott, J. (1981) *Action Research: A Framework for Self-Evaluation in Schools*. Cambridge: Cambridge Institute.

Hinton, S.E. (1967) *The Outsiders*. London: Macmillan.

Lister, I. (1991) 'Research on social studies and citizenship education in England.' In J.P. Shaver (ed) *Handbook of Research on Social Studies Teaching and Learning*. New York: Macmillan.

Mathieson, M. (1975) *The Preachers of Culture*. London: George Allen and Unwin.

National Curriculum Council (1990) *Curriculum Guidance Eight: Education for Citizenship*. London: National Curriculum Council.

Naidoo, B. (1992) *Through whose Eyes*. Stoke-on-Trent: Trentham.

NEAB (Northern Examination and Assessment Board) (1992) English GCSE syllabus. Manchester.

OFSTED (1994) *Spiritual, Moral, Social and Cultural Development*. London: OFSTED.

Orwell, G. (1945) *Animal Farm*. London: Penguin.

Smucker, B. (1977) *Underground to Canada*. London: Heinemann.

Stenhouse, L. (1973) *What is Action Research?* Norwich: CARE, University of East Anglia.

Swindells, R. (1984) *Brother in the Land*. Oxford: Oxford University Press.

Taylor, M.D. (1987) *Roll of Thunder, Hear My Cry*. London: Heinemann.

Troyna, B. and Hatcher, R. (1992) *Racism in Children's Lives*. London: Routledge.

PART FOUR
Teacher Thinking
Values, Knowledge and Action

CHAPTER NINE

Understanding the Role of Emotion in Anti-Racist Education

Phil Johnson

INTRODUCTION

When children come to school they have already formed partial theories – made up of both 'knowledge' and emotion – about the way the world works. Often those theories remain unchanged by our teaching. In my experience of nearly 30 years of multicultural education programmes, I have seen many students leaving school with much the same negative attitudes towards ethnic minority groups as they had when they started school. I argue in this chapter that their emotional commitment to prejudices formed early in life causes them to disregard our teaching. We social education teachers would have more impact on the racial and ethnic attitudes of children if we were to address that powerful emotional 'baggage' that the children bring with their 'knowledge' about groups. However, because of the tendency in the West to regard thinking as superior to emotion, we have only paid lip service to the role of emotion in learning, and in our teaching we have tended to overlook emotion. I suggest that we ignore emotion at our peril: we ignore it in our teaching so it ignores our teaching – and our teaching fails. Because our teaching does not address the feelings and emotions already associated with students' existing 'knowledge' of the world, those feelings and emotions cause the students to ignore our teaching.

Here I argue that values education and, more specifically, anti-racist education would be much more successful if in our teaching we took more seriously the role of emotion in children's past learning. I am suggesting a new focus to our teaching, not a new subject. We need to plan for that focus and to trial teaching strategies that involve children coming to an understanding of the influence of their feelings and emotions in their past learning, and coming to have more control over the way those feelings and emotions influence their learning. 'More control' does not mean anything like complete control. Nor does it imply that emotion is always detrimental to the learning process. We need to work with students to help them recognise, understand and direct the sometimes positive and sometimes negative role that emotion plays in learning. Metacognition may be a useful process for pupils to acquire in order to develop that increased control. In values education, a metacognitive approach means helping students learn more about how they learn values – including the emotional side of that – and then helping them to use that knowledge to improve their own values development.

What is the role of emotion in past learning and in our current 'knowledge'? Aboud (1988) suggests that emotion is important early in a child's life in the development of prejudices but is replaced by perception and then cognition as the dominant factor. I argue that emotion is still a significant factor at all stages, and the emotion that is involved in earlier learning remains a significant factor that teachers must later take into account. Take the example of children's 'knowledge' about groups in the community. Children learn through their families and their group memberships that 'our family is to be trusted', or that 'our religion is the one true religion', or that 'we should be proud of our nation, our ethnic group or our race', or that 'our gang is the greatest'. When they learn those things they are not just learning positive 'facts' or information about their own group and negative information about other groups. Most importantly, they are also absorbing positive and negative feelings and emotions about those groups. In those socialisation situations they are building their identity, their sense of their self in affective as well as cognitive ways. Their 'knowledge' about their selves and about those groups is a complex mixture of 'facts', ideas, understandings, beliefs, attitudes, feelings and emotions.

It has long been accepted that emotion plays a role in motivation to learn. It has been seen as important that children feel positively towards the subject matter being taught and that they feel confident about their capacity to master it. We have also been concerned, to some extent at least, about the need to 'start from where the children are at', to acknowledge the different levels of development, the different knowledge and skills that children bring to the topic at hand. However, we have not sufficiently recognised that before we can motivate children to learn, that is, to change their current knowledge or values, we have to help them reflect upon their existing emotions associated with that knowledge and values. In race relations education, this means helping our students make explicit their current feelings about other groups and helping them think about where those feelings have come from.

THE NATURE AND EXTENT OF RACIAL AND ETHNIC PREJUDICES IN AUSTRALIA

Australia is a very multicultural society built by successive waves of immigration since the British invasion from 1788 onwards. The Aboriginal people have lived here for at least 50,000 years. Their descendants now constitute about 1.5 per cent of the 18 million total population. In the nineteenth century the Anglo-Celtic majority established a White Australia Immigration Policy that was not expunged until 1972. After World War II, British migration was augmented by large migrations, initially from northern Europe and then from southern Europe and the Middle East. In the last two decades significant numbers of refugees have come from all the world's trouble spots, and migrants from Vietnam, and Chinese from a number of countries have added an important Asian influence especially in particular parts of the largest cities.

Vasta and Castles (1996) argue that racism is still common in Australia. All migrants and Aboriginal people report a range of racial discrimination and prejudice. There are many manifestations of this from the seemingly insignificant through to violence and the occasional racially motivated murder. The reputable Age-McNair Opinion Poll in 1966 found that 65 per cent of the 2063 sample thought current immigration numbers were too high, 88 per cent thought that the intake from Asia was too high and 34 per cent disagreed with multiculturalism. It should be noted that 61 per cent agreed with multiculturalism. This latter figure probably reflects the situation well: there may be less overt racism in Australia than in most nations. I find that children are very aware of the racism that does exist. Brenda says:

> Like if you're in Australia and you come from China, the Australians pick on the Chinese people... They reckon they don't belong here, this is Australia land... But it's wrong, like if the Australians say to the Chinese 'Why are you here?'. The Aborigine people can say that to the white people, 'cos they were the first ones to be in Australia.

This is sophisticated reasoning from an 11-year-old.

I suggest that it is useful to distinguish a modern, more subtle form of racism from traditional biologically-based overt racism. This modern racism is not so aggressively expressed, it is less obvious. Its practitioners can be middle-class and well-educated. They know that racial bigotry is not politically correct so they do not express it. Perhaps they do not feel that strong visceral reaction to minority group members that the overt racist does, but they are still likely to discriminate (generally subtly) against 'out-group' members while making the point that they are not racist. However, the negative effects of their discrimination against Asians and Aborigines is as powerful as that of overt racism.

In my view, subtle racists tend to be critical of minority group members, for example, for not accepting the dominant culture, for not joining dominant social organisations or, on the other hand, for trying to take over social organisations. They acknowledge the rights of individuals in theory, but in practice they are not comfortable with minority group members who choose to speak their own language or who retain their own culture within their own social organisations. They feel threatened economically, culturally, socially and/or psychologically. They are prepared to have 'outsiders' join their society so long as they assimilate, so long as they give up their own ways and take on those of the dominant group. Such people are unlikely to make an effort to meet the 'outsiders' half or even quarter-way. They cannot cope with the ideology or philosophy of pluralism or multiculturalism. Although they have strong feelings and emotions about the dangers of such philosophies and ideologies, they may argue quite rationally for their views, or they may keep their views quiet, unlike the overt racist who generally speaks out stridently.

I suggest two contributory factors in the development of negative attitudes and feelings towards other groups. First, a culture of 'them and us', that has been handed down the generations through socialisation, is deeply and emotionally ingrained into our core identity, and has not been much affected by the official policy of multiculturalism. The second, which I shall return to in a moment, is the failure of multicultural education to address negative emotions towards other groups.

In Australia multiculturalism appears to be working in that there is little ostensible conflict between groups. However, it is not operating in people's daily lives, as people from different ethnic and racial backgrounds have little to do with each other socially. There is informal or social segregation. This applies amongst my university students: most students from southern European, Anglo, and Asian backgrounds sit in separate groups in classes. The old factors that feed racism – ignorance and fear of the 'other' – are still operating. If we are to reduce the levels of this subtle racism and thus some of the potential for more overt racism, we have to find ways to make multiculturalism work in practice in people's daily lives. We have to create a society in which people not only live full lives within their own cultural groups, but also are open to – not just tolerating – the 'other'.

CHILDREN, RACISM AND EMOTION

I have found upper primary school-aged children show the capacity to think in surprisingly sophisticated ways, and they are prepared to grapple with complex and difficult social issues. They can think about how their ideas, feelings and values have arisen; they can think about their own role in constructing their values and about their potential to change their values in the future. Most of them are also surprisingly open to other groups. However, sometimes many of the same children who show such openness and flexibility in their thinking also show signs of negative beliefs, feelings and attitudes about other groups. Rarely do they articulate those negative views to their teachers.

In one study in four classrooms in two schools we looked at children's attitudes towards other groups by asking them to place on a map of their street which families they would like to live near them. They could choose only 12 from 20 surnames with nationalities appended. There were six families from Australia. One of those was additionally labelled as Aboriginal, while the other 14 were from 14 of the countries, including England and the USA, from which people have migrated to Australia. The children made a wide range of choices, including some surprises: more left out the English family than included them, but the families from China and Chile were clearly the least favoured and the Australian families much more favoured. Here I am not exploring the statistical significance of the data but I want briefly to share some of the children's thinking.

The children were interviewed about their choices and there was a range of very idiosyncratic reasons for choosing or rejecting a family, for example: 'because I didn't like their last name. I like the hard names', and: 'Well, I like Aborigines and my sister's best friend's mum is English'. It should be noted that many children made very positive statements and choices about diversity, but in each group we found a minority of children who were prepared to say something like Andy: 'Because they wouldn't suit me... Because they're different people and they eat different foods... Because they're all the countries I don't like', and David: 'These people do strange things like have a smell around the house... but they look a bit different... because they speak different languages and stuff'. And at the extreme is the statement from Michael: 'I hate, hate, hate Chinese people'.

In each classroom there were some children who appeared to be providing the politically correct answer, the answers they believed the interviewer or their teacher would want. David explained why he had left out his eight families: 'Cos most of them aren't Australian, and I just like mostly Australian', but then, perhaps as a politically correct afterthought, he added: 'But I put some kind of Chinese in'. In fact he had not included the Chinese and Vietnamese families. Stefan, when asked why he had left out the Murrays (the Aboriginal family), said: 'I didn't want four Australians living in the street so I just crossed one out'... Was it that he did not want to admit that he had deliberately left out the Aboriginal family? Wesley said he found the decision hard, 'so I just decided to take two off each one (the list was divided into four groups of five families). Strangely, in his 'random' mathematical selection, he excluded only one Australian family. Jane gave the impression of wanting to please us and her teacher with her comment: 'I didn't really want too many Australians, because I wanted it to be a bit different and learn new languages and that. But I still wanted a couple because it's someone to talk to'.

The written words can be interpreted in a number of ways, but with most of these cases, the body language and tone of voice indicated a child seeking approval or wanting to provide the correct answer. The interviewer said to Nick: 'Can you tell me about your drawings?' (they were somewhat stereotyped). He replied: 'Just funny drawings, not anything... That one (the Vietnamese), the ears are a mistake, but I don't know... Not because I think that Chinese people are bad or something, I was just being silly.' In their selections and their drawings some children were prepared to be more forthcoming than they were in their spoken comments. Perhaps their guard is down when they are working on their own.

Similarly, I have found that sometimes children will give the 'correct' responses for up to 20 minutes in an interview situation and then, perhaps as they relax more, they say something quite contrary to what they have been 'presenting'. An example is the case of the three boys who had been somewhat non-committal for the first 15 minutes of an interview, but then Mick says: 'Some Australian people are racist...like they don't like blacks'. When asked how he knows, he says: 'cos half of my brother's friends are like that...they tease 'em and that'. He does not want to repeat the words, but eventually one of the other boys says 'boongs' (a pejorative word for Aborigines). Another mentions 'nips', (a pejorative term for Japanese), but even then the discussion remains guarded for a few minutes. But as the discussion was coming to a close, all of a sudden Steve came out with the following: 'Sometimes the Chinese and Vietnamese should be grateful because Australia has got China town and everything and if you went over to there, they wouldn't treat you that way, they would just...like tease you and everything. They wouldn't have Australia land there'. Mick agrees and Paul says: 'They still want more'. Then Mick voices a common Anglo-Australian fear: 'They probably want to take over...the Chinese'. Dean says that they shouldn't come to Australia and Mick puts the terms: 'If they come to Australia, they should just be quiet, be thankful for what they've got and don't ask for more, and don't be greedy'.

Many children seem to decide that it is too difficult to argue with their teachers' strong anti-sexist or anti-racist agenda so they give the teachers the answers they want to hear. They do that partly to keep the teacher happy, not because they are convinced by the teacher's position. So often we teachers say things like: 'I don't want to hear that sort of thing in my classroom', so it is not surprising that children learn to censor their comments for us. In interviews I find they are more forthcoming but are still aware of their audience and the inappropriateness of some terms: 12-year-old Emma uses the pejorative term 'nips' for Japanese, but immediately apologises: 'Sorry...I'm just using the word that some people use'. In another school the interviewer asks about the sorts of people in Australia and Thao answers: 'Japan, China, Vietnam' and Di adds: 'Abos'. Thao's 'Di!!!' indicates that she is shocked that Di would use such a pejorative term. When asked why she picked up Di's term, she first says 'It sounds funny' but then she pointed to the tape-recorder. And when asked would she pick up Di for saying the same thing in the school-yard, she says that she would not.

Already at age 11 or 12 children's social views have strong emotional components linked to their personal, familial, social class, ethnic, and religious, identity. In not exposing those views to the teacher the children are also protecting their identity and, as a consequence, protecting their views from teachers' attempts to challenge them. However, the children's views may not be so strongly held as at adolescence or later, so, perhaps the end of primary school is a good time to explore alternative views with them.

The suggestions in this chapter are partly derived from the above work I have done with primary school children in a variety of Melbourne schools over many years. In some recent interviews I explored how metacognition might be applied to feelings and values. I asked the children to talk about their past and present thinking and feelings about groups in Australia. Several talked about their previous fears of black people or of Asians and of how they had changed, often through contact with individuals from different backgrounds. They suggested family, peers, the media, and contact with other groups as influences in the development of their beliefs and feelings. Interestingly they were also able to think about how those influences might have affected them. Sherie said: 'Umm...first influence you get of them...like if you go to kindergarten with a person who is...black who is really really mean to you...you think that – and that's the first sort of black person you've met – umm...you think that they're all mean...'.

I also asked the children whether, and if so how, they might be able to influence their own ideas and feelings in the future. Not surprisingly many children struggled to articulate their ideas for such questions, as would adults, but they worked at it... Emma said: 'If you could interact with another group or...see what they're doing or...like be with another group, then you might find out that they're really bad or they're really nice...then your feelings would change about them, or they could stay the same'.

I realised from the children's preparedness to struggle with those questions that, if we put the questions into an appropriate teaching context, that is, if we built them into integrated units of study, we might achieve worthwhile development in the children's values and valuing. Later in this chapter I report briefly on such a teaching unit that I am presently working on with a teacher.

The reader may want to refer to the work of Roebben (1995) whose concern is with training younger children in good emotional habits. My own belief is that older primary school children can be more intellectually (and emotionally) engaged in understanding the way their emotions are involved in their values and valuing. Roebben's approach may complement mine: his may be more suitable for the earlier years and mine for the later years. Let us look at emotions and feelings in more depth.

EMOTIONS AND FEELINGS: EVIDENCE FROM RESEARCH

Damasio (1994) puts the provocative hypothesis that not only is emotion involved in all decision making, but also that it is *essential* for decision making. He is saying that emotions or feelings help us make decisions. Those people who have damage done to the areas of their brain where their feelings are processed are unable to make even the most trivial decisions because they continue to think through all the possibilities. Ultimately emotion assists us to choose between the different possibilities. As Denzin (1984, p.242) put it: 'emotionality overrides cognitive doubt'. This relates to my point about the importance of affect in the further development of values.

On the other hand we do not want emotions to dominate our decision making. If we look at acts of racism, from acts of avoidance, discrimination, and vilification, through to acts of oppression and violence, the response to the outsider often seems to be automatically emotional with no thought involved. Many people react emotionally to the smallest manifestation of the stereotype of a minority group. Our work with children is designed to explore ways to help them become more aware of those feelings and help them to learn to intervene rationally in the emotional response to the racial or cultural stereotype.

Izard (1977) points out that not all emotions are automatic, that the emotions can also arise from our thinking about something, and in turn, emotions can affect both perception and cognition. She also points out that emotions have both an innate and a learned component, and that while there are a limited number of basic emotions, there are many cultural ways in which those emotions are expressed. It is important in our teaching to help children to recognise that those forms of expression have been learned through socialisation. Our teaching can also explore with students the extent to which we can learn to control both the innate and learned components of emotions.

Denzin's (1984) work adds a number of dimensions to our understanding of emotion and affect. He directs us to look at the experience of emotion much more from the inner perspective of the person experiencing it, asking us to consider its meanings to that person and how it works in his/her life. Denzin describes links between imagination, empathy, and emotionality that are very useful to explore with children in race relations teaching. He also makes explicit links between feelings and values, claiming that 'moral self-consciousness is at the core of the person' (p.83) and 'on the basis of emotionality, the person is moved to act morally' (p.240). He also recognises that emotions are learned and expressed in social situations.

Denzin also talks about the importance of self-justifications that provide information about how children link their emotions with their identity and their values. He points out that at least in western cultures, 'self-justifications may follow an emotional episode, may be expressed during emotionality, or may be offered beforehand, as preinterpretations' (p.53). Every teacher and every parent has heard many self-justifications from children (and from adults). It is important for teachers who are thinking about the role of the emotions in learning to see self-justifications as a window to the child's attitudes, feelings, emotions and values, and to their ideas about their self.

An example of a text for teachers that has taken account of the affective domain is Pike and Selby (1988). While they do not talk about how emotion has come to be involved in learning, they do provide many useful suggestions for allowing children to explore and develop their feelings. In the remaining part of this chapter I discuss strategies for educating against racism.

EDUCATION AGAINST RACISM

Teachers in schools with few ethnic minority children rarely see conflict in the playground or hear explicit racism amongst their students and so they assume that racism only occurs in schools with a larger mix of ethnic groups. However, if the above analysis of the nature and extent of subtle racism is correct, there is likely to be a significant minority of children at every school who have strongly negative feelings and views about other groups but who only express that very quietly in what I have described as a subtly racist manner. In such schools anti-racist teaching is still necessary but it has to allow children plenty of time to express their own views and feelings: we have to be patient while the children make the decision that it is OK in our classroom to say what they really feel and believe. Once those views and feelings are articulated the procedures are much the same as in schools where the children freely express explicit prejudice. Some of those procedures are to provide the children with exposure to a range of other views and to enable them to explore for themselves the implications for people and for society of those different views. Also we can help children recognise not only the range of feelings and emotions that exist in the community and in themselves about other groups, but also the effects of those feelings and emotions. We can also help children explore the causes of prejudices and the connections between prejudices, ideologies and behaviour.

I indicated earlier my belief that multicultural education has not been successful in Australia. There are still many children showing ignorance of, and expressing feelings of fear, uncertainty and hostility towards, other groups in the society (Cahill 1996), particularly towards Asians and Aborigines. When choosing the families as her neighbours, Laura made sure that the Aboriginal family wasn't included:

> I tried to leave out the Aborigine person because I've heard a few stories people have told about what happened to them when they had Aborigines living next door to them...the people in our grade they said they had Aborigines living next door to them and they threw the dog stuff over the fence and it landed on their little brother.

When asked had she met any Aboriginal people, she said she had not.

In a number of very different schools I have found children talking about the number of Japanese people taking over Australian jobs. That is strange because there are virtually no Japanese migrants in Australia (although there are many

Japanese tourists adding much to Australia's income). There is some confusion amongst the children. For example John says:

> The people I notice most nowadays are the Japanese and Chinese and a lot of Vietnamese...they live around here, they're everywhere... In one of the newspapers there was an article saying that, the headline was 'Japanese go home' because what it was, was Australians were saying that the unemployment rate was up because all the Japanese were coming over and walking into our jobs.

John appears to use 'Japanese' synonymously with 'Asian'. Linh says that the Chinese are seen in that way also... 'people tease me about being Chinese, even though I'm Vietnamese. Anyone who is Asian is Chinese to them'.

Multicultural education has tended to teach superficial 'facts' about other cultures and has provided positive experiences – 'food and dance' multiculturalism – possibly in the hope of developing empathy through the stomach! I agree with the English critics of multicultural education when they argue for a more direct anti-racist education. However, for that anti-racist education to be effective I believe we need to help our children learn more about (a) the culture of racism, (b) the socialisation processes through which they may have learned that culture, (c) the extent of ignorance between groups and the effects of that ignorance, and, as I have pointed out, (d) their own and others' feelings towards other groups.

METACOGNITION AS A PROCESS FOR LEARNING

I see metacognition as learning more about learning (especially one's own), and the application of that knowledge to improve one's own learning. It has two distinct but interrelated components: (a) knowledge of, and (b) control of, learning. It is a higher-order cognitive process that most people use occasionally, for example when they say 'let's think about where we went wrong and see how we can fix it'. Eleven-year-old Amy listened to the other girls talking for several minutes about the problems of Aborigines in Australian society when she said: 'You said that some of them, like have drinking problems and that, well how do we know?'. She is being metacognitive: thinking about knowing. The metacognitive approach that I am proposing is a planned, reflective approach to help our students understand and improve their own learning.

Brown and DeLoache suggest that the basic skills of metacognition include:

> predicting the consequences of an action or event, checking the results of one's own actions (did it work?), monitoring one's ongoing activity (how am I doing?), reality testing (does this make sense?), and a variety of other behaviours for coordinating and controlling deliberate attempts to learn and solve problems. (Brown and DeLoache 1983, p.282)

In anti-racist education these skills need to be adapted to help children to recognise, articulate and then develop their existing values, attitudes and beliefs, and of course, their feelings associated with all of these. So, if we were working with the children that I mentioned earlier who had identified their previous fear of blacks, we would explore where that fear came from, how it manifested itself and how it may have influenced their attitudes, beliefs and behaviour. Such an exploration with them would no doubt help other children identify their own fears or other feelings, and if they acknowledged those feelings, further processing could follow.

A fundamental skill involved in metacognition is reflection: the capacity to reflect on one's own thinking and situation. This involves self-awareness and self-questioning, and probably self-confidence and even some self-doubt. It requires the development of a capacity to systematically describe and analyse one's values, and work through one's approach to a values situation. Reflection can then lead to self-regulation and self-direction, and in the values situation, to some degree of 'self-control' and to acting on the basis of conscience.

Another fundamental skill needed when confronting a new values dilemma is the ability to recognise the situation as having a values dimension. For example, children need to be able to identify a situation of racist name-calling as involving values and they need to be aware of choices between possible behaviours. At this first stage they can learn to identify feelings that may be associated with the situation and its values dimension and also identify the feelings associated with the choices that can be made. They also need to be able to make predictions, for example, about the consequences of particular decisions to act.

As mentioned earlier, I am presently working with a teacher to develop a teaching unit exploring ways of helping children become more organised in their thinking, and articulate in their talking, about their feelings related to their beliefs, attitudes, values and valuing. If we can help children understand that their values have arisen in affect-laden social contexts (often through non-verbal socialisation), they may become more independent of their past socialisation. We want to see whether this process might help the children to improve their valuing and take more control over their subsequent values development.

The integrated curriculum unit of study will last for up to eight weeks and will utilise language arts, visual arts, music and drama to explore the issues with the children individually, in groups, and in the whole class. The children will learn to identify and describe emotion using cartoons, photographs and portraits. Mime and drama will help them explore the facial and bodily expression of feelings. They can use art and writing to process their thinking and feelings, and can write stories and poetry, keep journals, develop word lists, definitions, descriptions, and explanations. (See Dunlop (1984) for other suggestions for teaching about emotion.)

Traditional values-clarification approaches, but with an added emphasis on the role of emotion, can be incorporated into the proposed unit. Similarly, while Philosophy for Children (Lipman 1995) mentions emotions explicitly, and sometimes focuses on emotions in its programmes, it tends to treat the emotions using only philosophical tools. I want children to be able to do that also, but I think that they need to explore and learn about emotion in much broader and deeper ways before they can most effectively use the Community of Inquiry-type discussions that Philosophy for Children suggests. Such discussions have the children in a circle with the teacher playing a guiding role but allowing the children time and freedom to discuss issues in depth. Some of those issues can be the sort of questions I mentioned earlier, asking the children to think about how their feelings and beliefs have arisen, how they have changed, how they might change, and how the children might influence future changes.

CONCLUSION

If we can help primary school children to be aware of the ways in which ignorance and misinformation about other groups cause people to develop negative ideas and feelings, those children may be less likely to succumb to those perennial 'feeders' of racism as they grow older. The more children know about their feelings and how they have come to feel the way they do, and the more aware they are of inconsistencies in their beliefs, feelings and values, the more likely it is that they will want to and be able to change those beliefs and feelings, and improve their values and behaviour. If we can help children develop more understanding of their emotions, and thus more control over their emotions, we have reason to hope that they will be more confident and caring citizens of the future.

REFERENCES

Aboud, F. (1988) *Children and Prejudice.* Oxford: Basil Blackwell.

Brown, A. and DeLoache, J. (1983) 'Metacognitive skills.' In M. Donaldson, R. Grieve, and C. Pratt (eds) *Early Childhood Development and Education.* Oxford: Blackwell.

Cahill, D. (1996) *Immigration and Schooling in the 1990s.* Canberra: Australian Government Publishing Service.

Damasio, A. (1994) *Descartes Error: Emotion, Reason and the Human Brain.* New York: Grosset/Putman.

Denzin, N.K. (1984) *On Understanding Emotion.* San Francisco: Jossey-Bass Publishers.

Dunlop, F. (1984) *The Education of Feeling and Emotion.* London: Allen and Unwin.

Izard, C.E. (1977) *Human Emotions.* New York: Plenum Press.

Lipman, M. (1995) 'Using philosophy to educate emotions.' *Analytic Teaching 15,* 2, 3–10.

Pike, G. and Selby, D. (1988) *Global Teacher, Global Learner*. London: Hodder and Stoughton.

Roebben, B. (1995) 'Catching a glimpse of the palace of reason: the education of moral emotions.' *Journal of Moral Education 24*, 2, 185–197.

Vasta, E. and Castles, S. (eds) (1996) *The Teeth are Smiling: The Persistence of Racism in Multicultural Australia*. St.Leonards, NSW: Allen and Unwin.

CHAPTER TEN

The Teacher's Role in Democratic Pedagogies

Doug Harwood

INTRODUCTION

During the last 30 years, many 'active/democratic' approaches to teaching have been developed in primary and secondary schools, to encourage pupil participation in the processes of learning and decision making. This has raised questions about which role(s) teachers should adopt when teaching democratically and how these should be managed. This chapter will discuss the alternatives recommended by those working in this field and the contribution of research, including the viewpoints of children, to our understanding of such practice.

The concept of 'role' helps us to describe distinctive patterns of behaviour, both verbal and non-verbal. Although the issue of 'role' was at the forefront of the educational agenda in the 1970s, due to the controversy surrounding the 'neutral chairman' role (Humanities Curriculum Project 1970) and again in the 1980s in relation to political education (Carrington and Troyna 1988; Harwood 1986; Stradling, Noctor and Baines 1984; Wellington 1986), it has been neglected as a question for the 1990s. However, recent concern about how to educate children to be morally responsible citizens, alongside recent pronouncements advocating an increase in whole class teaching, look like bringing the issue back to centre stage. It is therefore timely to look at the various role options available to the teacher.

ALTERNATIVE TEACHER ROLE(S) FOR ACTIVE/DEMOCRATIC PEDAGOGY

Alternative 'roles' in the context of democratic discussion have been identified by Rudduck (1978; 1979); by my own work in the context of pastoral care (Harwood 1983) and political education (Harwood 1986); and by Tudor

(1993), in relation to the 'learner-centred classroom'. A summary of the teacher roles relevant to democratic teaching is presented in Table 10.1. A major issue is how far teachers should use 'instruction' to develop and explain their own personally held views and how far remain impartial when teaching democratically. To help analyse this question, the key roles of 'impartial facilitator', 'instructor' and 'devil's advocate' will now be identified, with illustrations based upon videotape evidence from the World Studies 8–13 Project. This project was set up in 1980 to help young people develop the knowledge and skills they need to live in an interdependent world (Fisher and Hicks 1985).

Table 10.1 Types of role available to the teacher in active/democratic pedagogy

Role	Description	Rate
1. Participant	Is free to express ideas, opinions and feelings just like any other member of the group.	
2. Devil's Advocate	Tries to stimulate participation by deliberately taking oppositional stances.	
3. Impartial/Neutral Facilitator	Chairs the discussion by organising and facilitating pupils' contributions and by maintaining rules and limits. Does not express personal viewpoint. Does not give positive or negative feedback after pupils' contributions.	
4. Instructor	Explains and clarifies relevant information, concepts and ideas. Asks task questions to assess understanding. Gives positive or negative feedback after pupils' contributions.	
5. Committed Instructor	Uses the instructor role, as above, in a sustained way, to propagate own viewpoint on controversial issues.	
6. Interviewer	Questions individuals to elicit their ideas, feelings and opinions.	
7. Observer	Observes the pupils during their discussion, but does not intervene.	
8. Absent Leader	Withdraws from the group after the initial organisation of work.	
9. Other?		

You might consider how often you use each of the above roles, using the scale:
0 = never; 1 = rarely; 2 = occasionally; 3 = often; 4 = most of the time; 5 = always.

1. IMPARTIAL FACILITATOR

This role involves the following types of behaviour:

(a) Impartial chairing, as when the teacher:

- (i) invites pupils to elaborate further upon statements, which may still be unclear
- (ii) redirects questions or issues to other pupils for comment or development
- (iii) invites pupils to agree or disagree with each other
- (iv) invites pupils to comment on or question what has just been said
- (v) clarifies or invites pupils to clarify what has been said as a basis for further discussion
- (vi) summarises the main trends of the discussion, as a stimulus for further reflection
- (vii) applies rules of democratic discussion.

(b) Asking open questions, as when the teacher asks questions to which there may be a range of possible alternative responses or which require genuinely creative thinking, rather than knowledge of a definitive answer.

(c) Neutral response, as when the teacher replies to a pupil's idea without indicating agreement or disagreement, as when receiving ideas, without further comment, during brainstorming.

(d) Introducing evidence, in the form of photographs, written materials, statistics etc., as a stimulus for discussion, rather than as facts which are beyond dispute.

Each of the examples that follows involves a different class of pupils.

Example 1

In the following illustration of these types of behaviour, the teacher is using the 'Jigsaw Photograph' activity. In this, a picture of a 'female worker in a computer factory in Thailand' has been cut into separate parts. Small groups of children, aged 12–13 years, have been given one part of the picture at a time and asked to make suggestions about its identity. The teacher brainstorms their ideas:

Teacher: Can you give me either a word or a question?
        (*Behaviour 1(b) open question.*)

Pupil: Microscope.

Teacher: Microscope, next?

(*Behaviour 1(c) teacher accepts the suggestion and writes it on the board without comment.*)

Pupil: Factories.

Pupil: Surgery.

Teacher: (*writing on board*) Next?

Pupil: Think it's a man.

Pupil: A scientist.

Pupil: A lady.

The teacher receives the children's ideas neutrally, without comment or question and acts as secretary for the group. At this stage, children are asked to refrain from questioning each other or raising disagreements, so that others will not be inhibited from offering their own ideas.

Example 2

At the end of the brainstorming, the teacher reads the short caption, which accompanies the picture: 'In factories all over the world, women are employed to do intricate and repetitive sorts of work. They work in a factory and do very careful things. Health conditions in factories like this one in Thailand, which manufactures microchips, are notoriously poor. Workers often have to retire early with severely damaged eyes' (*Behavior 1(d)*).

Teacher: Having gone through the picture, does anyone want to comment on the picture and what I have just read?
(*Behaviour 1(b) open question*)

Pupil A: Do they want to work in a factory?

Teacher: Can anyone answer that?
(*Behaviour 1(a) (ii) reflects question back to the group*)

Pupil B: They wouldn't want to work in those conditions.

Pupil C: But maybe they can't do anything else there. Maybe there are no other jobs for them to do.

Pupil B: I have read that people working in those places sometimes lose their eyesight. Sometimes, they only manage to work for two or three years.

Pupil C: But you can't live without money. They have to work there to survive.

Pupil B: But they will find it difficult to work, if they lose their eyesight.

Teacher: John [Pupil C] says that they have to work in those conditions to survive, whilst Anne [Pupil B] says they wouldn't want to work there because their health will suffer too much. What does anybody else think?

The teacher has refrained from intervening until now. However, s/he wants to widen the participation, so s/he summarises the main arguments and invites discussion (*Behaviour 1(a) (vi)*).

> Pupil D: I think that she might have a baby to look after or maybe she lives with her parents and they are very ill.
>
> Pupil E: She can't help it. She has no choice.
>
> Pupil F: Her friends might all work there and she wants to be with her friends.
>
> Pupil D: Some people in this country don't like their job, but they have to work. They don't want to but they have to.
>
> Teacher: You seem to be agreeing with John that they want to work there, because of the money and friends. (*Behaviour 1(a) (vi)*) Does anybody support Anne's view that they wouldn't want to work there? (*Behaviour 1(a) (iii)*).

The teacher is concerned that Anne (pupil 13), who first expressed concern about the conditions of work, is now isolated. She therefore tries to find support for her.

> Pupil D: I don't think factories should be like that.
>
> Teacher: What do you mean? (*Behaviour 1(a) (i)*)

The teacher has remained impartial, so that all the ideas have come from the children. S/he has attempted to look after the dynamics of the discussion, so that everybody has a fair hearing.

2. INSTRUCTOR ROLE

This role involves the following types of behaviour:

(a) Making task statements, as when the teacher states ideas, facts, opinions etc. in his/her own person or presents evidence from texts etc. as matters of fact, rather than as a stimulus to further discussion.

(b) Asking closed questions, as when the teacher asks a question to which there is a generally known and accepted factual answer.

(c) Asking leading or rhetorical questions, as when the teacher asks a question which includes, in its phraseology, clues as to the preferred answer, or asks questions which invite agreement with the teacher's viewpoint.

(d) Explicitly agreeing or disagreeing with the pupil's ideas or opinions, as when the teacher replies 'That's right' or 'I agree with what Joan has just said'.

(e) Suddenly changing the focus of the lesson unilaterally.

The 'committed instructor' role applies when the teacher uses the above forms of instruction to propagate her/his own viewpoint in a sustained way.

Example 3

A teacher has just read aloud the passage about the female worker that was read in Example 2 to a different class.

Teacher: Why do you think people want to work in this factory, even though it is unhealthy? (*Behaviour 1(b) open question although the context is narrowly defined.*)

Pupil A: They wouldn't want to work in those conditions. They work there because it's the only chance they've got.

Teacher: So you are saying they wouldn't want to. They work there because it's the only chance they've got. Because there are no other jobs (*Behaviour 1(c)*). What other reasons? (*Behaviour 1(b)*).

The teacher reflects back pupil A's answer, but does not then invite any further discussion before asking for additional ideas.

Pupil B: For the money.

Pupil C: They've no experience of anything else.

Teacher: There might not be any opportunities to work. There may not be jobs that pay that sort of money.

The teacher elaborates slightly on the children's ideas and thereby confirms that they are acceptable, as they stand, rather than a topic for discussion (*Behaviour 2(d)*). S/he goes on to act as instructor, by developing the point further.

> The money is important, for example, if you were offered a job to work in a shop and one shop offers you £2 and another one offers you £3, what one would you choose?...and if it was horrible to work for the £3 and nice to work for the £2, which would you choose?

The teacher raises the issue of choice, but does not facilitate any discussion.

> You have to make a choice. I mean, it's probably a bit like you coming to school and although you might not like school, at least you see your friends every day at playtime. That's probably true in the factory. She'll see her friends every day, because she goes to the factory every day. (*Behaviour 2(a)*).

The teacher has contributed a long task statement, including the new idea of friends and work. S/he now suddenly changes the focus of the discussion.

> Someone brought up something about good eyesight. It actually says here that the woman will probably have to retire early with severely damaged eyes *(Behaviour 2(e))*. Can anyone explain that? *(Behaviour 2(b) this question focuses on factual information rather than values.)*

Pupil D: Eyes are strained due to staring, so they are damaging their eyes.

Teacher: Can you understand that? *(Behaviour 2(d) The teacher implies agreement and confirms this by elaborating the point further.)*

> It's like staring at something day after day doing the same thing. There are rules in this country about using computers... 20 minutes' work then 10 minutes off... Perhaps she has to work to get enough money. She has no choice. But perhaps after two or three years, she won't be able to do this job. She'll be unemployed. She probably can't do other work. Its a very short time to be earning money *(Behaviour 2(a): the teacher's own viewpoint is very evident)*. Do you think, knowing that, that she wants to work in this factory? *(Behaviour 2(c))* What makes her have to work in this factory? *(Behaviour 2(c))*

Pupil B: Money.

Pupil E: Family. Maybe she's got a family.

Pupil F: Friends are there. That would make it nicer for her.

The teacher has acted as the instructor, by using question–answer strategies and his/her own statements to develop the key ideas of the lesson. It is interesting that the children have repeated some of the points already introduced by the teacher. S/he seems to have been very influential.

3. DEVIL'S ADVOCATE

This role involves the following types of behaviour:

   (a) Deliberately making provocative statements to stimulate debate.

   (b) Deliberately asking provocative questions to stimulate debate.

Example 4

After reading the passage outlined in Example 2, a teacher asks:

Teacher: Would you like to work in a factory like that? *(Behaviour 1(b))*

Pupil A: No. It might make me go blind.

Pupil B: No. You have to work such long hours.

Pupil C: It would be awful just sitting there all day.

Pupil D: You have to concentrate so hard. It would ruin your eyes.

Teacher: Does everybody agree? (*Behaviour 1(a) (iii)*.)

Pupils: Yes!

Teacher: Well, I don't agree. I would work there. I could see my friends every day. I could support my family. I could use the money to buy a hi-fi system and have good holidays (*Behaviour 3(a)*). Why shouldn't I work in the factory? (*Behaviour 3(b)*.)

The teacher makes statements that may not reflect his/her true feelings, in order to challenge the pupils' thinking (*Behaviour 3(b)*).

Pupil B: 'Cos you might lose your eyesight.

Teacher: Well, at least I could have a good time whilst I had my sight. If I couldn't earn money, I couldn't have a good time (*Behaviour 3(a)*).

Pupil C: Wouldn't you be too tired to have a good time?

One problem with the Devil's Advocate role is that the discussion can become polarised. An alternative would be for teachers to present the new arguments through other forms of evidence, that is, via a comic strip, article, story etc., so that they do not appear to be their own views. Similar problems can occur when the teacher adopts the 'participant' role. The teacher's views might either become too central to the discussion or be accepted too uncritically by the pupils.

MANAGING THE TEACHER'S ROLE

As well as deciding which alternative(s) to adopt, teachers have to decide how best to manage their role in the democratic classroom. Four main strategies can be identified: the 'fixed role', the 'flexible role', 'role hierarchy' and 'role sequence' approaches.

The fixed role

The 'fixed role' means that the teacher remains consistently in just one role when leading democratic discussion. For example, the Humanities Curriculum Project (1970) proposed that, because 'the teacher could not be an arbiter of truth or warranter of knowledge' when dealing with controversial issues, s/he ought to remain consistently in the role of neutral chairman and not state her/his own views (Stenhouse 1983, p.168). Similarities between this position and the teacher's role in Lipman's 'Philosophy for Children' project have been identified (Lane and Lane 1986). The advantages of the 'fixed' impartial role are that it provides consistency for the children, provided that its rationale is explained beforehand. It offers pupils space to provide ideas and practise skills for themselves and gives the teacher the opportunity to observe and manage the process. The disadvantages are that it creates difficulties for the teacher when children seem unable to cope with the novelty of the situation or lack the necessary skills to discuss democratically.

The flexible role

The 'flexible' approach to role management suggests that the teacher should always be free to switch roles, to respond to the immediate needs of the situation. Thus, for Stradling *et al.*, there are 'no universal prescriptions... Different circumstances require different methods and strategies' (1984, p.11). This means that, if the situation demands it, teachers should be free to state their own views. The advantage of the 'flexible' approach is that it allows teachers to respond creatively to the unexpected demands of the classroom. The disadvantage is that the teacher's change of role can be used mainly to serve the teacher's short-term self-interest, at the expense of longer-term objectives (Harwood 1983). It can also appear to be unpredictable and inconsistent in the eyes of the children.

The role hierarchy model

I have suggested previously (Harwood 1983; 1986) how flexibility can be accommodated within a hierarchy of preferred roles (see Table 10.2). I argue that, in 'active/democratic' pedagogy, the teacher's main role should be that of 'impartial facilitator', so that space is provided for pupils to contribute their own ideas and skills. However, there will be times when the pupils genuinely are unable to move forward their discussion and learning without help. When this happens, the teacher should consider changing role to demonstrate the skills which seem to be lacking. This model combines elements of both the 'fixed' role, in preferring the 'impartial' position, and of 'flexibility' in allowing role to be changed in special circumstances. However, the teacher is warned against changing role too frequently, especially to positions which are more comfortable and familiar. Ideally, teachers should approach role changes cautiously, in partnership with the children and with full awareness of potential costs as well as benefits. The role of 'sensitive facilitator' in 'Student-Centred Learning' is close to the 'hierarchical' model (Brandes and Ginnis 1986, p.169), whilst 'World Studies 8–13' similarly recommends that the teacher's 'own opinions and values *really* ought not to feature' (Steiner 1993, pp.74–5).

Table 10.2 A hierarchy of roles for the teacher in active/democratic pedagogy

I would try to adopt these roles **often**.	Impartial Facilitator	To provide maximum opportunities for pupils to make their own contributions.
	Observer	But only when the discussion does not need my interventions.
	Absent Leader	When the pupils are preparing for general discussion, it is better not to be present, unless invited.
I would **occasionally** adopt these roles.	Instructor Devil's Advocate	But only when pupils genuinely cannot provide their own ideas, concepts and critical perspective.
I would only **rarely** adopt this role.	Committed Instructor	But only when extremist (such as racist or sexist) positions are being left unchallenged.
I would **never** adopt these roles.	Participant	Teachers cannot be equal participants, because of their authority position.
	Interviewer	It is unfair to focus upon one individual within the group setting.

The role sequence model

Whereas the 'flexible' and 'hierarchical' models assume that role changes will be unpredictable, the 'role sequence' approach suggests that the management of role can follow a planned sequence, matching the developing needs of the participants. Some who argue that teachers should be free to present their own views, nevertheless acknowledge the effectiveness of neutrality in creating space for pupil-to-pupil interaction in the early stages. I have thus identified the 'advocate' role, in which teachers ensure that all views are expressed before arguing in favour of their own position (Harwood 1986). One might question how far such control of the timing of the agenda is truly democratic. I have also identified a 'declared interest' role, in which teachers state their own views at the start, so that pupils can judge their bias during later stages. Egan (1986) has described a 'sequential' model in the field of counselling, which can be adapted for the 'debriefing' stage of democratic groupwork. In this, the teacher's role changes to be compatible with different stages in the 'helping' process. The stages are: *the expressive stage*, during which the teacher acts as an 'impartial facilitator' in order to help pupils to find their voice; *the cognitive stage*, during which the teacher encourages deeper understanding, by asking more challenging questions (catalyst role) and offering new interpretations and theoretical perspectives (instructor role); and *the action stage*, during which the teacher helps pupils to identify and evaluate alternative action plans, whilst remaining non-directive in relation to the eventual decision.

THE PUPIL'S DEMOCRATIC RIGHTS

Harber and Meighan (1986) have argued that pupils should be involved in decisions about their teacher's role, as a fundamental right of citizenship. Teachers also have rights and responsibilities arising from the authority placed upon them by the wider community. A transactional approach involving the sharing of viewpoints by pupils, teachers and other adults would be the best solution, although differences in power and authority may be difficult to manage. There are other potential difficulties: children may initially have a greater preference for a dependency relationship based upon instruction than the teachers, especially when external assessments are involved. They will often have no experience of the new pedagogy upon which to base their choice. For this reason, teachers should discuss their rationale for changing role with their pupils, before implementation. Where pupils and teachers have no previous experience of the new pedagogy, they might agree to experiment with the approach for an agreed period of time.

RESEARCH FINDINGS: DOES THE TEACHER'S ROLE MAKE A DIFFERENCE TO CHILDREN'S CONTRIBUTIONS TO DISCUSSION?

It is important that decisions about role management should be based upon the study of classroom behaviour and outcomes, rather than just rhetoric. In a recent review of research (Harwood 1997), I found that the 'impartial facilitator' has advantages over the 'instructor' role in encouraging pupils' democratic participation, as follows:

- 'the extent to which teachers use forms of direct instruction is negatively related to the amount of interaction between the students' (Cohen 1994, pp.28–9)
- increased talk by the teachers correlated with low levels of pupil-to-pupil and pupil-initiated talk, whereas the opposite was the case when teachers made greater use of 'impartial chairing' (Harwood 1989, pp.191–2; 1997, p.80)
- 'impartial chairing' correlated with 'extensive evidence of increases in speculative confidence in students and also of increments in reading comprehension, vocabulary and pupil self-esteem' (Stenhouse 1975, p.50)
- the adoption of the 'impartial' role enabled pupils to 'move from one stage of thinking ability to the next highest one, during the course of the interview' (McNaughton 1982, p.274)
- the range of roles assumed by pupils increased when the teacher was acting as 'impartial chair' (Harwood 1989, p.192)

- 'a significant improvement in formal reasoning and creative reasoning' (Lane and Lane 1986, p.265) and in reading and mathematics (Lipman 1985, p.39)
- the 'impartial' role correlated with more elaborated and extended verbal contributions from the pupils, especially when the teacher used chairing skills to manage the interaction (Harwood 1997, p.65).

THE PUPILS' VIEWPOINT

The reactions of children can be a crucial influence on the teacher's choice of role. If pupils' basic preferences are not being met, they will usually find ways of communicating their dissatisfaction. There have been few studies of children's views specifically about the role of the teacher in active/democratic pedagogy. Rudduck (1979, pp.18–21) included pupils' comments, which expressed a wide range of views on their experience of the neutral chairing approach of the Humanities Curriculum Project. However, there is a need for more work in this area.

I undertook the following study shortly after the end of the Gulf War (Summer 1991). At the time, there had been uncertainty as to whether pupils should be taught about the war in school. I carried out both group interviews and questionnaire research in five schools (one rural; two inner-city; two suburban), with the same small groups of 9–11-year-old children, selected by their teacher. One school had a predominantly Moslem population. I concluded the interviews with questions to elicit children's views on the role of the teacher in classroom discussions about the Gulf War. Throughout the interviews, I maintained an impartial role. The teachers' and pupils' names are fictitious.

Children's views on their right to discuss political issues

The children were almost unanimous that they should have been allowed to discuss the Gulf War in school (34 positive responses out of 37 questionnaire returns). A range of reasons were given, in which the idea of children's rights figured strongly.

Interviewer: Some people have said that schools shouldn't really talk about the Gulf War. How would you reply to them?

Pupil: They are completely wrong.

Interviewer: Why do you say that?

Pupil: It affects us as much as anybody else.

Pupil: We have a right to speak about it more than some adults.

Pupil: Well, if our country is fighting for it, then we have a right to know.

Pupil: We have a right to know because we are also involved as well as adults.

Nevertheless, the children were sensitive to the problems of dealing with the issue in class:

Pupil: If there are people in this school who have dads there, I don't think it should be discussed because it upsets them.

Pupil: They should have the option whether they should talk about it or not.

Pupil: There is a girl in our class and her dad's name is Hussein and it is hard for her because they keep taking the mickey out of her.

Pupil: We never used to say his last name because we might upset her.

Pupil: She is a Moslem, so you felt that anything you said might be wrong.

Children's views on the role and influence of the teacher

Interestingly, some felt that discussion was better if you had an adult present:

Pupil: What you say to your friends and what you say to an adult is completely different.

Pupil: You need an adult to keep your views within reason, because if I spoke with this lot, we would just say 'Oh, we are going to blow up the Iraqis'.

This view correlates with recent research, which found that the quality of children's discussion improved when the teacher was present as facilitator to the group (Harwood 1995).

One child even felt that if views were expressed too strongly in the presence of the teacher this might lead to punishment:

Pupil: If the children go really mad and say 'Why did they start the war? Why did Saddam Hussein start the war? Why did that man with the big, massive moustache and big head start the war?', then we'd be put in DT [detention].

In relation to the role of the teacher, there was general agreement that the teacher should facilitate and listen to the pupils' opinions:

Interviewer: What role should the teacher take in discussions about issues like the Gulf War?

Pupil: The teacher should appreciate other people's views and listen to their views.

There were mixed views as to whether teachers should express their own opinions or remain impartial. Some children tended to support the practice, which they experienced themselves with their own teacher:

Pupil: Have it in different parts, like Mrs Smith tells us what she thinks about it and then we discuss it and then somebody like you comes in and asks us questions.

Pupil: Well, they (teachers) should first ask the children's opinion and then say 'Well, my opinion is this', because if not the children will say 'Oh yes, that's my opinion as well'. Miss Jones does it. First she asks your opinion and then she tells you what her opinion is.

Most children did think that teachers should express their point of view:

Interviewer: Some people think that teachers should not give their opinion on political issues. What do you think of that?

Pupil: They should, so that we get to know more about them...what they think.

Pupil: We should discuss it [i.e. what the teacher thinks]. It's good that we discuss it, because we get more of a view.

Pupil: If Miss Jones didn't give her opinion, I would think she didn't care at all, because she knows what it is like to be in a war.

Interviewer: Say the teacher felt that Saddam Hussein was right to go into Kuwait, should the teacher explain that to you?

Pupil: She should say 'Well, I believe that he should have gone into Kuwait, but you are entitled to your opinion'.

Other children felt that teachers had a democratic right either to declare their views or be silent, as they wished.

Pupil: Make it more open. Everybody should feel more free about the school.

Pupil: If she does not want to at all then she should say 'Well, I would not like to say my opinion for certain reasons, but you can say your opinion'.

Pupil: They have got a right to not say.

Pupil: About the teacher, if she doesn't want to give her opinion, well, it is up to her...

However, this child went on to say that...

if she didn't for about half an hour, I would put my hand up and say 'what is your opinion?' and then she might have to say her opinion, because sometimes teachers won't say anything because they don't feel like it.

At the same time, the children were clear that they did not want teachers to propagate their views too strongly:

Pupil: I don't appreciate a teacher coming round and saying 'Oh well, this has happened and this is the view you must have'.

There was also evidence that some children did not want teachers to express their own point of view. In this sample, it was the Moslem children who felt that the teacher's views would be too biased for them to lead discussion on the Gulf War fairly.

Pupil: If the teacher would tell us the reasons, they could tell us the wrong things. I would listen to my parents, not the TV.

Pupil: How could you trust the teachers to tell you the truth?

Pupil: They [i.e. teachers] might not like us supporting the other side.

Pupil: I would just close my ears, if the teacher tried to explain it.

Others were aware that the treatment of the Gulf War in school and in the media might have been biased:

Interviewer: Did you discuss any reasons why Saddam might have been right?

Pupil: No, we only discussed one side.

Interviewer: Do you think you should have been taught about how Saddam had thought about it?

Pupil: Yes.

Pupil: I think we should have gone into it in much more detail.

Pupil: They blanked out some details.

Pupil: The television is biased.

For other children, the teacher's viewpoint seemed unproblematic and therefore could be highly influential. Some valued the teacher's viewpoint more than that of other children:

Pupil: Like Miss Jones knows more than us. She was in the Second World War and she knows what it is like. Miss Jones is a really good understanding teacher. That is why she is really good at it.

Pupil: If [we hadn't] seen it on the news, *with the teachers telling us,* we might not have thought that the Iraqis did not want to fight.

CONCLUSION

It is evident from the above that there was no clear consensus amongst the pupils about which role teachers should adopt when controversial questions are being discussed in the classroom. Some children genuinely want to hear the teacher's opinions alongside their own and other views and do seem not to be too influenced by them. Others, in this case the Moslem children, distrust the teacher's bias and do not want to hear the teacher's views on matters about which they themselves already have strong opinions. There are other children who can be too strongly influenced by what the teacher has to say. This presents the teacher with a difficult dilemma, in which it might be impossible to satisfy everybody. In these circumstances, it is important that the teacher should openly discuss all the possibilities with the children and arrive at a mutually acceptable decision.

Finally, the experience of participating in these interviews with children demonstrated to me that young pupils are very capable of engaging in sophisticated democratic discussion, when this is facilitated by an adult, acting impartially. This, alongside the research evidence already cited, suggests that teachers should encourage pupils at least to experiment with the 'impartial facilitator' role. As two children replied during the interviews:

Interviewer: I haven't given my opinion. How do you feel about that?

Pupil: You listen to us and we are having quite good fun, so we really didn't notice.

Pupil: It is good what we are doing today. We are all listening to each other instead of the teacher just standing there talking about it.

REFERENCES

Brandes, D. and Ginnis, P. (1986) *A Guide to Student-Centred Learning*. Oxford: Blackwell.

Carrington, B. and Troyna, B. (eds) (1988) *Children and Controversial Issues*. London: The Falmer Press.

Cohen, E.G. (1994) 'Restructuring the classroom: conditions for productive small groups.' *Review of Educational Research 64*, 1, 1–35.

Egan, G. (1986) *The Skilled Helper: A Model for Systematic Helping and Interpersonal Relating*. Monterey, California: Brooks/Cole Publishing Company.

Fisher, S. and Hicks, D. (1985) *World Studies 8–13: A Teachers' Handbook*. Edinburgh: Oliver & Boyd.

Harber, C. and Meighan, R. (1986) 'Democratic method in teacher training for political education.' *Teaching Politics 15*, 2, 179–187.

Harwood, D.L. (1983) 'Leader-roles in pastoral groupwork.' *Pastoral Care in Education 1*, 2, 96–107.

Harwood, D.L. (1986) 'To advocate or to educate? What role for the teacher in political education in the primary years?' *Education 3–13*, 14, 1, 51–57.

Harwood, D.L. (1989) 'The nature of teacher–pupil interaction in the Active Tutorial Work approach: using interaction analysis to evaluate student-centred approaches.' *British Educational Research Journal 15*, 2, 177–194.

Harwood, D.L (1995) 'The pedagogy of the world studies 8–13 project: the influence of the presence/absence of the teacher upon primary children's collaborative groupwork.' *British Educational Research Journal 21*, 5, 587–611.

Harwood, D.L. (1997) 'Teacher roles in "World Studies" democratic pedagogy.' *Evaluation and Research In Education 11*, 2, 65–90.

Humanities Curriculum Project (1970) *The Humanities Project: An Introduction*. London: Heinemann.

Lane, N.R. and Lane, S.A. (1986) 'Rationality, self-esteem and autonomy through collaborative enquiry.' *Oxford Review of Education 12*, 263–275.

Lipman, M.A. (1985) 'Philosophy and the cultivation of reason.' *Thinking, The Journal of Philosophy for Children 5*, 4, 33–41.

McNaughton, A.H. (1982) 'Cognitive development, political understanding and political literacy.' *British Journal of Educational Studies 30*, 264–279.

Rudduck, J. (1978) *Learning through Small Group Discussion*. University of Surrey: Society for Research into Higher Education.

Rudduck, J. (ed) (1979) *Learning to Teach through Discussion*. Occasional Paper No. 8. Norwich: Centre for Applied Research in Education, University of East Anglia.

Steiner, M. (1993) *Learning from Experience: World Studies in the Primary Curriculum*. Stoke-on-Trent: Trentham.

Stenhouse, L. (1975) *Introduction to Curriculum Research and Development*. London: Heinemann.

Stenhouse, L. (1983) *Authority, Education and Emancipation*. London: Heinemann.

Stradling, R. Noctor, M. and Baines, B. (1984) *Teaching Controversial Issues*. London: Edward Arnold.

Tudor, I. (1993) 'Teacher roles in the learner-centred classroom.' *ELT Journal 47*, 1, 22–31.

Wellington, J.J. (ed) (1986) *Controversial Issues in the Curriculum*. Oxford: Blackwell, 149–168.

CHAPTER ELEVEN

Economics, Environment and the Loss of Innocence

Martin Ashley

Dear '1015',

I am very concerned for the rainforest. Every second, 40 trees are destroyed or harmed. It isn't just any forest – it deserves to live. The rainforest contains the most animals out of any forest. The plants and trees give us oxygen. Some of our medicines also come from the rainforest. I hope you can understand my concern. The rainforest needs our help.

Has environmental education succeeded? Is this the voice of the environmentally educated child? There can be little more destructive of the goals of children learning to participate as environmental citizens than such continued outpourings of the pleas of the powerless. This chapter is about empowering environmental citizens. In it, I shall explore the very important link that exists between the environment and economics. If environmental citizens are to be empowered, they need access to all the facts, and that includes economic ones. I shall argue that environmental education isolated from economic and citizenship education is in constant danger of being mere rhetoric. I shall further argue that such education runs the risk of 'burn-out' so that the concern shown by the 11-year-old writer to '1015', the Saturday junior supplement to *The Times* newspaper, is a spent force by the age of 14.

INTRODUCTION

The 1980s, as the decade of gestation of the National Curriculum, was a decade which saw the repression of many initiatives such as political education, multicultural education, global education and world studies that had previously flourished (see Griffiths and Troyna 1995). The justification for this repression, most notably associated with education secretary Kenneth Clarke (Graham and Tytler 1993), was that the curriculum had to be 'neutral' or 'value free'. That no one political viewpoint should be advocated above any other sounds superficially to be a noble sentiment until it is realised the degree to which the 1995 National Curriculum, through omission and other subtle techniques (see Ashley 1997), does precisely that. Readers will have to decide for themselves whether the desire to preserve children's economic innocence which I am about to describe can be ascribed to conspiracy theory or whether it is teachers themselves who contribute to a taboo on the loss of economic innocence almost as strong as the taboo on the loss of sexual innocence.

It seems to me that it sometimes suits adults to maintain the distinction between the supposedly innocent world of children and something often referred to as the 'real world'. In the world of childish innocence we have *Blue Peter*, baby seals that we don't like being clubbed to death and rainforests that 'they' are cutting down. Come the end of childhood innocence, however, and the 'groundswell among young people of concern for the natural world' referred to by our recent junior education minister Angela Rumbold in her preface to Curriculum Guidance Seven (Environmental Education) is swept away by the incoming flood tide of 'economic reality' and the need to secure a job which will bring suitable material rewards. Indeed, the poll carried out for Radio One prior to the 1997 general election indicated that the economic reality of employment prospects was the number one issue for first-time voters. What has happened to all the baby seals?

In the 'real world', economics, the environment, ethics and politics are part of the seamless whole that so inspired the proponents of the integrated or holistic approach to the primary curriculum. However, the ethical relationship between environment and economics is an uncomfortably close one which is discussed in some depth by Sen (1987). It is easy to demonstrate that the environmental abuse in Third World countries which causes us so much concern in the West is associated with an economic ethic that is driven by the assumption that the lowest price for the Western consumer is the primary, if not the only, good. Sen is concerned to put the record straight on this issue. It is not economics that is at fault: it is the ethical standards we apply to our economics. I would argue not only that Sen is right, but that the separation of the study of social and natural environments from the study of economics and human behaviour leads almost inevitably to the ethical impoverishment that so concerns Sen. How can an environmental education that results in a hypocritical attitude to rainforest destruction or the exploitation of children in bonded labour be justified?

A possible answer to this question is that some of the accepted ethical foundations of economics and the environment may well be too unpalatable, certainly for young children. Perhaps if we began to investigate the cost of a chocolate bar we might find that workers on cacao plantations in developing countries are cruelly and ruthlessly exploited. We might even find that in the real world of economic and political power, young children are amongst the first to be exploited for labour in developing countries. Children, after all, come fairly near the bottom of the hierarchy of economic power. How ready are we to 'discover facts not well known to the consumer' and square the ethical attitude we like to imagine we have towards the environment with the demands of fair trade? (See Clough and Holden 1996). Perhaps it is better not to ask. To spoil our own children's enjoyment of chocolate is perhaps as much an attack on childhood itself as it would be to tell a class of six-year-olds that Santa Claus is a lie.

At the time of writing, the *Guardian* has just added its voice to the growing sense of alarm concerning the disillusionment of the 18–25 age group with our political system. 'Swampy', the last of the A30 road protesters, has been extracted from his tunnel by the authorities and is digging a new one under the site of the proposed second Manchester Airport runway. I suspect that 'Swampy' and his associates were not amongst the university students polled for Radio One who regarded their employment prospects as the most important issue of the recent election campaign. The frequency with which environmental concerns are the subject of single issue politics is yet another pointer towards a fragmented curriculum which has failed to link environment, economics and citizenship.

We cannot treat the environment as though it were a different subject to economics or indeed citizenship and it is ironic that primary schools, once the bastion of the holistic approach to education, may in some cases share the guilt for this. I am concerned less with Swampy than with Richard, the 14-year-old author of this quotation:

> I don't want to hear anything more about the environment because I learned everything I need to know about it at primary school.

Richard, a 14-year-old pupil in a rural comprehensive school, is an intelligent and articulate boy and more likely, in my view, to end up as a university student looking for a 'good job' than as an unemployed single issue campaigner. The research which I shall describe shortly suggests that my claim that Richard is representative of the 'mature flower' of the approach which presently pertains in many primary schools may be justified.

I asked him whether, on a field trip, he would rather participate in an option on wildlife or an option on energy and pollution. Predictably, he said he'd rather have the wildlife option. He said that this would be fun and interesting and that he didn't want to know about negative things such as pollution. Surely, I said, pollution was an important topic? What would the world be like by the time he was my age? Did he worry about that? Yes, he replied. But he'd learnt all he needed to know about pollution at primary school. He knew that we should cut down on energy and he was fed up with people like Friends of the Earth going on about using cars less. He knew that too, but the idea just wasn't practical. People lived too far away from work, too many people lived in the country and worked in the town...

Some promising understanding of economic geography. So did he care about the environment? Yes he did, and if somebody came up with a sensible, useful suggestion about what he could really do, he'd do it. What might this be? I wondered. We began to talk about political processes. Did he know what the Chancellor of the Exchequer did? Yes, he did. Was there enough money from taxes to pay for all the things we'd like in our schools and hospitals, to have the army we'd like, to pay for environmental protection? No, there wasn't. So how would Richard like the Chancellor to prioritise public spending? Try to maintain hospitals and schools, spend less on defence and more on combating pollution was his reply. We discussed defence. He was fairly insistent that a big army advertised one as a potential aggressor and resulted in more rather than less global conflict.

Here is evidence of untapped potential. Richard has some appreciation of the way in which the values of our society are made explicit through processes of economics and politics. Although he has not studied economics as a subject he has, as Jahoda (1981) suggests is likely in children from the age of 11 upwards, a developing mental capacity for economic reasoning. Given that Richard's perceptions are more intuitive than the result of explicit teaching, we might legitimately expect a lot more. Richard's claim that he 'learnt all he needs to know at primary school' is alarming and ought to concern any committed, reflective teacher. The introduction of the English National Curriculum has undoubtedly raised standards in some areas in some schools. I have argued elsewhere (Ashley 1997) that the old Plowden style 'topic' approach of primary schools achieved little in the way of serious rigour for the subjects of science and geography and, paradoxically, resulted in an even less rigorous approach to environmental education.

Moscovici (1984) has discussed how science, which attempts to explain the commonplace in terms of abstract concepts, works in opposition to the social framework of environmental education. His arguments are well supported, not only by Richard's statement, but also by the results of my own research which is described below. Uzzell, Rutland and Whistance (1995) warn of the hypocrisy in advocating democracy in certain fragmented parts of the curriculum (for example 'education for citizenship') whilst presenting detached and essentially undemocratic solutions in other fragments (p.174). Richard needs a curriculum that will equip him with the competences of a global citizen of the twenty-first century and this means a curriculum that is more skilfully constructed than ever before in order to achieve coherence and interconnectedness.

Richard needs the knowledge, understanding and maturity of insight that will reinvigorate mainstream political processes and lead beyond the present split between single issue campaigning and cynical distrust of mainstream politicians. This means a curriculum which, whatever the legitimate demands of particular subjects, has an holistic overview which is able to clarify values and clear away the historic debris which allows us to imagine that we have ethical concerns for the environment and the world's underprivileged majority whilst simultaneously promoting a contrary economic hegemony. Why then is it that the National Curriculum Orders for science exclude mention of economics in relation to scientific ethics and the environment until Key Stage Four (ages 14–16), and then mention it only as an almost incidental topic? Why do we have a curriculum that was encouraged by the recent education secretary Kenneth Clarke to be 'objective' and 'value free', and that is now criticised for not teaching values?

THE PROCESS OF VALUES CLARIFICATION

The notion of a 'value free' curriculum is spurious and dangerous. No curriculum is value free. Watson (1993) quotes Harris (1988) in support of her view that the nul curriculum, that which '...exists by reason of the fact that it does not exist...is what is conveyed by omission, avoidance, bypassing, as well as ridiculing, criticising and putting down...' (p.20) is never neutral. Ignorance is never neutral. A curriculum which, by its prescriptions, causes learners not to know something, or not to realise that something they do know can be understood differently, has the effect of actively promoting a certain viewpoint or set of values. This is precisely what happens with our present National Curriculum. As I shall discuss shortly, without the process of values clarification, without a commitment to an ethical base to our teaching which ends economic innocence, we run the risk constantly of teaching, by omission, all sorts of dubious and dangerous values with regard to the environment.

The psychologist Derek Wright (1971) introduces us to the two very useful terms of operative and expressed values. These are potentially powerful analytical tools which can help us to clarify our thinking and perhaps encourage us to look afresh at the ethical foundations of our behaviour towards other societies and the environment. Operative values are those values that we can observe a person has by noting his or her behaviour. For example, if a man spends a lot of money on an expensive sports car and then spends a lot of time polishing it all Sunday afternoon, we might observe that the man operatively values cars. Alternatively, a man might spend a lot of time with his family. He might, in spite of a busy schedule at work, make a point of allocating time to play with his children. In this case, of course, we would observe that the man operatively values his children. 'Family values' for this man are operative and the defining of what is meant by family values in this context does not present too great a difficulty, since they relate to an observable behaviour.

The second kind of values are called expressed values. These, as the name suggests, are values which have been inferred, not from the observation of behaviour, but from what a person has said. If a person expresses the opinion that rainforests are valuable and that 'they' ought to stop cutting them down, then we have an expressed value. It is possible, of course, that we would be able to observe that the person who expresses this value devotes a lot of care and attention to avoiding the purchase of any products derived from exploitation of the rainforests or their peoples, and that this person covenants some of their income to a charity working to support rainforest conservation. Clearly we could then note that this person also operatively values rainforests.

One problem is that we talk about resource depletion but we don't talk about how much resources are actually worth. Our reluctance to discuss economics is causing us to teach, by omission, the idea that the price of a resource is the price of the human labour involved in obtaining it. We are teaching, by omission, that it is acceptable to consume more and more resources by reducing the costs of labour inputs. Such an approach leads to economic innocence or economic illiteracy.

EMPOWERING ENVIRONMENTALLY AWARE CITIZENS: A LESSON FROM RESEARCH

Real and significant changes in our approach to environmental sustainability are, in my view, more likely to be achieved through adjustments in economic priorities at the level of national government than through the single issue campaigning of the 'eco-warriors'. The research project I am about to summarise describes the degree to which the operative values of children conform to the values taught by the nul curriculum and unwittingly reinforced by the children's media. The research was undertaken a full two years before the 1997 general election, yet the economically operative values shown by the children, many of whom could have written the rhetorical letter to *The Times*, are uncannily similar to the economic agenda which dominated the election. Environment was not an economic priority in the election campaign. Neither was it an economic priority of the children in the research. My argument is that real progress in environmental education will only be made when the environment is set in its proper social, economic and political context and we begin to educate for a willingness to pay for environmental quality.

Four hundred children participated in the project. They were drawn from four schools selected to sample the end of primary school (aged 11) and the end of lower secondary school (aged 14) in urban and more rural locations. Questionnaires were circulated to the children which gathered the following data:

- knowledge of two environmental issues (transport and waste recycling)
- scientific understanding of the same two issues
- intention to act in response to the knowledge and understanding.

Economic data were gathered on the children's willingness to pay for a range of public welfare benefits which included:

- various aspects of health services
- sanitation and water supply
- educational and library services
- environmental protection
- access to the countryside.

Questionnaires were also completed by the children's parents which gathered data on the children's freedom to act in accordance with their expressed intentions and the parents' perceptions of their children's attitudes and behaviour towards the environmental issues.

A sample of 45 of Year 6 pupils (aged 10–11) was then selected for detailed study the following year (their first year of secondary schooling). The study consisted of observations of the children's operative values in relation to the environmental issues (i.e. the way the children actually behaved in practice in relation to transport, waste recycling and the use of open space) and structured interviews which explored the relationship between values expressed on the questionnaires and values observed to be operative from the children's behaviour. Analysis of the interviews allowed a detailed examination of the relationship between expressed and operative values to be made.

The economic data derived from the whole sample of 400 children revealed a set of priorities which is remarkably similar to the economic priorities that constitute the main areas of concern during general elections (the 1997 election being no exception).

Table 11.1 summarises the results.

Table 11.1 Children's economic priorities through willingness to pay (percentage of children willing to pay)

Health and sanitation	Ambulance	84.9 per cent
	Fresh water	78.3 per cent
	Doctor	74.7 per cent
Education	School	60.6 per cent
	Public library	45.6 per cent
Environment	Pollution control	57.9 per cent
	Conservation of river	31.4 per cent
	Access to countryside	28.3 per cent

These results seem to demonstrate that the intuitive economic values of the children are remarkably similar to the economic values of mainstream politics. Health and education are high priorities; conservation of the countryside is, in economic terms, a marginal consideration. However, 57.9 per cent of the sample were prepared to pay for the control of atmospheric pollution. Translated into voting intentions and eventually the economic priorities of the ruling political party, these figures might lead initially to increased political pressure to control emissions of pollutants into the atmosphere.

By a similar token the loss of countryside and wild places, valued by a minority, is likely to continue as the economic priorities of government take their inevitable course. These data are reflected in the relative proportions of the current electorate placing environmental concerns as one of their main economic priorities and are certainly reflected in the economic and environmental options offered by the main political parties. They give little indication of impending change in spite of the rhetoric of Agenda 21, which proclaims, for example: 'governments should strive to update or prepare strategies aimed at integrating environment and development as a cross-cutting issue into education at all levels within the next three years' (Agenda 21, chapter 36).

Of immediate concern to teachers is the indication from the study that approximately 75 per cent of the children had a high level of knowledge of what was considered 'good environmental behaviour'. For example, most children knew that, to be helpful to the environment, one 'ought' to walk or cycle to school, and that one 'ought' to take the train or bus as the next best option. Similarly, a large majority of the children knew that one 'ought' to recycle certain articles and a very high majority were able to discriminate between different types of waste, recognising materials that would biodegrade quickly and materials that presented long-term disposal problems. When the scientific understanding of the justifications for these 'oughts' was examined, however, the scores were considerably lower, scores of around 45 per cent being typical. Significantly, no correlation was found between knowledge of 'oughts' and understanding. In other words, increasing the level of scientific understanding would seem to have little effect upon attitude.

This relationship was confirmed by a complete lack of correlation between understanding and intention to act in that the intention seemed unrelated to the knowledge or understanding held. In other words, a child might display quite a high level of scientific understanding yet express minimal intention to act upon this knowledge. Similarly, a child might express a strong intention to adopt a 'pro-environmental' behaviour, yet possess little or no understanding of the scientific reasons that might justify the behaviour.

Twelve-year-old Jonathan might be regarded as one of the most 'environmentally committed' of the children taking part in the research. He cycles to school, recycles waste, is one of the most active members of the school's environmental project and a keen supporter of the county otter survey team. It was found by the research project that neither Jonathan nor any of the other pupils who operatively valued cycling did so because it was 'good for the environment'. Their reasons for cycling ranged from convenience (it was quicker) through having a new bike and/or gaining a degree of independence to health and enjoyment. Jonathan, in interview, talked with enthusiasm about the day when he would be old enough to own a motorbike. He did not seem to connect his own environmental rhetoric with his real life. Motorised transport is something most boys aspire to own and peer pressure and media images undoubtedly play a significant role at least as much as the simple fact that, as Richard recognised, we live in a society whose economic basis has created an infrastructure of car dependence. Very likely Jonathan will get to his future college or place of work much more quickly and conveniently by motorbike or car when he grows up and enters the 'real world'.

Jonathan was also overheard, during an otter recording expedition, to say that this was 'the best school trip I've ever been on'. The circumstances which precipitated this remark were that he and a friend had fallen in the river and ended up having a water fight. It is very important to report things in context and there is a familiarity about this context which connects very much with Richard's world view, which is that canoeing and water sports are 'cool' whilst going on country walks with aged parents is distinctly not the thing to do. Eleven-year-old Simon might be commended for his honesty and frankness in stating 'I know my mum's car's bad for the environment, but it's warm and comfortable so we still use it'. Simon was a member of a class where the pupils were encouraged to be honest and to express their own views. He was not required to assent to the 'approved teacher viewpoint' (in this case that we should aim to use cars less).

We are back to the problem of the chocolate bar. We would be ill advised (and joyless) to make Jonathan feel guilty for dreaming about motorbikes or falling in a river and having a water fight. It is wrong to deny children their childhood. It is even more wrong, however, to deny them access to the knowledge and understanding that they will need to become active environmental citizens of the twenty-first century. The issues are not complex and the needs are clear. We have to educate within a paradigm where discounting the environment is not an unwritten assumption, a fact or even value perspective to be taught by omission.

How, for example, is the Lake District National Park to be preserved from destruction through over-use by tourists? This issue should long since have overtaken traditional studies of hill farming as the most pressing item on the agenda. The quality of ideas and discussion generated by lower secondary pupils I have taught when discussing the issue of whether we should have to pay to enter the park has been outstanding. It has certainly clarified values. Christopher, aged 11, wrote:

> I do not think it is fair to charge people to come in. The people who value the park the most might be poor people who wouldn't be able to come, so we should all pay through our taxes.

Emma, aged 12, maintained:

> If we insist on people walking, we would be keeping the disabled out. We would be willing to pay to use a park and ride scheme.

It is interesting how these children react to values clarification through a concern for human needs. This is very much in contrast to the 'they should stop destroying the rainforests' rhetoric.

A little economic understanding can transform children's interest in the energy debate too. We might question the censorship of this issue exercised by the present National Curriculum. At primary school, children are not taught that the electricity they use in the home is directly related to the 'pollution' they are familiar with from the children's media and which children, as the 'environmentally aware' members of our society are imagined to be against. Children at upper primary level are taught that electricity is to do with batteries, bulbs and buzzers. They are not taught that it is a means of transferring vast quantities of energy from power stations which have enormous environmental costs.

Children in the lower secondary school are taught about different energy sources but not about their relative costs. Neither are they taught about how much energy is contained in a so-called 'unit' of electricity that can be purchased for a mere eight or nine pence. The result is that a realistic assessment of the energy problem is impossible. The debate is excessively influenced by media-induced emotional hype such as the 'Chernobyl fear' factor rather than a sober assessment of the dire economic and political factors which were the principal cause of the Chernobyl catastrophe (Shlyakhter and Wilson 1992). Before I introduced economic and political insights into my teaching I had to content myself with Kate's comment:

> I don't remember what the Hinkley Point nuclear power station is but I'm against it because the cool people are against it.

Peter's comment was no more enlightened:

> If you don't like a nuclear power station you can knock it down and put up some windmills instead.

After introducing an economic element, I found these comments more encouraging. Matthew, aged 13, wrote:

> We should definitely save energy, but no-one will listen because energy is so cheap. We should bring the price up.

Thomas, also 13, added:

I think nuclear energy could still be used, but only if we invest more money on research. We have to pay a price for safety.

It seems to me that Matthew and Thomas may be more likely than Kate and Peter to respond positively to such possibilities as taxing energy and giving incentives to insulate homes. This confirms the need for debates focusing on the choices which must be made between conservation and unlimited material consumption.

CONCLUSION

The economic ignorance surrounding many other environmental issues such as waste recycling, transport, materials and manufacturing is so profound, and yet only a little reorientation in favour of ending economic innocence might achieve an enormous amount. I have given the example of how the introduction of simple economic concepts raises the level of sophistication of children's participation in debate on nuclear power. Why cannot a maths lesson be taught in the context of a breakdown of costs in a simple product? Such a lesson could then introduce the possibility of a slight increase in the cost of the product in order to enhance environmental protection. Would children be prepared to pay this cost? Would they be prepared to pay a little more for their break-time snacks? Would they be prepared to buy 'fair trade' chocolate bars? Would they be prepared to pay a little more for a school trip if the revenue went into protecting the environment? These are the questions teachers need to ask and, as I have argued, they are not complex. Nearly all teachers I know are fully capable of dealing with them in a competent, professional manner.

We must ask ourselves, then, why there seems to be a reluctance to do so. Is it because teachers have never considered the possibility, have never thought to question the ethical basis of our economic behaviour? Is it because teachers have some built-in antipathy to the whole notion of 'economic and industrial understanding' which dismisses anything perceived to have a remote connection with industrial capitalism as 'something we'd rather not talk about'? Perhaps we are just afraid to ask the questions? Suppose we asked the children to prioritise their economic aspirations? Suppose we asked them which they'd rather have, clean air or fast cars and they said fast cars? Maybe there is a secret fear that the economic system of fast cars and fast food palaces has already captured the souls of our children and that we teachers are powerless to do anything about it?

We should be wary, though, of an 'environmental education' which itself treats the environment as a 'consumer good'. The 'environment' can become a place only to be 'consumed' by scouts on camping and canoeing trips. Wild animals can become objects only to be 'consumed' by children belonging to wildlife clubs. Who is to say that the rights of citizens who wish to 'consume' the pleasures of camping or watching badgers are to take priority over the rights of citizens who wish to 'consume' the pleasures of motorcycle scrambling or simply driving along motorways? It is surely our clear duty as teachers to ask the questions, whether or not we have personal feelings or even a fear of the answers. It is only by opening the debate and giving children the skills to articulate and reflect upon the values with which they are growing up that we can arrest the decline in our environment. We need to remember that it was the arrival of human values and human economic systems that disrupted the evolutionary self-sustaining mechanisms of nature. It is time we stopped playing with the symptoms and grappled with the cause.

REFERENCES

Ashley, M. (1997) *Value as a Reason for Action in Environmental Education*. Unpublished PhD thesis. Bristol: University of the West of England.

Clough, N. and Holden, C. (1996) 'Global citizenship, professional competence and the chocolate cake.' In M. Steiner (ed) *Developing the Global Teacher: Theory and Practice in Initial Teacher Education*. Stoke-on-Trent: Trentham Books.

Graham, D. and Tytler, D. (1993) *A Lesson for us All. The Making of the National Curriculum*. London: Routledge.

Griffiths, M. and Troyna, B. (eds) (1995) *Antiracism, Culture and Social Justice in Education*. Stoke-on-Trent: Trentham Books.

Harris, M. (1988) *Women and Teaching*. Paulist Press.

Jahoda, G. (1981) 'The development of thinking about economic institutions: the bank.' *Cahiers de Psychologie Cognitive 1*, 1, 55–73.

Moscovici, S. (1984) 'The phenomenon of social representations.' In R. Farr and S. Moscovici (eds) *Social Representations*. Cambridge: Cambridge University Press.

Sen, A. (1987) *On Ethics and Economics*. London: Blackwell.

Shlyakhter, A. and Wilson, R. (1992) 'Chernobyl: the inevitable results of secrecy.' *Public Understanding of Science I*, 3, 251–259.

Uzzell, D., Rutland, A. and Whistance, D. (1995) 'Questioning values in environmental education.' In Y. Guerrier, N. Alexander, J. Chase and M. O'Brien (eds) *Values and the Environment: A Social Science Perspective*. Chichester: John Wiley and Sons.

Watson, B. (1993) *The Effective Teaching of RE*. London: Longman.

Wright, D. (1971) *The Psychology of Moral Behaviour*. Harmondsworth: Penguin.

CHAPTER TWELVE

Questioning Identities
Issues for Teachers and Children

Ian Davies and Micheline Rey

INTRODUCTION

The purpose of this chapter is to explore the ways in which teachers and children can learn about identities. Discussion of these ideas draws from debates within intercultural education and citizenship education as well as those from the teaching and learning of history. It is not assumed that the ways of working with adults would always be the same as those employed with children.

Following the raising of some conceptual issues, the first section relates to work with student teachers and experienced teachers who were encouraged to investigate identities through their own family histories. A purpose of this discussion is to develop teachers' thinking so that they are informed and confident to cope with such issues with children. The later sections of the chapter relate to the ways in which identities (including national and European) can be investigated by pupils in classrooms.

CONCEPTUAL ISSUES IN INTERCULTURAL EDUCATION

Much of what is described here builds on the writing and practice of Micheline Rey (e.g. Rey 1991; 1997). She has explained that using the word 'intercultural' means emphasising the prefix 'inter': interaction, exchange, opening up. It also means giving proper weight to the word 'culture': ways of life, representation and understanding of the world, behaviours including the establishment of relations with people and how we sense and feel. It is vital to recognise the importance and meanings of the interactions between individuals and groups in different places and at different times. There are two key aspects: the term 'intercultural' affirms explicitly the reality of interactions and interdependence as well as ensuring that these interactions contribute to mutual respect and the formation of cohesive communities rather than accentuating relations of domination and attitudes of exclusion and rejection.

Intercultural education relates closely to certain models of education for citizenship. In three recently developed frameworks, intercultural education would seem to relate most strongly to multiple citizenships (Heater 1990); maximal citizenship (McLaughlin 1992) and post-national citizenship (Rauner 1997). A full discussion of these models can be found in Fouts (1997) but essentially these forms of citizenship stress the importance of identities which recognise interdependence, an escape from the negative constraints of nation states, an embracing of the practices associated with the achievement and celebration of human rights, participatory democracy and equality. This approach is vital for while there is evidence of apathy among young people and adults there is at the same time a:

> climate of intolerance, aggressive nationalism and ethnocentrism which expresses itself in violence against migrants, people of immigrant origin, and minorities such as gypsies. (Council of Europe 1996, p.21)

QUESTIONING IDENTITIES THROUGH AN EXPLORATION OF TEACHERS' FAMILY HISTORIES

Teachers and others who work with children cannot do so without preparation. They need to understand the issues themselves prior to engaging with children. Work undertaken at the universities of York and Geneva has focused on diversity and interdependence through an exploration of personal histories. Some details from experiences at the University of York can be used to highlight certain issues. Most of the people in the groups were students although some staff have also become involved. A variety of graduate students were involved on different occasions: those training to become history teachers as well as those, largely from overseas, who were reading for higher degrees.

The sessions had a number of key elements. Introductory work concentrated on the need for students to understand the importance of migration throughout history and throughout the world. The various classifications of migrants were explored with an outline of the categories of immigrant workers under various status denominations, asylum seekers (waiting for authorisation or rejection), statutory refugees (according to the United Nations Convention of 1951 and the Protocol of 1967) and others (the most numerous at present) who are often not accepted under any category. The purpose of that exploration was to question the meaning and the effects of categorisations and to analyse attitudes to 'others'. Often, status (high or low), our administrative and social situation (whether it is accepted or rejected), social class, religion or ethnic group etc. hinder true communication and affect our relationships. These categorisations influence our judgments, our attitudes and our reactions to people, especially when they are (im)migrants or members of minorities.

The work explored identities through the participants' experience of migration. The exercise aimed to show that, although students often think that migrants, foreigners or those from minority groups are marginalised because they are 'different', we are, after all, not so different from them. Students were invited to realise that their families have experienced the same kind of migrations and difficulties including rejection. Those families have also been enriched through migration. All of us (migrants and those who think of themselves as non-migrants) have the same needs, the same feelings and deserve the same consideration.

The nature of individual and collective identity is an important area for students to consider. Investigations within their families, or later, with the group, allowed them to realise that the experience of migration – not always an easy one – strongly influences identities and that loyalties are plural, dynamic and related to the behaviour of others. It was intended that this exercise would help them to approach these issues with sensitive and intelligent professionalism in their relations with parents and children.

The students were given background reading about migration (e.g. Rey 1991) three weeks before the session itself. Students were encouraged to read this article closely, and to gather information about the migrations of members of their own families. It was made clear to them that they would be asked to present their findings to the full group of students and so sensitivity would need to be exercised in terms of the selection and presentation of material, and also in the reactions to those presentations by peers and tutors.

Individually and as a group the students were helped to analyse the consequences which the migratory movements had on the members of their family. They were asked to research:

- date of birth, date of death, gender
- nationality(ies), naturalisation(s)
- use of languages, acquired languages
- migratory movements (internal/external)
- motives and reasons for migration (e.g. political, economic, professional, personal)
- consequences of the migration (e.g. linguistic, cultural, economic, health, identity support).

They were then asked to consider:

- experience of elements of 'break-up' as compared with continuity, and change as compared with permanence
- experience of change in family and social relationships
- variations in male and female experience

- influence of the nature of the reception on the social integration of the migrants, on their further movements and future identity choices
- how each person lived through the migration period and how they look back on the experience
- interrelation between personal life stories and the social, political, economic, cultural context of the migration.

This allowed for an evaluation of their own perceptions of migratory movements through the life of their family, and raised questions to explore as a group.

The very great extent of migration immediately became apparent. This was true both geographically and temporally. Drawings by students and tutors on maps of the United Kingdom, Europe, and the world showed extensive migratory movements for three periods: before 1945, between 1945 and 1969, and finally since 1970. One person was able to comment on family history which extended back to at least 1245, and many told of events from the nineteenth century.

Migration associated with political movements and war were much in evidence. UK students discussed links with former colonies and commonwealth countries with many contacts, specifically with Australia and Canada. Some families had worked in South America and in Africa and comments were made on the impact of independence movements. The Taiwanese and Chinese students referred to the political situation in and around 1949 and its lasting consequences. The development of communism in both Europe and elsewhere and the subsequent moves by families to escape from or embrace these developments was apparent. The influence of war as an aspect of politics was immediately evident and students had obtained a large amount of information relating to the conflicts of both world wars as well as to events on a smaller scale. The experience of fighting, the home front and the aftermath of war were all vividly reported.

Language was another very important area. One student discussed the total of seven new languages that had been acquired by only four members of her family as a result of migration. Others spoke less positively about the experiences of learning languages as part of the process of migration:

> Problems of migration are everyday life in my family. Of course, because our English is poor. For instance, my five years old daughter goes to school but cannot speak English at all. I feel that the factors which affect the identity of my family originate from language while they originated from economy in my home country. I feel that in social relationships my behaviour is not assigned a high symbolic value because my English is poor. Actually I don't feel like an immigrant but in England under culture shock I have realised that the integration of my children and generally

speaking second generation of migrants is very important but a difficult task.

Economic circumstances were a significant factor for many participants. Some students' families had only recently undertaken migration voluntarily as opposed to being forced to escape from unemployment, whereas others had moved in order to gain high status professional positions in the law, medicine and business. Many of the students had undertaken very recent migration (either internal or from overseas) to continue their studies. The economic aspirations associated with such migrations were clear. In the UK contacts with Ireland were very noticeable, and led many students to discuss the economic (and political) links between the United Kingdom and Eire. The famine of the 1840s played a role in the migration of a number of families. One commented that his family had split at the time of the famine, with one half wanting to stay on the land they had held for centuries, while the other half decided to go to Australia and take everyone in the village with them. So bitter was the quarrel that those who stayed behind changed the spelling of their name to disassociate from those who went; but few of those who stayed survived.

Gender issues were discussed as for some families a pattern of females following males had occurred while for others less stereotypical developments had taken place. A number of people noted the importance of the male searching for work which led to the movement of females and then of whole families. The students commented that the session had made them think more deeply about many aspects of history and about the issues involved in migrations. It had done so in a stimulating way which as one said made them realise that 'we are all migrants'.

We had intended that this experience would encourage these future teachers to have a more open and co-operative approach to pupils and parents coming from various communities (linguistic, cultural, ethnic etc.) and to be better prepared to develop intercultural education in the classroom. Perhaps the experience would have been richer and the dialogue more intercultural with more varied groups. However, when overseas students are involved caution is needed as one of the main concerns throughout their time within the UK may be to meet the challenge of integrating with the host community. Having permission to live in a country is not the same as being accepted (Curtis 1995).

QUESTIONING IDENTITIES IN THE CLASSROOM

The discussion so far draws the attention of teachers and others to key issues both in terms of professional development and, more directly, for the education of children.

We are, however, not recommending a simplistic approach to exploring identities in schools based on the use of pupils' family histories. A discovery of family history for children may be even more sensitive than it is for adults. The main purposes of the above example are to show teachers how the experiences brought about by migration are so crucial to our identity and common to all.

We would recommend a variety of different approaches to raise issues about identities with children. A simple, positive and commonly used example (something similar can be seen in Pike and Selby 1988, p.120) allows children to question some of the different facets of their identity by asking them to label the petals on a flower to illustrate the different 'people' contained within each individual. The following example was drawn with little or no guidance from an adult. The question 'who am I?' was posed and children were allowed to show on the petals some of the aspects of their identities which they felt to be important. The drawing below, completed by an eight-year-old pupil from a North Yorkshire school, shows that different identities have been recognised and would possibly allow for more complex work to take place with the guidance of the teacher.

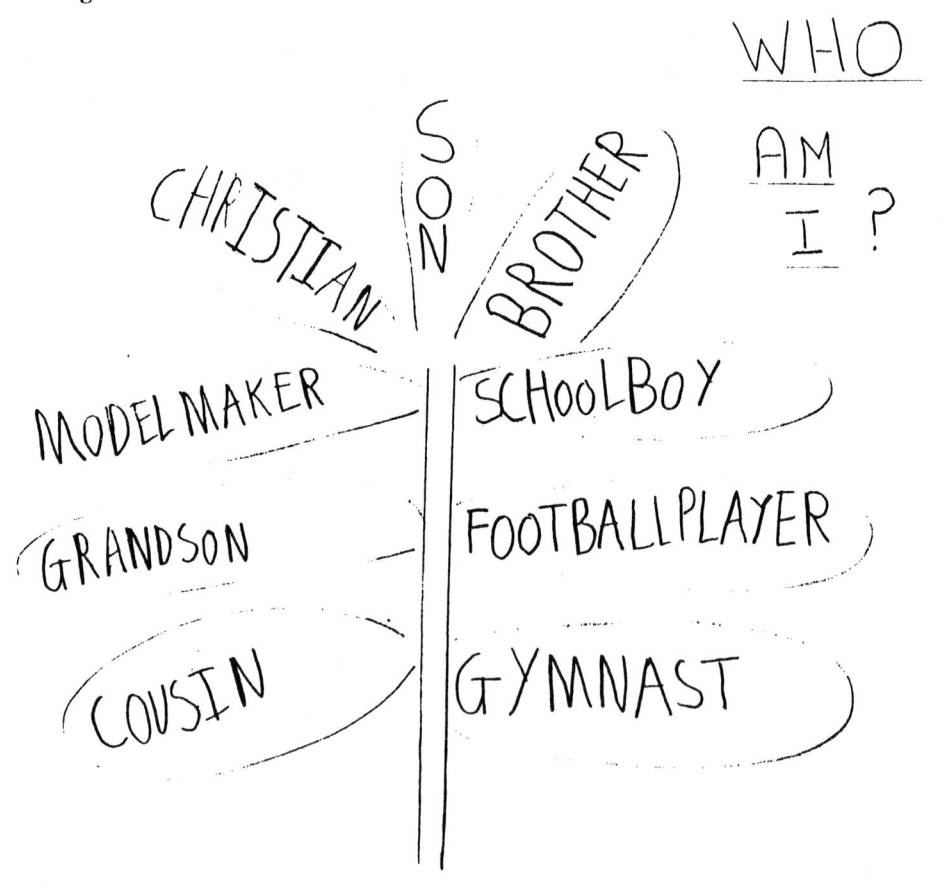

Figure 12.1 Who am I?: a drawing by an eight year old boy

Much of the context of what is shown below suggests relating the work to history education although many other areas could be used. There are key decisions to be made in three main areas: access, content and process.

Access

It is often assumed that education is somehow a closed world or that identities can only be questioned when there are migrants from overseas present in the school. These simplistic assumptions need to be challenged. Increasingly projects are taking place which are based on discussion groups of pupils from different countries. E-mail facilities make this straightforward. There are also possibilities associated with exchanges and visits and people from the local community can be invited to speak with children about experiences in the past.

Content

History can be characterised very narrowly. At the moment there are calls for history teachers in the United Kingdom to pay more attention to national identity. We would suggest that it would be more useful to ensure that appropriate coverage of the interactions of countries and people are included. Teachers should ensure that at least three aspects of the past are studied: different ways of life within the home country; different ways of life in the wider world; and the interactions between people within the home country and communities in the wider world.

Process

Pupils should have opportunities to work alone and in co-operation with others. They need to be able to examine history, how history has been made and what purpose history is expected to fulfil. While it is important that children learn relevant knowledge and concepts, it is also important that they begin to understand the significance of power relationships in their own society to the construction of history they learn. They need to question the place given to dominant and minority groups. In this respect they will be beginning to engage with the real business of being an historian.

QUESTIONING IDENTITIES IN THE CLASSROOM: ISSUES AND EXAMPLES FROM HISTORY EDUCATION

We will now begin to explore more precisely the ways in which identity has been affected by what has been called the 'invention of tradition'. These activities link directly with the investigations suggested for teachers of their own histories as revealed through migration. We suggest that teachers consider the pros and cons of the following as a model rather than something to use uncritically.

The myths of the past often hold us firmly in their grip. In the British context this can be seen, for example, in statements by John Major in the 1997 general election campaign when he referred to 'a thousand years of British history'. Britain has, of course, existed for a relatively brief historical period, much shorter than a thousand years, and despite the rather monolithic official view of the nation that has been enthusiastically promoted there is great evidence of diversity and interdependence. This diversity and interdependence is revealed by the personal histories discussed above.

The model described below allows for an examination of the ways in which traditions are being invented in contemporary Europe. In general terms the advice of Bracey (1995) is useful when discussing the history of one particular country:

1. The place of Britain should be seen in a European and world context.

2. Britain has always been a diverse society.

3. Regional diversity should be understood.

4. Different interpretations of Britain's history should be understood.

5. Different versions of events should be considered.

For work more explicitly on contemporary Europe pupils could ask:

- What sort of European tradition(s) is/are being developed?
- Is it one that we should feel happy with?
- Are certain people/issues/areas being excluded?
- Can the developing traditions be improved in any way?
- What are the differences between invention and spontaneous generation of tradition?
- Should we seek consciously to develop tradition and if so in what ways?

Teachers might wish to read work in two main areas to prepare for their teaching on the themes associated with the invention of tradition. In terms of historical understanding probably the best book available is that edited by Hobsbawm and Ranger (1987). Others, such as Gathercole and Lowenthal (1994), are also very useful. Relevant work from the field of history education is curiously rather difficult to find but with 'interpretations' being declared as one of the key elements of the National Curriculum in England and Wales for pupils aged 5–14 (with associated official guidance e.g. SCAA undated) and with articles beginning to explore its meaning (Davies and Williams 1998) there is perhaps some hope that more relevant activities will be developed for the classroom in the near future. The following quotations show some of the official advice that has been given in England and Wales in an attempt to clarify the nature of 'interpretations'. The National Curriculum Council (1993) argued that there are three threads which can help teachers plan work about interpretations:

- Interpretations combine fact and fiction, imagination and points of view
- Interpretations are dependent, if they are of historical worth, on evidence
- Differences between interpretations can be explained by reference, among other things, to purpose and intended audience, and to the background of the author of any interpretation (NCC 1993, p.50)

Further guidance suggested five key questions which teachers could use:

- Which parts of the interpretation are factual and which parts are views or imagination?
- How plausible is the interpretation?
- How far are these views supported by evidence? How selective has the use of evidence been?
- What was the purpose and intended audience of the interpretation?
- How far was the interpretation affected by the background of its author? (Adapted from NCC 1993)

SCAA has identified four broad stages of progression in pupils' understanding of the evaluation of interpretations:

- Recognising that there are different interpretations and representations of the past
- Describing and giving reasons for different representations and interpretations
- Describing and analysing interpretations
- Analysing and evaluating interpretations in relation to their period (adapted from SCAA undated).

The above may help teachers consider the issues associated with the presentation of images designed to represent Europe in the past and today. As a result, for teachers wanting to explore with their pupils what it means to be British (or European), the following activities are suggested. These have attempted to represent a particular interpretation of the past and show how traditions can be invented. Of course the content of these activities would need to be varied according to the cultural origins of the children in the class.

Activities

1. The quotation referred to above from John Major could be set against other interpretations such as a map of the developing United Kingdom with dates of the invasions by, for example, Angles, Saxons, Jutes, Vikings, Romans, Normans

and with dates and origins of monarchs such as William III (i.e. William of Orange), the Hanoverian Georges, and the links between the current royal family and Greece, Germany and Russia. The five key questions given above posed by the NCC in 1993 could be used to focus pupils' work.

2. The 'story' of recent European integration from the British point of view could be presented by using one of the many texts already available. This will give the pupils some more recent historical context than that supplied from the activity mentioned above and also continue to raise questions (superficially at this stage) about the specific version of the past that is being invented. Normally, textbooks focus on a few key events (e.g. Treaty of Rome; Britain's entry into the EEC), provide a few often-used dates and briefly discuss the question 'should Britain join?'. This, of course, ignores other Europes (e.g. Council of Europe; the former eastern Europe), other data (such as the accounts of working-class men and women) and other forms of co-operation such as those associated with leisure rather than 'high' politics.

3. Pupils could then be asked to consider the following list as examples of what is often used in the promotion of a particular identity. Pupils could give at least one example for each of the items in the list. Pupils should then reorder the items to show their relative significance (most significant first, least significant at the foot of the list). The list could contain some or all of the following (in brackets are examples of what might be used if one was focusing on British identity):

- special days marked for celebrations (e.g. St. George's Day)
- flags (Union Jack as an amalgam of some of the national symbols of Britain)
- passports (the 'old' British passport)
- music ('Land of Hope and Glory'; the national anthem; 'Jerusalem')
- statues (examples from any town or city, perhaps use Nelson's column in London)
- place names (Waterloo Station, Trafalgar Square etc., i.e. names of famous battles against other Europeans)
- monuments (examples from any town or city, perhaps use Admiralty Arch in London)
- famous individuals (Churchill probably the most commonly used example)
- uniforms (cubs, guides and scouts' uniforms could be used here as well as adult military uniforms)

- rituals (everyday examples could be used such as birthday parties with special emphasis on the ages of 18 and 21, but other examples such as the use of language in the House of Commons can be instructive)
- sporting occasions (major events probably most useful with the Ashes trophy or the FA cup final providing many examples of symbolism)
- famous institutions (the choice of certain institutions rather than others – churches being more significant than trade union buildings, the position of certain buildings with some occupying prime sites)
- parades and other mass gatherings (the ceremonies on 11 November in central London and elsewhere to commemorate recent wars)
- common sayings/mottoes (many examples could be given here – *hon y soit qui mal y pense* would be a national example)
- often-used pictures which represent Britain (Buckingham Palace and other royal buildings and symbols are probably the most commonly used examples).

The above commonly used symbols and processes often represent a particular view of a Britain which stresses armed forces, has engaged in war within Europe, values particular types of people (usually avoiding references to, for example, young female black individuals or groups), is firmly based in the south rather than the north, honours the traditions associated with monarchy at least as much as those relating to democracy, has links with former members of the empire, and emphasises national elements strongly.

4. Pupils could then examine a number of contemporary sources showing some of the significant features and some of the symbols of the European Union. For each of the sources pupils could explain the message that they think is being conveyed. Four key and commonly used symbols could be used: the 1995 map of the European Union following the expansion to 15 members; the flag of the EU; the new passport for British citizens; and the celebration of 9 May as Europe Day (this has been chosen to commemorate the Schumann Declaration in 1950 in which he proposed the placing of coal and steel production under a common High Authority and argued that it would be 'a first step in the federation of Europe' and that it would make war between France and Germany 'not merely unthinkable but materially impossible' (McCormick 1996, pp.48–9). If possible it would also be useful to let pupils listen to at least some of the European anthem, 'The Ode to Joy', from Beethoven's Ninth Symphony. Again, pupils could be asked to consider the tradition that is being invented before our eyes. It is true that the symbols used in the documents published from Strasbourg, Brussels and Luxembourg are often determinedly inclusive (for instance a spider's web has been used in Commission of the European Communities (1992) to represent 'creativity, perseverance, a sense of organisation, control of equilibrium and a common will' (p.10)). But the flag

with only 15 stars, the passport with the British emblem so prominently emphasising the nation, the choice of 9 May with a special emphasis on France and Germany, and the use of a particular sort of music can be discussed by pupils.

5. Pupils could then be asked to consider the many different Europes that exist and to develop their own versions of symbols which could represent them. Among the many that could be mentioned attention could be drawn to:

- a geographical Europe which highlighted major rivers, mountains, plains
- an economic Europe with many different forms of production based on a wide range of natural and imported resources
- a cultural Europe with many languages, forms of music, art
- a scientific Europe with different traditions associated with medicine (including homeopathy), physics, chemistry and other natural sciences
- a political Europe which gives due attention to existing nation states but also incorporates regional and local government
- a political Europe in which some of the main issues are highlighted (transport, the environment, unemployment etc.).

One could give many more examples. The point is that by the end of this work pupils would have had an opportunity to explore the way in which tradition is invented, applied some of that thinking to their own country and then to the European Union, before developing their own view of the potential symbolic representations of the many different forms of Europe which currently exist.

CONCLUSION

Although the issues involved are complex we have tried to show what could be done. The first necessary and very positive step is to realise that these complexities have to be considered. Teachers and others who work with children have to explore their own perspectives and we have suggested that one appropriate way for them to do this is through examining their own histories which reveals the reality of intercultural exchange. Not all activities for adults are suitable for children and so we have suggested that for pupils, teachers move the focus of the work away from the individual and on to the way in which symbols are used and traditions invented, thus helping pupils understand the development of specific identities. Pupils should have the opportunity to deconstruct some of the symbols that are currently in use and to develop others. In so doing we would help prepare pupils for their role as adults in ensuring that new representations of nationality acknowledge peoples' multiple identities and are more inclusive and open than in the past.

REFERENCES

Bracey, P. (1995) 'Ensuring continuity and understanding through the teaching of British history.' In R. Watts and I. Grosvenor (eds) *Crossing the Key Stages of History: Effective History Teaching 5–16 and Beyond.* London: David Fulton.

Commission of the European Communities (1992) *European Union.* Luxembourg: ECSC-EEC-EAEC.

Council of Europe (1996) *History Teaching and the Promotion of Democratic Values and Tolerance: A Handbook for Teachers.* Strasbourg: Council of Europe.

Curtis, A. (1995) *Language, Learning and Support: Overseas Students at a British University.* Unpublished D.Phil. thesis. University of York, U.K.

Davies, I. and Williams, R. (1998) 'Interpretations of history.' *Teaching History.*

Fouts, J. (1997) 'Models of citizenship.' Unpublished paper. Seattle Pacific University.

Gathercole, P. and Lowenthal, D. (1994) *The Politics of the Past.* London: Routledge.

Heater, D. (1990) *Citizenship: The Civic Ideal in World Politics, History and Education.* London: Longman.

Hobsbawn, E. and Ranger, T. (eds) (1987) *The Invention of Tradition.* Cambridge: Cambridge University Press.

McLaughlin, T.H. (1992) 'Citizenship, diversity and education: a philosophical perspective.' *Journal of Moral Education* 21, 3, 235–250.

McCormick, J. (1996) *The European Union: Politics and Policies.* Oxford: Westview Harper Collins.

National Curriculum Council (1993) *Teaching History At Key Stage 3: History.* York: NCC.

Pike, G. and Selby. D. (1988) *Global Teacher, Global Learner.* London: Hodder and Stoughton.

Rauner, M. (1997) 'Citizenship in the curriculum: the globalization of civics education in anglophone Africa 1955–1995.' In C. McNeely (ed) *Public Rights, Public Rules: Constituting Citizens in the World Polity and National Policy.* New York: Garland Publishing.

Rey, M. (1991) 'Migration and intercultural education: genealogical studies in teacher training.' In H. Barkowski and G.R. Hoff (eds) *Berlin Interkulturell: Ergbnisse Einer Berliner Konferenz Zu Migration Und Padagogik.* Berlin: Wissenschaft und Stadt Colloquium Verlag.

Rey, M. (1997) 'Human rights education and intercultural relations: lessons for development educators.' In J. Lynch, C. Mogdil and S. Mogdil (eds) *Education and Development: Tradition and Innovation.* London: Cassell.

SCAA (undated) *The Assessment of Interpretations and Representations and the Use of Sources in GCSE History Examinations.* London: SCAA.

CHAPTER THIRTEEN

New Teachers Talking Citizenship
Europe and Beyond

Veronica Voiels

> If I think of myself as a citizen of the world, not just a Dutch citizen then I truly feel as though I am a person in the fullest sense.
>
> Being a European citizen means reducing the importance of my British identity.
>
> Any curriculum which is solely based on 'national knowledge' can never effectively teach about democracy and human rights.

These contrasting statements were made by three students training to be teachers in Britain and the Netherlands. The students were participating in an intensive course on 'Education for Citizenship' and, as part of my own research, their knowledge and beliefs about this area were elicited at the beginning and again at the end of the course. The argument in this chapter is that teachers' knowledge and beliefs are significant to the way they structure children's learning in this field. This includes the role of the teacher in helping children to understand and make sense of their own identities, and their responsibilities as participants in society.

The interviews reported on reveal varying degrees of knowledge and indeed some confusion about citizenship. This was particularly evident where students reflected on national versus European identity, and where they considered classroom practice. The findings are important to our understanding of teachers' personal and professional development.

INTRODUCTION

The argument that teachers' knowledge and beliefs directly affect their professional behaviour is not new. Bennett, Wood and Rogers (1997) provide a useful summary of recent research in this area. They refer to Richardson's work (1991) where she investigated the relationship between teacher thinking and classroom practice. Her research team found that 'most categories of reading practices could be predicted accurately from teachers' beliefs' (p.20). Similarly work by Thompson (1992) indicated 'a high relationship between teachers' beliefs about mathematics and their actual practice' (p.20). Little has been done on the relationship between teachers' knowledge and beliefs about citizenship education and their classroom practice. This chapter aims to examine student teachers' thinking and make suggestions about the personal and professional development needs of all teachers.

My own view is that citizenship education is an integral part of the personal, social and moral development of children, helping them to develop a sense of their own self-worth and to respect and appreciate others regardless of cultural differences. Furthermore citizenship education is a means whereby children can learn about their democratic rights and responsibilities and how to become involved with their own local community whilst being aware of the wider context of Europe and the world.

If we require teachers to consider social, moral and personal education within the context of global citizenship, then it is important that student teachers be given the chance to think through and acknowledge their own beliefs and values in this field. Nias identifies the 'substantial self' of the teacher, which is a set of 'self defining beliefs, values and attitudes...and is highly resistant to change' (1989, p.203). Her work with newly qualified teachers concludes that teachers have their own sets of values, that these affect deeply how and what they teach, and that these are discussed neither in their initial training nor in the staff room. In spite of this, in Britain we expect teachers 'to accept a wider range of responsibilities – moral, social, affective, physical as well as cognitive – for their pupils than is the case in many other countries... (p.205). If this is the case, then it behoves us to examine the views student teachers hold about their identity, and to provide appropriate opportunities for them to develop self-awareness so that they may then deal with these areas with children (Voiels 1996).

My enquiry involved student teachers in England and the Netherlands. I wanted to investigate their knowledge and beliefs about citizenship education and how well their training had prepared them to teach this. I was interested to see if there were any differences between the Dutch and English student teachers in their attitudes towards and perceptions of citizenship. Dutch students were chosen as they had also had a National Curriculum imposed within the previous ten years, but one very different from the English and Welsh National Curriculum, as citizenship as a theme runs throughout all subject areas in Holland (Holden 1996).

METHODOLOGY

I used four organising questions with each group of students. The first question focused on their general understanding of themselves as citizens and the second on their identity as European citizens. The third question focused on their perceptions of the knowledge children would need as an essential aspect of education for citizenship. The fourth and final question was asked after the end of the course and was used to elicit and evaluate students' understanding of education for citizenship as a result of the intensive course. After responding to each of the questions, students were encouraged to discuss their responses and elaborate on these. Discussions were recorded and categories derived from the 140 responses.

FINDINGS

Student understanding of citizenship

Question One: citizenship and personal identity

The first question asked each student teacher to fill in a personal card completing the sentence 'To me being a citizen means...', followed by discussion. It was evident from the responses that for both British and Dutch students, certain aspects of citizenship were more important than others.

Citizenship was expressed as:

- belonging to a community (34 per cent)
- contributing to the community and taking responsibility for others (24 per cent)
- providing rights, support and protection (20 per cent)
- personal identity and freedom (13 per cent)
- national identity (5 per cent)
- being part of a global community (4 per cent).

Overall, then, a feeling of belonging was a key factor in students' personal understanding of citizenship, with contributing to the community and taking responsibility also being seen as important.

Individual statements reflected the importance of community:

To me, being a citizen means:

- being an individual with my own beliefs, but yet having to conform to some degree
- being part of a large group but within that large group being an individual who can contribute to the group and also expect support from the group when needed.

A high proportion of these student teachers recognised the importance of taking responsibility for others, saying that citizenship involved 'working with others to make our lives easier' and 'sharing responsibilities in caring for others in the community'.

For some students national identity was an important issue and being a citizen meant 'belonging to and being involved with my country' or 'being part of a community of a certain nationality and having responsibility for it'. However others included reference to the global dimension of citizenship. One stated that being a citizen meant 'being a member of a community, not confined by culture, language and boundaries'. Others stated simply:

- I am part of society and mankind.
- I belong to the entire community, city or the world.

Question Two: citizenship and a European identity

The second question invited students to respond to the statement 'To me being a European citizen means...'. Again groupings were derived from 118 student responses. These categories which emerged were quite different from those of the previous question.

European citizenship was expressed as:

- being part of a wider community (20 per cent)
- having wider responsibilities and an awareness of the needs and resources of the community of Europe (16 per cent)
- having the benefits of being part of a European community (18 per cent)
- freedom of access to Europe and ease of travel within it (17 per cent)
- different to citizenship as previously defined (18 per cent)
- the same as citizenship previously defined (11 per cent).

Student statements showed that their notion of community as defined in the previous exercise was extended. They made reference to being part of 'a more diverse community' and having 'a wider identity than Northern Irish Catholic' or 'being a citizen with a wider scope'.

Many statements referred to cultural diversity and differences. For these students being a European citizen meant:

- keeping rules and respecting cultural differences
- appreciating other laws and being more aware of other cultures
- awareness of other cultures within a large community.

It is interesting to note that many British students viewed participation in Europe as an opportunity to engage with another culture rather than including British culture within European culture. One strongly represented aspect was that being a European citizen meant taking the initiative in gaining knowledge, information and understanding of European affairs. One student summed up this combination of responsibility and potential:

> The welfare of these other countries has to be taken into consideration. We can come together as a bigger community and fight for our rights '*en masse*'.

Many of the Dutch students clearly stated that there was no difference between being a citizen and being a European citizen as the experience and principles were exactly the same:

> It is the same as being a citizen in the Netherlands but with a wider scope.

> It means the same as being a Dutch citizen.

However, some of the replies from the British students revealed an indifference to the notion of being a European citizen or difficulty in giving a personal meaning to it. This was shown by blank replies or such statements as 'it does not mean a lot to me'. Some British students feared 'losing their identity'. For some being a European citizen meant:

- having my British identity taken away and being exposed to many things which as a country we might not have believed in before
- loss of authority from the European government always changing British laws.

Another added, 'we have enough troubles with our own country, why take on more?'.

Of particular significance were the responses of students who were British citizens of African, African-Caribbean or Asian origin. They expressed strong feelings about personal identity and the extent to which citizenship was related to issues of racism and social injustice. They wanted to discuss the roots and origin of personal identity: whether it was based on the country of one's birth and family background or whether it transcended any kind of cultural conditioning. One student stated:

> Citizenship is nothing to do with me as a person. I am who I am regardless of where I was born.

Question Three: what children need to know

The third organising question asked student teachers to identify the knowledge they thought children ought to be taught if they were to be educated for citizenship. As before, student statements were recorded for subsequent collation and analysis.

The responses from the British and Dutch students to this question are listed separately on this occasion to show the marked difference in response. Again, suggestions are shown here in an order which reflects the emphasis given.

Suggestions from British student teachers:

Children need knowledge about:

- the democratic process, what it is, what it means, where it comes from
- differences between cultures, and the right to be different
- the law, including laws pertaining to children and young people
- the history of the society they live in
- the effect and consequences of rules.

Suggestions from Dutch student teachers:

Children need knowledge about:

- the parliamentary system, including human rights, duties
- different interpretations of citizenship
- global issues and the political and economic systems of the world
- the 'pros and cons' of European membership
- the Dutch system of government
- laws about prejudice and discrimination
- the cultural and historical background of minorities
- the great religions and religious and cultural differences
- the position of one's own country in relation to the rest of the world.

In discussion both groups felt strongly that they would need to teach about other cultures if their pupils were to be able to fully understand and locate the key concepts of citizenship and related areas of democracy, human rights, social justice and global responsibility. They also realised that this had implications for their own level of knowledge about these issues, a point which particularly concerned many British students.

A further concern shared by many students was the level of emotional and intellectual maturity that would be required of their pupils to deal with issues of citizenship. For them their main challenge was to find ways of making these issues accessible to children of all ages.

Student understanding of citizenship education in relation to classroom practice after the course

Question Four: Citizenship education in practice

This final question was part of an evaluation of a taught course which included a focus on knowledge and beliefs related to citizenship education. In the course students had undertaken practical activities using ranking exercises, Venn diagrams to sort statements, simulation exercises, time-lines and other tasks which required students to articulate their beliefs and defend their value statements. Textbooks and children's literature were also used to link citizenship education with curriculum content. Throughout this process the tutors also modelled activities for the classroom.

At the end of the course, students were required to complete the statement 'As a teacher, I can develop citizenship in my classroom by...'. They were thus invited to consider their future role as teachers and the ways in which they could create a classroom environment in which the principles of democracy, social justice, human rights and global responsibility would be experienced by their pupils. Responses fell into two main categories:

1. Teaching methodology and underlying principles:
    - encourage lots of group work and social interaction
    - have discussions on what children would like their school to be like
    - create opportunities to help children develop skills in defending their rights
    - deal directly with issues of law and justice
    - encourage children to air their views without fear
    - create time for discussion and debate
    - use role play to encourage empathy with people and children who have had their rights taken away
    - give them the facts about global responsibility with no secrecy
    - teach about other cultures and religions
    - open up the process of teaching and learning.

2. Relationships between teachers and pupils:
    - encourage equality for girls and boys
    - help children appreciate that each person is different
    - make sure they listen to each other
    - try to let them help each other
    - encourage children to respect one another, especially those with disabilities.

In discussion many students said they could see how children could experience democracy, justice, and human rights in the everyday life of the classroom. Some of the primary students were clearly surprised that establishing classroom rules for the purpose of keeping order in the classroom could with some careful consideration and modification be developed to teach children the principles of democracy and justice. A wealth of practical suggestions suggested that the students felt more confident to begin to implement citizenship education in the classroom than they had at the beginning of the course.

DISCUSSION AND IMPLICATIONS

One notable feature of this investigation was the lack of confidence that the British students felt initially in discussing democracy and related issues of social justice, human rights and global responsibility. They commented on their own lack of political education, a perception borne out by Davies (1994) and a recent survey reported on in the TES (*Times Educational Supplement* 1996). The Dutch students were more confident in discussing these issues and appeared to have greater awareness of areas of the world where democracy and human rights were not respected. This could be due to the fact that civics has always been a compulsory part of the Humanities Curriculum in Dutch schools, and citizenship is now central to their National Curriculum.

In addition some British students indicated a lack of commitment to developing a European identity, whilst others saw membership of the EU as being just about possibilities for travel. This was in sharp contrast to the Dutch students who were much more 'at home' with the notion of European citizenship.

For black British students there was a further dimension: that of personal identity, its origin and the role of the state in protecting this. For all students the global dimension of citizenship only emerged after they were asked specifically to reflect on global issues and responsibility.

It would seem from the third question (about the knowledge children require) that the Dutch students were able to articulate more precisely the needs of the learner. While all students felt that children should learn about democracy, laws and cultural differences, the Dutch students were more explicit in making reference to minorities, prejudice and religious differences.

The final question, asked after the course, suggested that earlier concerns about the ability of children to assimilate the historical and cultural knowledge necessary for an understanding of citizenship and human rights had been allayed. Students' own understanding of citizenship had increased and they had come to appreciate that both the curriculum and the way they ran their classrooms provided opportunities for citizenship education.

The findings suggest that student teachers are often hesitant about defining citizenship and hence need time to explore these issues if they are to be able to teach for citizenship in the classroom. British students in particular would appear to need more information about how democracy works and about the nature of Britain's role within Europe. The global dimension of citizenship needs to be made explicit for teachers and pupils as it is not automatically seen as part of citizenship education.

There are implications too for what is taught in schools (both primary and secondary) as certainly the British students did not appear to have had any input on citizenship in their formal education. The Dutch students' greater knowledge may stem from the requirements of their teacher education course or be influenced by the requirements of their National Curriculum.

It would seem from the above that the opportunity to explore and discover sources of identity should be an aspect of citizenship education in schools. But a first stage must be to ensure that our future teachers are conversant with the issues. They need to have explored what citizenship means to them personally, to have discussed issues of social justice and human rights and to be able to articulate the role of the teacher in educating for national, European and global citizenship.

CONCLUSION

A significant feature of the responses to Question One showed how 'belonging to' and 'being part of' a community were seen as essential aspects of citizenship. Student teachers need to understand more explicitly the nature of community through various theoretical perspectives in sociology and history as well as how they might create a sense of community with the children in their own classroom. If we acknowledge that students' beliefs and thinking about such issues are important, then we must make time for discussion of these areas on courses in Initial Teacher Education. This is a significant recommendation when the move is towards a skills-based approach, with emphasis on traditional curriculum areas. Neither the newly introduced Career Entry Profile nor the new standards for QTS (Qualified Teacher Status) include reference to beliefs, knowledge and understanding in this field. This should be a matter of concern to any educators involved in personal, social and moral education or education for citizenship.

Furthermore the difference between the British and the Dutch students' knowledge about citizenship and global issues highlights the need for students to be taught explicitly about democracy, human rights and global responsibility. Within this the European dimension needs particular attention if we are to foster a commitment to the European community from our teachers and their pupils.

Such teaching needs to be at both a practical and theoretical level. Students need sessions where the links between knowledge, beliefs and personal action can be made explicit. This can allay fears that the area of citizenship is 'too difficult for young children' or too abstract a concept. Such sessions need to show how citizenship begins in the classroom, how it involves issues of fairness and justice which even very young children can understand, and how a global dimension can also be included from the very beginning. The responses of the above students indicate what is possible after a short intensive course, where students were given time to discuss, to challenge each other and to partake in the kind of active learning methods they could replicate in their own classrooms.

Beyond this there are implications for the British National Curriculum. Students will not take citizenship seriously until it is an explicit part of the curriculum which is delivered to all children. Recent government initiatives indicate that this may happen in the near future. SCAA (School Curriculum Assessment Authority) (1996) has suggested that one way to improving social, moral and spiritual education may be through explicit timetabled sessions on education for citizenship, noting that Britain is one of the few countries where citizenship is not already an important part of the curriculum.

Such a change to the curriculum would require much in-service work for practising teachers. More research needs to be done on teacher thinking in this area so that appropriate courses can be designed. It may be that practising teachers share the confusion felt by British student teachers about personal and European identity; it may be that they too feel citizenship education is too abstract and too daunting an area for young children in particular. This chapter is a first step in identifying the thoughts and beliefs of student teachers and indicates that even a short intensive course can help students clarify their thinking and can contribute to their personal and professional development. Such work now needs to extend to practising teachers and as a result to our children, if we are to educate them for active participation as citizens of Europe in the next century.

REFERENCES

Bennett, N., Wood, L. and Rogers, S. (1997) *Teaching Through Play: Teachers' Thinking and Classroom Practice.* Buckingham: Open University Press.

Davies, I (1994) 'Whatever happened to political education?' *Educational Review 46,* 1, 29–36.

Holden, C. (1996) 'Enhancing history teaching through a human rights perspective.' *Evaluation and Research in Education 10,* 2 and 3, 113–127.

Nias, J. (1989) *Primary Teachers Talking.* London: Routledge.

School Curriculum and Assessment Authority (SCAA) (1996) 'Education for adult life: social, moral and spiritual education.' Discussion paper, No. 6, London.

Times Educational Supplement (1996) 'MPs act on sinking interest in citizenship.' 7 June.

Richardson, V. (*et al.*) (1991) 'The relationship between teachers' beliefs and practices in reading comprehension and instruction.' (*American Educational Research Journal 28,* (3), 559–586.

Thompson, A.G. (1992) 'Teachers' beliefs and conceptions: a synthesis of the research.' In: D.A. Grouws (ed) *Handbook of Research on Mathematical Teaching and Learning.* New York: Macmillan.

Voiels, V. (1996) 'The inner self and becoming a teacher.' In M. Steiner (ed) *Developing the Global Teacher.* Stoke-on-Trent: Trentham Books.

PART FIVE

Case Studies from European Primary Schools

CHAPTER FOURTEEN

Children's Newspapers
Meeting Other Minds

Geoff Anderson

INTRODUCTION

> Me and Emma go on camp with the Guides like the Russian children. (Victoria)

This child had been involved in creating a collaborative newspaper with children in her own class and in Russia. In so doing she gained knowledge of what some Russian children do, and found similarities with her own lifestyle.

This chapter sets out to explore how primary teachers can enable children to compare their own experiences with those of others and thus develop their understanding of the world around them.

Through such active engagement children can develop positive attitudes which motivate them to acquire key skills and concepts as young citizens. The more involved children are in these shared experiences, and the more their contributions are valued, the more they feel able to take an active role in questioning, challenging and influencing their own lives. In turn, this gives children the confidence to tackle controversial issues relating to the values and morals of the local and wider community. Sharon, like Victoria, also learnt about other children's lives, this time after reading a contribution from a child living in the Gambia:

> I have learnt that this girl cooked for all her family and I was very surprised.

She gained in her knowledge, and furthermore was challenged in her perceptions of childhood.

Both Sharon and Victoria had contributed to a newspaper which involved children from different countries. It is the purpose of this chapter to explore a small project through the experiences of the children, teachers and student teachers involved. The premise is that if one can address issues of importance to young people in different social and cultural settings through shared writing and reading, then these children will be acquiring the knowledge, concepts, attitudes and skills appropriate for their role as active citizens in an increasingly global society.

Teachers wishing to develop programmes focusing on different cultural and social settings can draw on resources already available to support the study of contrasting localities. These are plentiful and many are of good quality, prompted by the demands of the National Curriculum. However these lack a personal element with which children can really interact. Such personal contacts can be established by working with agencies such as the Central Bureau (1994), local twinning groups, or informal contacts through parents.

Furthermore as systems of communication improve and become more accessible, links become potentially greater in scope. Approaches well documented in Beddis and Mares (1988) are further explored in more recent material such as 'Children around the world: linking to learn' (National Primary Centre 1996), where it is confirmed that new information technologies increase motivation for contact between schools. The Globe newspaper project described in this chapter may well benefit in time from such advances in technology. However, even without the Internet or e-mail, the children in the current project were involved in 'meeting other minds'. Indeed the fact that this was achieved with limited resources only serves to emphasise the vast potential to be realised in years to come. In discussing the project I show how children gain from being challenged in meaningful interchanges of personal experience, and from being encouraged to deal with the real and often controversial issues of being active young citizens.

BACKGROUND

The Curriculum Guidance (National Curriculum Council 1990) set out a list of components for Education for Citizenship. Three broad areas were outlined:

- the nature of community
- roles and relationships in a pluralist society
- the duties, responsibilities and rights of being a citizen.

These were seen in five 'specific, everyday contexts' (p.5):

- the family
- democracy in action
- the citizen and the law
- work, employment and leisure
- public services.

Various authors (for example Morrison 1994, and Gilbert 1995) have criticised not so much the components of this guidance as the means of interpreting these for teaching and learning. Gilbert, for example, maintains that the approaches are inadequate and do not reflect the contemporary world. The Globe project set out to redress this situation, focusing on the following three aspects of education for active citizenship.

1. Developing children's sense of identity within a global perspective

Anna Craft (1995) makes valuable links between the development of 'senses of self' and the potential within education for citizenship. Mares and Harris (1987) confirm that children's attitudes towards other peoples and places around the world are based on certain stereotypes and prejudices. They conclude that there is a need to find a strategy within the curriculum for encouraging and fostering positive attitudes from an early age. One of the purposes of the Globe project was thus to provide opportunities for children to learn about the lifestyles of other children and in so doing to come to new understandings of their own identity.

Biott and Easen (1994) emphasise the important role teachers have to play in selecting appropriate contexts and in actively engaging children in such work. In particular they recommend collaborative groupwork as a vehicle for increasing awareness of self and others.

2. Developing children's collaborative skills

Children have regularly used their own 'in-house' journals to develop writing skills and to share ideas. Liz Slater (1992) demonstrates the benefits not only of writing in various forms but also of children discussing amongst themselves the content and format for an audience. This collaborative aspect is picked up by Burns and Housego (1996) who argue 'that children have got to learn to relate to all kinds of people in life, and group work of this kind is an ideal opportunity for such social learning' (p.65). They cite a case where children were able to make editorial decisions together and discuss analytically how the group was working.

A higher level of collaboration is possible if children are given ownership of the subject or content of the material to be published. If this material raises controversial issues such as bullying or prejudice, then 'just as cycles of hostility can be created, so too can cycles of friendship through the use of interaction to break down stereotypical thinking' (Biott and Easen 1994, p.200).

3. Developing children's skills in conflict resolution

Discussions of this kind will sometimes lead to disagreement within a group of children. For this reason there is potential for using collaborative activity to develop strategies for 'conflict resolution'. Rowe and Newton (1994) offer guidance for teachers by providing a series of stories written to raise a rich variety of issues. This confirms the value of a story as a powerful medium to motivate children and engage them in critical thinking. Basil Singh (1988), in writing about the process of modifying one's values, confirms the importance of the individual reflecting on the framework of value assumptions within which one is living.

INTERNATIONAL LINKING

Newspapers with an international dimension have been produced for some time. 'Fax! Junior', published in Grenoble, brought together in one issue in 1993 for example, children from France, Great Britain, Italy, Holland and Germany to share experiences related to common themes such as health, community services and the environment. The Internet now offers opportunities to collaborate internationally by electronic mail. British Telecom's Campus World is one of a number of educational packages allowing children controlled access to the World Wide Web. Users are able to collaborate, publish and access material in an ever faster way. As technology develops and reduced costs make the equipment more available, the scope for conferencing on-line becomes more realistic for more schools.

'Citizenship Through Newspapers' (Newspapers in Education 1995) is a teachers' pack designed to promote local newspapers as a source for examining the eight components of citizenship as defined in Curriculum Guidance 8 (National Curriculum Council 1990). The National Primary Centre (1996) publication cites an inter-school newspaper produced by children in Scotland, Malaysia and Spain. The benefits in such links include the breaking down of barriers for pupils and opportunities for collaboration between both children and teachers.

The Globe project aimed to bring the elements discussed above together to develop the skills of citizenship and to raise issues relevant to young people.

THE PROJECT

A group of primary teachers helped to create the format for the first Globe newspaper. In order to give the children a range of accessible material to write about and share it was felt important to draw on personal experiences. This enabled meaningful comparisons to be made. Among the themes offered were 'Our School', 'The Local Environment' and 'Favourite Recipes'. Five countries were represented (France, Scotland, Russia, The Gambia and England) involving nine teachers. In the English schools there were opportunities for student teachers to work with the children. In writing for the newspaper the children were required to share ideas, to make decisions about content and to select appropriate ways of presenting the material.

Among the contributions received from other schools was the one from a pupil from Gunjur in The Gambia, the subject of Sharon's earlier comment:

> A Recipe Benachin...
>
> My name is Bintou A. J. Jassey. I cook for my family. I have to do this because I am a girl. Before cooking, you buy onions, pepper, two cups of oil, some Maggi (stock cube), potatoes, sweet potatoes, pumpkin, pepper, aubergine, bitter tomatoes and fish. First of all you gut and descale the fish. Then you slice it so that it has diagonal cuts across its sides. You chop the vegetables and heat the oil. Then you fry the fish in the hot oil and also the vegetables. Of course, you must cook rice to eat with the meal. Rice is the staple diet of The Gambia. I cook this on my other fire whilst the fish are frying. I have to wash the bowls, cups, plates, everything. I then divide the food into different bowls for different parts of my large family. We eat from communal bowls, using usually our hands or sometimes a spoon. Cooking is difficult because I have to do everything by hand, like pound the pepper, tomatoes, etc. in a big wooden pestle and mortar. I also have to cook on an open fire. It takes a long time.

The English children were fascinated to read about the worlds of other children. This reflected what seemed to be an intrinsic desire to find out about new places and a curiosity to compare common themes, particularly those relating to what other children do. Nick, from Great Bedwyn, announced:

> I liked the bit about The Gambia – they have a mosque in the school and families eat together from one bowl.

Paul, like Sharon, registered a sense of surprise:

> I didn't know that a child would have to cook for her family. I felt quite sad that a child has to cook for her whole family, and then clear up.

This to some extent confirms Cullingford's (1996) findings related to perceptions of other cultures that 'the immediate outlook shared by all the children is negative. Africa is associated with famine and poverty; but even more importantly with a primitive way of life'.

But what of Rachel's thoughts in the same class?

> A Recipe Benachin taught me something I did not know because I do not cook for my family. The article made me feel very lazy because she did all the cooking and I do not do any...

Here's a sense of respect and personal inadequacy, far removed from the pity identified by Cullingford. Still more revealing is Carly's understanding and acceptance...

> There was one thing that I didn't know was that a girl had to cook for her family. I thought – when I saw it – her mother was lazy but that's just the way the family runs.

This range of comments raises challenges for the teacher. Here are very different interpretations of a contrasting image of childhood. The role of the teacher is clearly crucial in handling the discussion and moving beyond the 'surprise' shown by Sharon. There are also issues here to do with the children's own past experience and home influences. Inexperience of cooking could result from existing roles within the children's own families, including gender stereotypes. It may well be that in some cases children in the UK will regularly cook for their family. So differences in experience undoubtedly occur *within* a class as well as between this and another culture. Indeed it may be possible to address sensitive issues of comparison within a class precisely because they have been raised through common exploration of more distant situations. Sensitivity is therefore required in guiding the children to use this altered concept of childhood to reconstruct and develop their understanding.

This exciting potential for exploring more sensitive issues, both locally and in a wider context, provided the impetus to develop the newspaper still further. Globe II was produced with the involvement of 20 teachers in seven countries (France, Scotland, Russia, The Gambia, Iceland, Italy and England). Student teachers were again involved in the English schools. If children, through their collaborative writing and reading of the first Globe, could acquire some of the skills of citizenship (for example personal and social skills) then a way could be found in the second Globe newspaper (Globe II) to develop further the more challenging concepts. The idea of children doing this through sharing stories was the solution. The means by which the whole writing process developed again involved the collaborative interactive skills for citizenship mentioned earlier. In addition for Globe II, however, there was the potential to reflect these within each story. The children could move on from the earlier factual, comparative lifestyle approach, and explore a more creative style of communication.

Influenced to some extent by the tradition of French *'bandes dessinées'* which was naturally familiar to at least one of the Globe's schools, the idea of comic strip stories grew. Here was a format that enabled children from different cultural and linguistic backgrounds to share ideas accessibly. The key role of illustration lessened the need for words: the words that were used could be interpreted through visual clues. The links with citizenship were further developed in the themes of the stories. It was decided to frame these within a scenario that addressed 'a problem, a solution', thus giving scope for exploring 'controversial issues upon which there is no clear consensus' (National Curriculum Council 1990, p.14). This allowed children the freedom and the challenge to decide what 'a problem' might be. For some it related to feelings for others; for example, the French story was about friendships (Figure 14.1) and the Icelandic story about stereotypes (Figure 14.2). For others it involved environmental concerns; for example an English story was about car pollution

(Figure 14.3) and an Italian story about the conservation of dolphins (Figure 14.4).

Figure 14.1 Friendship (French children)

1. How do you like living in a snowhouse?
2. Why do you think I live in a snowhouse?

Figure 14.2 Stereotypes (Icelandic children)

Figure 14.3 Car pollution (English children)

Figure 14.4 Conservation of dolphins (Italian children)

It was apparent that some problems identified were common to several countries. Pollution and conservation were the most popular themes. Problems connected with relationships were also quite frequently used. In the case of the English schools, the student teachers reported discussions which led to votes being taken to select a group's problem. One group drew suggestions out of a hat. One student described how the opinions of her group regarding new traffic schemes changed as the discussion progressed in the light of points put forward. Discussions of 'a solution' presented another challenge. The solutions themselves were wide-ranging. The younger children tended to be more realistic in their ideas. 'Put more rubbish bins in the playground,' said Matthew. Older children tended to offer more imaginative suggestions, for example 'that the council have community cars that people can borrow/hire when they need to go on long journeys or on holiday'. In a few instances the mechanisms for finding solutions were shown in the stories, reflecting the key role of the teacher. For example, talking through a problem with bullies provided a forum for finding an answer in the Scottish story (Figure 14.5).

Figure 14.5 Problems with bullies (Scottish children)

Interestingly, in one of the Italian schools, circle time was used as the means for sharing problems and reaching solutions (Figure 14.6). The Italian children explained...

> A solution has been offered by our teachers who made us the proposal to have a weekly meeting in order to talk about our problems in a group. That has been called the CIRCLE TIME. Through an active listening to each other and a discussion we try to face and to solve together some of the problems which trouble us. Not always we succeed in finding a real solution to our difficulties, but we feel that discussion in a group helps us a lot. We are no longer alone and we are aware of our great value.

Figure 14.6 Circle time (Italian children)

In reading the finished newspaper, one group of English children provided some personal interpretations on the stories. Controversial issues seemed to be those that are 'massive', that can 'spread all over the world' (Christopher). Litter was given as an example because 'the world would get filled up with it' (Nicole).

'Difficult' problems seemed to centre on personal relationships. Bullying and unkindness were offered as examples. At this age (nine or ten), the children's concept of 'difficult' may still be self-centred. Perhaps the fact that mechanisms do exist to recycle rubbish presents this as less of a problem than dealing with anti-social behaviour at school, for example. In discussing the *way* the stories reached solutions, the children needed to see the *processes* for decision making. Litter was seen initially as requiring personal action. Children commented:

> You can pick it up and put it in the bin.
>
> You could put up some posters.

By using the example of the Italian 'circle time' the children saw discussion as a crucial aspect of resolution. They compared this readily to a council meeting or parliament. 'Have a conference' was one response. The children were prompted to reflect on why this might be fair, mentioning rules and procedures, for example suggesting that they should not shout out, should 'tell ideas and discuss' and should 'decide by voting'. The children also explored an alternative scenario which might arise if their efforts to persuade someone to take action were not successful. This led to conflicting views:

James: You might protest.

Christopher: You don't protest.

Nicole: You might get into trouble.

The solutions in the stories prompted discussion of the value of these, both in real and emotional terms. Drought was dealt with by 'getting water to countries that haven't any'. This was broadened to developing countries in general, 'making things equal by giving things to people that haven't got it'. On being asked whether these people can give anything themselves, 'kindness' was the reply. This led to a discussion on links between wealth and friendship. The children here had explored concepts prompted as well as provided by the stories, but needed guidance in this by the teacher. The stories clearly attracted children by their appearance as comic strips. The use of French or Italian in some did not seem to deter the readers. 'You can guess what it means by the pictures,' explained one child.

DISCUSSION

The value of the two newspapers in terms of 'meeting other minds' needs to be seen in relation to their particular focus. The first Globe was essentially a collaborative activity that resulted in the sharing of aspects of daily life. Here were children and teachers engaged in imparting local knowledge for the benefit of an audience of interested readers. In return these children had the opportunity to compare their ways of life with those of others. The children were learning to listen to their peers, to appreciate points of view, to consider an audience, to select material fairly, to take on individual responsibility, to contribute towards a shared goal, to respect differences and to show understanding of other situations. Here was evidence of children developing skills identified earlier as necessary for active citizenship, namely a sense of identity within a global context and the ability to work collaboratively.

Globe II allowed children to develop these skills further. Children were encouraged to explore issues of common interest and concern, even if these proved controversial. The term 'empowerment' as used, for example, by Morrison (1994) may seem far away but small steps can be important ones, and, within the limits of the comic strip format, powerful mechanisms for posing and answering key problems were nevertheless rehearsed. In creating their accounts children had a personal medium through which to explore social and moral issues. Certainly if personal experience already provides the raw material for such stories – and themes such as friendship, rules and law, property and power, community and environment are part of all young lives – then one need look no further to begin the process of this exploration. Rowe (1993) centres his discussion of education for citizenship around the concept of fairness. He believes that young children should be challenged 'to see their rights and responsibilities in their social and moral context and to develop a personal view about their fairness' (p.62). Again, what better context than one derived from the children's own experience? In facing a threat to their local environment (Figure 14.3) the children tackled problems in a legitimate way, using acceptable means to modify anti-social behaviour.

In addition, a major thrust of the Globe project was to encourage children to look beyond their own lives. As has been seen, developments in information technology can help here: links with real people in more distant localities are no longer dependent on exchange visits or the postal service. Welford and Wickham Primary School, one of the English contributors to the Globe project, has regular home pages on its Website and attracts links from around the world. It recently hosted a visit by pupils from a school in Norway that it 'met' through the Internet. Regular interactive school-based projects are also set up by the school through an organisation called Kidscape, which has its own site on the World Wide Web: countries such as Brazil and Spain also contribute. Gunjur, the village in The Gambia, has for some time had its own fax machine, a facility that some of the project's other schools lack. It is nevertheless important to continue involving partner schools through more traditional means. Technology should be seen as an enabler and not an excluder; and the postal service, is, after all, indispensable for exchanging 'real' material.

A government-led National Forum for Values in Education has called for people to 'accept diversity'...'work co-operatively with others'...'develop a sense of self worth'...and 'understand the place of human beings in the world' (the *Guardian* 1996). This chapter has shown how these aims are achievable through international linking and has demonstrated the crucial role of the teacher in providing opportunities for children to share their experiences. The Globe project has shown that the process of active citizenship can begin through 'meeting other minds'.

REFERENCES

Beddis, R. and Mares, C. (1988) *School Links International.* Avon County Council/Tidy Britain Group, Schools Research Project.

Biott, C. and Easen, P. (1994) *Collaborative Learning in Staffrooms and Classrooms.* London: David Fulton.

Burns, C. and Housego, E. (1996) 'The pleasures and pains of collaborative writing.' *Education 3 to 13,* 24, 2, 60–67.

Central Bureau (1994) *Strategies and Resources for the European Dimension in Education 4–18.* London: Central Bureau for Educational Visits and Exchanges.

Craft, A. (1995) 'Cross-curricular integration and the construction of self in the primary curriculum.' In J. Ahier and A. Ross (eds) (1995) *The Social Subjects within the Curriculum.* London: The Falmer Press.

Cullingford, C. (1996) 'Children's attitudes to developing countries.' *Primary Practice 6,* 41–46: National Primary Centre.

Gilbert, R. (1995) 'Education for citizenship and the problem of identity in post-modern culture.' In J. Ahier and A. Ross (eds) (1995) *The Social Subjects within the Curriculum.* London: The Falmer Press.

Guardian (1996) 'Schools' code also aimed at public: the paper in full.' 31 October.

Mares, C. and Harris, R. (1987) *School Links International.* Avon County Council/Tidy Britain Group, Schools Research Project.

Morrison, K. (1994) *Implementing Cross-Curricular Themes.* London: David Fulton.

NCC (National Curriculum Council) (1990) *Curriculum Guidance 8: Education for Citizenship.* York: National Curriculum Council.

Newspapers in Education (1995) *Citizenship through Newspapers, Newspapers in Education.* Leicester: Centre for Citizenship Studies.

NPC (National Primary Centre) (1996) 'Children around the world: linking to learn.' *Practical Issues in Primary Education, Issue 16.* Grampian, National Primary Centre.

Rowe, D. (1993) 'The citizen and the law: teaching about the rights and duties of citizenship.' In E. Baglin-Jones and N. Jones, N. (eds) *Education for Citizenship.* London: Kogan Page.

Rowe, D. and Newton, J. (1994) *You, Me, Us!* London: Home Office.

Singh, B. (1988) 'The teaching of controversial issues: the problem of the neutral chair approach.' In B. Carrington and B. Troyna (eds) *Children and Controversial Issues.* London: The Falmer Press.

Slater, L. (1992) 'Writing newspaper stories.' In R. Bain, B. Fitzgerald and M. Taylor (eds) *Looking into Language.* London: Hodder and Stoughton.

CHAPTER FIFTEEN

Children and the Supermarché[1]

Jean Pierre Branchereau

As Europeans continue to forge new relationships world-wide, there is a need for this to be reflected in the attitudes and awareness of children in school. Their ideas about citizenship need to extend from the level of their own community/town/city to a broader concept embracing Europe and the wider world. As a starting point children living in 'developed' countries need to become aware that they are participants in a global network of economic exchanges. They need to be able to place themselves in what geographers have called the world system (Dollfus 1990, p.551). They need to understand how economic activities are affected, shaped and determined by the process of continuing globalisation.

This world system can be seen as a model with a centre and a periphery. The centre comprises three poles, representing the more affluent markets of North America, Europe and Japan. The peripheral elements are placed in hierarchical relationships depending on their closeness to the centre. For some the experience is one of integration, for others one of control and domination. These elements all contain economic, social and cultural domains. These are separate to each element area but are linked by movements of people (migration), wealth (commerce) and information (media).

An activity described in this chapter raises questions about the integration of the French consumer within this global system of exchanges. A class of 25 children (aged ten years) participated in a project 'Mapping out the origin of products sold in the supermarket'. It led pupils to consider issues such as the effects of their own environment, the cost of labour in the 'developing' countries and the cost of the transportation of goods. These questions are fundamental to understanding that the development of richer countries is closely linked to the de-

---

1 This chapter was translated by Gerard Poulet of the University of Exeter.

velopment or exploitation of poorer countries and to an appreciation of the concepts of development and underdevelopment.

THE EVOLUTION OF THE CONCEPT OF DEVELOPMENT IN THE TEACHING OF GEOGRAPHY IN FRANCE

The concept of underdevelopment has emerged in the years following World War II in the context of colonial empires and the Cold War. School geography up to then implicitly expressed recognition and justification of the attitudes prevalent in this context. Textbooks for history and geography, such as the well-known Lavisse in France, justified the French presence (the colonial empire) and used the term European towns (French colonial) in contrast to 'native' towns (Lavisse 1940, p.184). During the period of decolonisation the concept of underdevelopment shifted towards the concept of the Third World, with implicit reference to the Third Estate in the French Revolution (Cordelier 1989). Development was seen as possible either by imitation of the models of capitalism or socialism or else through the adoption of a model of non-aligned development. The content of the geography curriculum taught in schools reflected this shift as is evidenced by the emphasis on the difference of the peoples and cultures living in these regions.

The economic recession of the 1970s, the end of the socialism in many countries and the opening up of new economic borders have seen the concept of 'development' take the place of that of 'underdevelopment'. Thus in textbooks the term 'developing country' has replaced 'underdeveloped country' as a way to show respect for the peoples of these countries. In the same way the terms 'shanty towns' and 'slums' have given way to such phrases as 'peripheral districts of spontaneous habitat'. However, the effect has been to describe the reality of towns in 'developing countries' in a rational way that distances the emotional response. The effect at one level is to name a 'shanty town' as a scientific observable object, a product of a kind of natural evolution, an instance of spontaneous determinism in the evolution of the city. The effect at another level is to depoliticise the process and conceal its harshness.

Other terms are equally misleading. The terms 'tigers' and 'dragons' are used to depict the growth of some industrial countries in Asia, terms which blanket over the phenomena of underpaid labour and violation of human and children's rights. A revealing case study for geography, social and moral education programmes is presented by the activities of the shoe manufacturers Nike who have moved to Asia to find cheaper labour. Similarly the story of the manufacture of footballs for the forthcoming World Cup provides another example – we have narrowly escaped this competition being played with balls sewn by children. Again studying information on the labels of goods for sale will allow children to become aware of the networks and structures in the world system and of the need to develop solidarity between producers and users. It is important to note that at present the information on labels does not tell us whether or not the price reflects the exploitation of human or child labour.

'MAPPING OUT THE ORIGIN OF PRODUCTS SOLD IN THE SUPERMARKET': AN ACTIVITY WITH CHILDREN

The focus on this activity is not made because it is innovative or special but because it raises questions about 'development' which need to be explored in greater depth with the children in subsequent work. As a mapping activity it meets many of the requirements of the French National Curriculum including the following:

Objectives

Cognitive objectives (knowledge):

- locations in France, Europe and the wider world
- the place of France in the global system.

Methodological objectives (skills):

- conducting a survey
- organising simple/original research activities
- use of atlas and identifying locations on a map.

Behavioural objectives (attitudes):

- developing the habit of reading labels from a geographical and consumer's viewpoint.

(Ministere de L'Education Nationale 1995)

In this case study 25 children aged ten years visited a supermarket as part of a geography project and collected data about the origins of the products on sale. They then returned to the classroom to sort and analyse the information using maps of France, of Europe and the world. There were a number of interesting points which emerged during this process. As they looked at the origins of flowers and vegetables for sale they began to appreciate the interplay between climactic conditions and competitiveness within the European market and to discover the possibilities offered by the use of greenhouses in the north. Pupils also began to learn about the significance of new markets opening within the Iberian peninsular and in central and eastern Europe.

Discussion

For the purposes of this chapter we will focus on the discussion related to data placed by the children on the world map. This data led to two conclusions. At the time of the survey in the month of May some food products (pineapples, grapefruit) came from the southern hemisphere, from South America and Africa. Thus the young city dwellers from western France became aware that they were dependent in their own food consumption on the produce of 'developing' countries. Additionally it was demonstrated that other goods – car accessories, tools and toys – are imported from South East Asia, China and Taiwan. This led to a discussion about the economic basis of these exchanges. They were intrigued to learn that in spite of the costs of transportation to France, items such as these are still competitive on the French market. They were surprised that this was made possible not just through cheap transport by sea for durable freight but also by the low cost of wages and in some case the employment of child labour.

Through these activities the pupils learnt something of the basis of trade between France and numerous other countries, including in the Mediterranean, tropical areas and the wider world. They began to understand how climactic conditions and relatively low labour costs in some regions have created conditions of mutual dependency between the so-called 'developed' and 'developing' countries.

However, the issues raised in the first section of this chapter remain unresolved in this practical classroom context. What explanation should the teacher offer for this continually evolving state of affairs in which inequalities prevail? We have already seen how the concept of 'underdevelopment' had shifted firstly towards a new notion of 'unequal development' and of plurality within the Third World and then towards a new broader category of 'developing country' which understates the difference in the material and economic conditions experienced by workers and consumers. The danger is that pupils might understand that such visible inequalities are seen to be justifiable because they are necessary to the process of economic development. We might call this teaching a 'pedagogie de l'acceptation', a means to teaching an unquestioning acceptance of the status quo, an old ideology reappearing in a new guise.

The argument here is that whilst a study in a supermarket is good in some respects, an uncritical approach to studying the origins of goods might inadvertently lead to undesirable outcomes. If pupils are to come to understand the significance of their participation as consumers in the global economy we must ensure that our teaching does not obscure and blanket over the realities which follow long periods of colonisation and domination. Thus the study needs to be a starting point for the teacher and pupils to look more broadly at:

- the effects of the global economic system on developing countries
- the effects of the practice of cash crops, and of the use of new farming equipment and agro-chemicals
- the distribution of wealth across and within societies
- the balance of power in global trading relations and initiatives to encourage fair trading.

An approach suggested by Buck and Inman (1995) which looks at the inequalities between developed and developing countries is included in Table 15.1. This table includes questions which can be raised to encourage pupils to go beyond a superficial analysis of information about foodstuffs. Questions such as these are essential for children living in 'developed' countries to become aware of how they participate in a global network of economic exchanges. They provide opportunities for the teacher to extend children's understanding and knowledge of their experience as consumers at the supermarket.

Table 15.1 Food and sustainability

Key questions	Concepts	Key ideas	Learning activities
Who produces the food?		The manufacturing, processing and distribution of food Agriculture (subsistence and intensive) Gender, age, class, geographical location and 'race' of producers	Case studies of range of food producers from local to global
How does what we eat affect others?	Equality and inequality	Growth and effects of fast food industry across societies Economic, political and social effects of world markets on developing countries	Research activity based on case studies of fast food industries e.g. MacDonalds
How does what we eat affect other species and the physical world?	Sustainability	Deforestation Pressure on land Effects on oceans and seas Changing methods of animal rearing Use of agro-chemical	Group research tasks on different aspects e.g. oceans and seas, land use, animal rearing, deforestation, hedgerows
Does everybody have enough to eat?	Justice Scarcity	Differences of income between people, groups, societies Notions of absolute and relative poverty in developed and developing countries	Analysis of range of evidence e.g. statistical data, media, photographs, test imony drawn from range of societies
Why do some groups and societies have less to eat than others?	Poverty	Unequal trading relations between developing and developed countries Population growth in poorer countries and communities Poverty and unemployment	Simulation games and role play exercises around trading
How can we sustain a better future for all?		More equal trading relations Redistribution of wealth within and across societies More sustainable food production Access to and control over technology	Presentations from groups arguing different positions Making of newspapers presenting different viewpoints

Source: Buck and Inman (1995)

REFERENCES

Buck, M. and Inman, S. (eds) (1995) 'Citizenship education.' In *Adding Value? Schools' Responsibility for Pupils' Personal Development*. Stoke-on-Trent: Trentham.

Cordelier, S. (1989) *L'Etat du Tiers-Monde*. Paris.

Dollfus, O. (1990) *Geographie Universelle*. Paris: Reclus-Hacette.

Lavisse, E. (1940) *Histoire de France*. Paris: Colin.

Ministere de L'Education Nationale (1995) *Programmes de l'ecole primaire*. Paris: CNDP.

CHAPTER SIXTEEN

Consumers as Citizens
Children Working Together Across Europe

Marta Utset, Maria Villanueva and Carmen Gonzalo

> I did not know that my favourite food had so many additives.
> If they are no good, why do manufacturers use them?

This is a very simple and at the same time a very complex question. It epitomises the contradictions of our consumer society and demonstrates the need for consumers, including children, to be informed and made aware of their role as citizens. The above question was, in fact, a primary school child's reflection on the work she had been doing with pupils from four European countries in the project we describe in this chapter.

We want to present the work of this project to demonstrate to teachers across Europe the possibilities which now exist for collaboration. Previously money from Erasmus/SOCRATES (via the EU) had only been available to teachers and students in secondary and higher education. This has now changed to enable primary school teachers to meet with each other, to plan work together and thus to allow children from different European states to work together on common themes. Whilst the children may not meet in person (unlike the teachers) they may meet through fax, e-mail and the exchange of work on a common theme.

The objectives of the European project we describe were twofold: to introduce a European dimension in primary education and to develop in children a sense of citizenship, so they can begin to experience active membership of a new European society. In order to help children to achieve these objectives, teachers jointly developed a module on food to be studied in the four schools. This module set out to ensure that children were encouraged to reflect on the meaning of their own actions and on their rights and duties as citizens. Having evaluated the first year of the project we feel that this type of collaborative work between teachers and children of different European countries could be an excellent way of developing European citizenship.

INTRODUCTION

The European Union Treaty signed at Maastricht states that the Community must actively contribute to education by means of a series of actions to be developed by member states. COMENIUS now offers such opportunities for work in schools.[1]

The programme offers a courageous challenge: it encourages European children to work together on interdisciplinary activities of common interest and gives teachers the opportunity to collaborate, discuss and reflect on common issues and professional concerns. That is why this initiative should be warmly welcomed. Within COMENIUS (Action 1), partnerships can be developed between schools of at least three European countries focusing on collaborative European Educational Projects. Responsibility for co-ordinating the partnership lies with one of the schools who may have assistance from an Institute of Teacher Education.

In this context, primary school teachers from four countries across Europe decided in 1995 to form a partnership co-ordinated by Bellaterra Primary School, Spain. This school is located in the metropolitan area of Barcelona in Catalonia, an autonomous region in the north-east corner of the Iberian peninsula, bordering with France. The school is attached to the Faculty of Education of the Universitat Autonoma of Barcelona (UAB), and there is a well-established tradition of collaboration between the school and the faculty. Teacher trainers, student teachers and primary teachers benefit from this close work.

The school was helped in finding partner schools by tutors at the UAB. They decided to contact schools where there would be some commonalities but also sufficient contrast to make the work interesting. The partners eventually chosen were the Edmundo de Amicis Primary School in Pievetorina, Italy, a school in the Appeninnes; La Bressola School in Prades in the Catalan region of Roussillon, in the south of France; and the Kokko Ala-Aste in Kauhajoki, Finland. The four are state primary schools, the first two rural. It is worth noting that the teaching language in both Bellaterra and La Bressola schools is Catalan, whilst English is used as a common language of communication between the other schools. We present in this chapter the work that has been developed at Bellaterra Primary School during the project's first year and an outline of the intended work for the next three years.

---

1 Further information on SOCRATES and COMENIUS programmes can be obtained from: Technical and Assistance Office (TAO) Socrates and Youth, 70 rue Montoyer, B-1040, Brussels, Belgium; Central Bureau for Educational Visits and Exchanges, Seymour Mews House, London W1H 9PE, United Kingdom.

THE PROJECT RATIONALE

> How can we involve European opinion in a process of community decision making where consumers are considered as citizens?
> (Bonino 1996)

One of the main aims of education is to foster reflection upon, and knowledge and understanding of, the major issues and concerns of the society in which we live, and furthermore to develop in children the participatory citizenship on which that society depends. The Union Treaty and the post-1989 changes in Europe have increased the interest in how teachers might prepare themselves and young people for the new challenges of European citizenship. Whatever the problems and contradictions of these processes, teachers are educating the citizens of Europe, and we believe that the only way to build a desirable Europe is to take into account cultural diversity and to establish an intercultural dialogue. The future of Europe must be built on the basis of human rights and democracy; it must be seen as a shared place and not as a new fortress.

Shennan (1991) states that the principal aims underpinning a European dimension in education can be summarised in the language of values and attitudes. We need to help pupils develop respect and tolerance towards other people, a sense of responsibility and a co-operative disposition. Co-operating in a transnational project is one practical way of meeting these aims.

Starting from these aims and considering that children are a vulnerable target group for messages sent by consumer marketing, the project partners decided that food and consumerism should be the focus in the four schools linked in the project. We wanted to relate social and environmental issues, to explore the political and cultural dimension of everyday life and to allow children to consider their role as European citizens. The theme was also selected because of its potential for children to be actively involved.

Consumer education has been introduced in different ways in Western societies and its underlying philosophy has, in many ways, run parallel to related current consumer movements. The main focus of the 'first wave' of the consumer movement in the immediate post-war period was information and value for money. Today, this is no longer central to the issues that consumers face. Ralph Nader's *Unsafe At Any Speed* (1991) can be considered the exponent of a second stage in the philosophy of the movement. His argument is that we cannot trust large corporations to look after our interests, and so we must help defend the individual consumer. In the 1990s, a new wave of consumer consciousness has emerged both from environmentalism and from the development of a wider sense of citizenship. Key questions for the ecologically and ethically minded consumer are not only the economic or qualitative aspects of goods and services, but also their long-term impact on the health of the global environment.

PLANNING THE PROJECT

In the preparatory meeting, we outlined the main aspects of the project and decided that it was important during the first year for us as teachers to have as much contact as possible in order to familiarise ourselves with the characteristics of each school and their ways of working. In this way we would be able to define and develop the modules of work with our classes and to monitor the progress of this work. Three meetings were planned, each one in a different school, with all necessary contact being made by mail, telephone or fax.

During the first of the three meetings, we agreed the basic content, objectives and method of working, bearing in mind the curricula of each country, each school's educational projects and the final target group which was children across the whole primary age range. We chose food as the central focus for children's work as an issue that could help teachers in deepening children's understanding of the significance of their more common actions in everyday situations. This focus would allow for reflection on many different aspects. As can be seen in Figure 16.1 the general plan had three clear dimensions: environmental, health and consumer education with 'FOOD' lying in the centre.

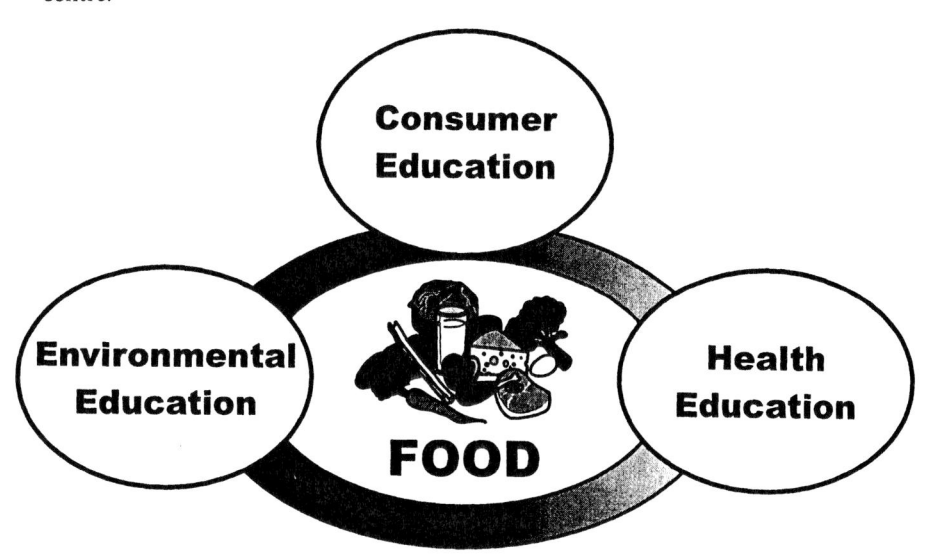

Figure 16.1 Food

We agreed that the work would be developed in the schools in cross-curricular modules taking place over a school year, with only one class being targeted in the first year. These modules could be modified and adapted according to the needs of each school. The initial challenge was thus twofold: to find stimulating activities that would enable children to explore issues fundamental to an understanding of food and consumerism, and to structure these activities so that children would be encouraged to make links between being a responsible food consumer and their role as citizens.

During the three meetings we worked on designing the broad conceptual framework as shown in Figure 16.2. The first year module has come out of this and has been developed in each school. We will now describe the work which was undertaken at Bellaterra Primary School as a result, this school being the project-co-ordinating school.

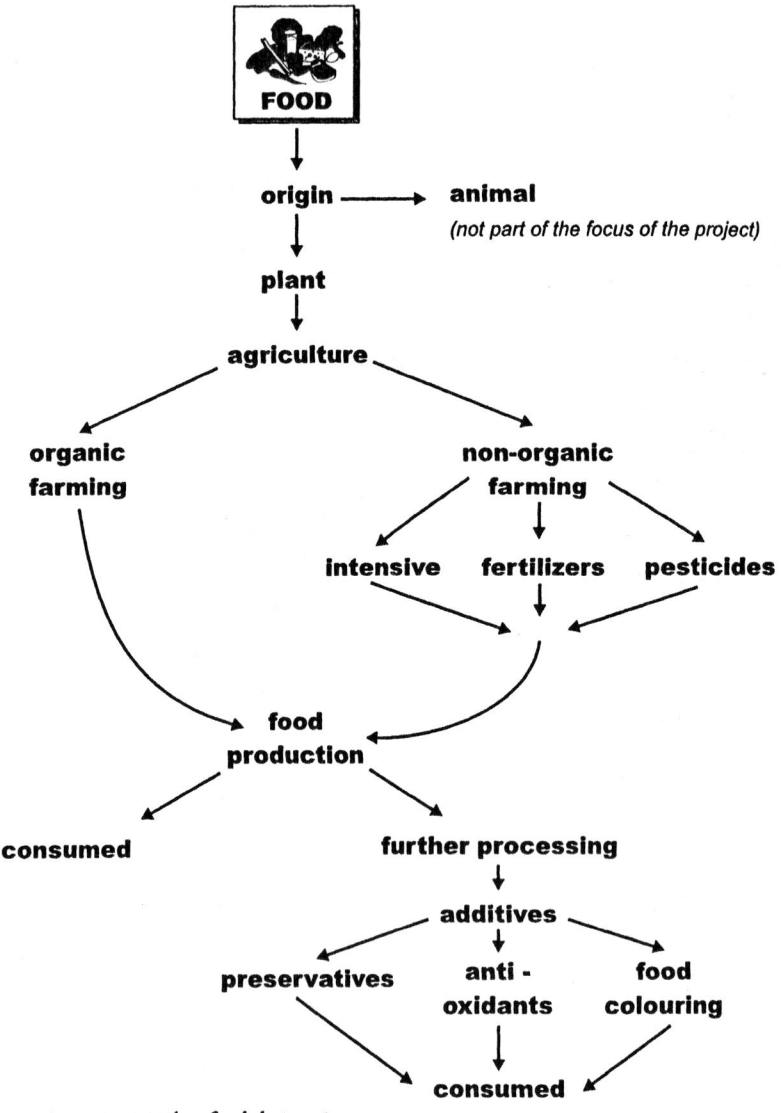

Figure 16.2 What food do I eat?

WORKING WITH PUPILS AT BELLATERRA PRIMARY SCHOOL

We taught the first module 'Food: Origins and Processing' during the summer term 1996, with a group of 25 boys and girls aged 11. It was intended that the module would be covered in ten units of 90 minutes each. It was divided into three phases: an exploring or discovery stage, the introduction of key questions and ideas and a final assessment stage. The aim of the unit was to make clear to children the variety of origins and processes undertaken in the production of food and to raise pupil awareness of the impact of their decisions as consumers of such foods. During the unit, students worked in different ways: in small groups, as a whole class, in pairs and as individuals. Children were encouraged to get information from different sources (reading texts, watching videos, attending an expert lecture etc.). At the same time they had to work on writing texts, designing mental maps, debating ideas and presenting information to the class.

Phase 1: Exploring pupils' previous knowledge

> Imagine that society decides that our diet must be composed of more and more synthetic and manufactured foods and less and less natural foods in order to provide food for the world population. What would you think of this?

We used this question to introduce pupils to an imaginary but possible situation as a way of finding out their initial responses. Students had to reflect upon the issue and write down the first ideas that came into their heads. These were then discussed. In general, they had definite ideas and were very sure in their opinions. However, at the same time they expressed radical but contradictory statements:

> No, I wouldn't like it, because natural food is healthier than processed food.

> Yes, I agree, because not everybody can eat natural food due to the different climates of the world.

The second part of the activity was aimed at finding out what they meant when they talked about natural or processed food so we handed out two lists of foods and processes for children to link together. They were then asked to produce a conceptual map of the links. These activities demonstrated that the children had particular difficulties with many of the technical aspects of the food processing. For instance, none of them understood the word 'pasteurisation', and most of them had problems when trying to relate additives to the effect they had on food.

Phase 2: Key questions and ideas

Having clarified the main issues that arose, the children then made a list of 15 kinds of food they had in their kitchens and classified them according to their animal or vegetable origin. This indicated first, that they knew much more about food of animal origin, due to a topic the previous year, and second, that they had many and common concerns about products which they identified as 'industrial': crisps, popcorn, packet soup etc., and of sweets or drinks such as Coke. We decided to focus on food derived from plants and went on to explore the various ways of producing food, including cultivation and processing, relating these to their impact on health and the environment. Each group was given different information on pesticides, pest control substances, use and abuse of nature, biological agriculture, world food production, farmers, pollution, etc. Each group then became responsible for finding out and explaining to the others its own bit of information.

Having completed this activity, pupils were then clearer in their conceptual understanding about fungicides, natural enemies of plants, watering systems, and environmental pollution including its impact over distance. The children were amazed at some of the things they discovered:

> I didn't know that the penguins that live in Antarctica can be contaminated by chemicals from crops in Europe.
>
> I was surprised to know that farmers can make fruits grow before time and that they can give them beautiful colours.
>
> If I were a farmer I would try to avoid products that may damage people.

We then invited a biologist who used pictures, slides, and overheads which complemented the information they had received from textbooks. We were aware of how the children were able to make use of this new vocabulary and how easily they understood the technical language of the biologist.

Our next step was to follow food from the fields to the shops where we find it ready to be bought. Through watching a video on agricultural systems, they were able to see different kinds of crop growing, harvesting and transportation to shops. They also saw how to preserve foodstuffs to enable them to be safely transported and different sanitary controls. We asked pupils to collect as many product labels as possible from the products they usually consume: doughnuts, yoghourts, sweets, coffee, canned products, jam. We wanted to know the place of origin and the additives of each product. Using a chart which explained kinds and functions of additives, the children began to realise that they consume products with many unnecessary additives: in particular the ones that alter colour, taste and smell. There were spontaneous reflections: 'why do makers use these additives?' with some pupils deciding that 'their only use is making the product more attractive for the buyer'. Others, however, thought they were useful because they preserved foodstuffs for a long time:

In my family we only go shopping once a week.

It is important to use additives. They help food to be taken to countries which haven't got food.

You can modify the way a product tastes but they aren't always necessary.

The children were then asked to rethink their previous conceptual maps and to write individually about the origins, processing and transport of particular foods and the impact of these on the environment. Figure 16.3 summarises the teachers' thinking as a result of the children's work.

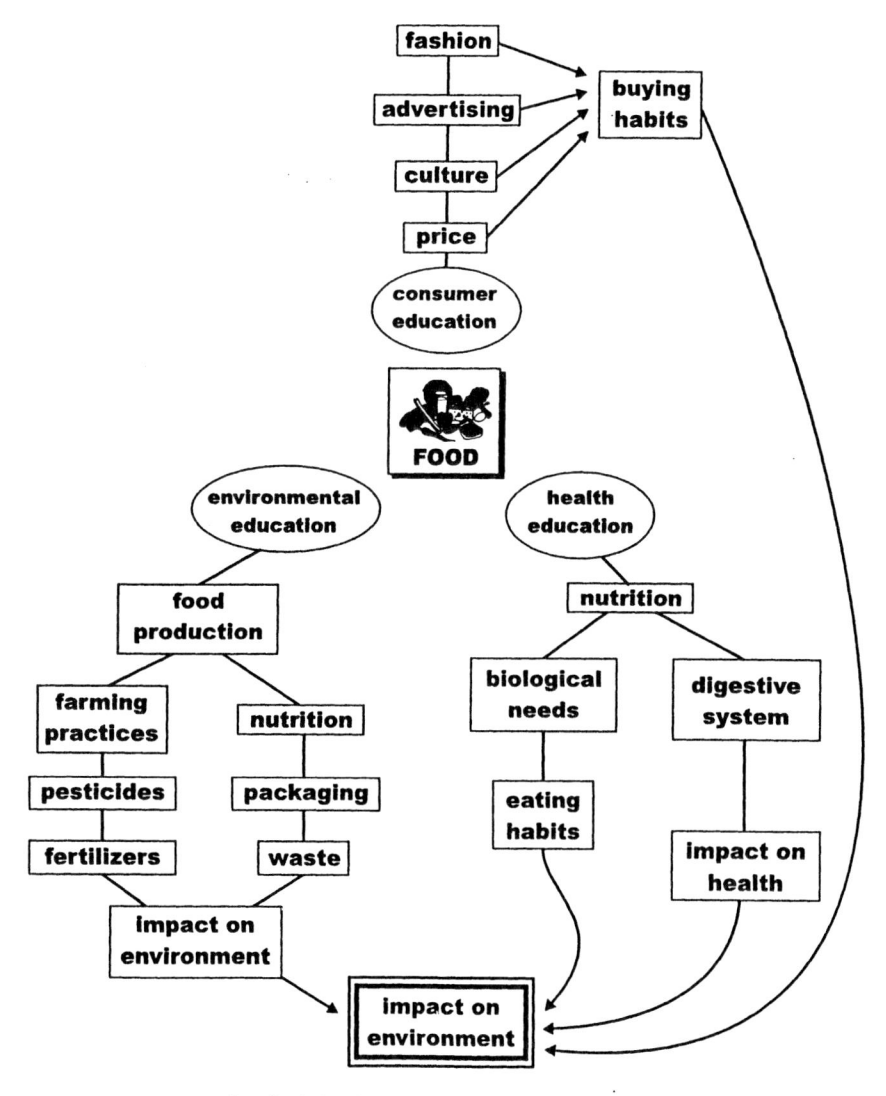

Figure 16.3 What food do I buy?

Phase 3: Assessment of the work

We organised a debate to discuss again the initial question of the unit. We did not pretend to arrive at an agreement but stressed that each child should be able to argue for his or her own personal opinion after listening to other people's ideas. A comparison of their opinions with those expressed in the initial activities showed that the children were better able to link concepts, had a more integrated knowledge of the issues and were better able to evaluate the advantages and disadvantages of various aspects of food processing:

> Farmers should find the balance of natural and artificial systems.
>
> They have invented more additives than we need.
>
> Scientists should go on investigating to find products that don't damage soil and plants, animals, people.

In addition they realised the importance of being informed about what they buy instead of being attracted by beautiful packages. In fact they were beginning to think as active food consumers, taking into account the impacts on the environment and on their health of the production, processing and distribution of food.

We wanted to end the unit with an evaluation by the pupils. They were asked to assess all the activities they had done and to highlight those pieces of information or ideas they found most interesting and new. They made comments such as:

> I didn't know that pesticides contaminate.
>
> I was surprised to know that farmers can make apples grow faster and make them more beautiful.
>
> I've learned to decode the numbers and letters of labels.

HAVING IN MIND FRIENDS IN EUROPE: THE OTHER PROJECT PARTNERS

We had decided that in the first year of the project the children in the four schools would work on the same content and materials, with a similar methodology, but that they would not exchange their work. We did this as we felt it was necessary first to create the kind of atmosphere which would facilitate the work for the future. We thought that they should get to know each other through different methods of contact, using the working meetings to meet each other's teachers.

At the beginning of the work children in the four schools were told about children in other European schools doing the same project as them. They were told that their teachers wanted to collaborate in this work so that they as children could be helped to know each other and to understand better the unity and diversity within their European environments and cultures. During the first two weeks children exchanged letters, photographs and pictures so they got to feel closer. From time to time, either spontaneously or at the teacher's request, we mentioned our friends and they pointed out similarities and differences. Some of these related to ways of eating or the harvesting time of the year: they realised quickly why Mediterranean countries were more similar in these aspects. On the other hand they reflected upon the fact that Finnish children did eat fresh fruits and orange juice in winter, thanks to transport systems or processing techniques. The children are now very excited at the idea that during the second year of the project they will actually exchange their own materials and activities with the children of the Italian, French and Finnish schools.

THE NEXT STAGES

The work done this year and the reflection on it has been the foundation for the planning of the next two years of the project. All partners have visited the four schools, met teachers and children and have extended the project's outline so that it can become in each case a whole school project. The plan for the next two years requires two things: first, that the experience is adapted and made relevant for all children of all ages so that all pupils are able to work with their respective teachers on the module, and second, to link the children through the exchange of materials, comments and suggestions about the work done. The contact between teachers will continue to be as frequent as possible and should include, in one way or another, all participants in the project.

In the second year, three meetings have been planned to discuss, fix and follow up the work. In each case the host school must plan and take responsibility for all aspects of the visit, and whenever possible, the meetings should be attended by different teachers to reinforce the idea that the whole school is involved in the project. Children who have already been involved in the project in the first year will continue to exchange information about themselves and their countries and this year in particular will say more about their way of life, costumes, feasts and traditions. In addition, they will start sharing materials related to the project. It is expected that on the teachers' visits to the schools they will bring with them their own pupils' materials and hand them out, personally.

In the third year pupils will intensify their links. There will be a further exchange of materials and common activities, and the emphasis will move to the children providing answers to the comments, questions and explanations that they request from each other. It is hoped that the children will reflect upon the joint project and try to understand each other's points of view with particular reference to the underlying values and attitudes.

During the final year teachers will review the units of work, modify them if necessary and help schools accept the challenge of integrating these cross-curricular themes into the curriculum.

The last of the meetings will be used to evaluate the work done and to arrive at conclusions both at the school level and as a partnership between schools.

CONCLUSIONS

> The study of the issues has made me reflect on many things, for example: I have discovered that sweets have many additives and they are not good. Now I don't eat as many as before.
>
> When I go shopping with mummy I look at the labels of the things she is buying. If they are not clear, I ask her not to buy them.

These are small examples but they show the impact of the module's work: children have been made aware of the importance of being informed in order to make decisions. This awareness has been shared with many of the families, although it has to be said that some mothers did complain, albeit in a friendly way, about pressures from their children when shopping. Another aspect of the work has been the global dimension, which has been complex and often seen as controversial. Working on such controversial issues has certainly contributed to children's development as citizens and has helped them to act upon opinions shaped by values.

So far all partner schools agree that the experience of linking children has been a very positive one. As has been said before, communication started with meeting the teachers of the other schools. Boys and girls have also lived the experience of sending and receiving letters and news from foreign friends. Most communication has been in the children's mother tongue which has required a great deal of thought on the part of the children. For instance, children have found it easy to communicate with Italian and French friends, because of the common Latin root of each language. However, communication with Finnish children has been more problematic. They even found their names surprising! In fact, they have come to appreciate the need for a different but common language and now also use English as a medium. For this reason, English has become the common language of the teachers' meetings.

Other areas of the curriculum also had a part to play in this project. For example the children were surprised at the very beginning to find that in two different countries with two official languages, children had the same mother tongue: Catalan. History had some lessons for these children. However, It can be said that the main achievement of this communication process has been that children have lost their fear and prejudice of other languages and have started to show a receptive and open attitude to transcultural communication. Recognising and accepting differences is the first step for the new European citizenship.

For teachers, the experience of the first year has been a very positive one. They have been able to plan the work for the whole project, and the discussion process has enriched them from a professional point of view. But even more important than that has been discovering the real meaning of working together, teachers and children, with a European dimension.

As a general conclusion it can be said that the experience of the project has been, essentially, a learning process for all the participants. It endorses the notion that education should be the vehicle for the achievement of attitudes and values for a desirable Europe in a just world, and shows that the active processes of analysis, discussion and decision making will engage teachers and children in a more active citizenship.

REFERENCES

Bonino, E. (1996) 'La Europa del consumo.' *El País*, 5 February.

Nader, R. (1991) *Unsafe At Any Speed*. London: Knightsbridge Publishing Company.

Shennan, M. (1991) *Teaching about Europe*. London: Cassell.

FURTHER READING

Edwards, J. and Fogelman, K. (1993) *Developing Citizenship in the Curriculum*. London: David Fulton.

Gonzalo, C. and Villaneuva, M. (1996) 'Geography and values education.' In F. Buffet and J. Tschoumy *Choc d,mocratique et formation des enseignants en Europe*. Lyon: Presses Universitaires de Lyon.

Guix (1996) 'La visiç educativa d'Europa.' Vol. 230. Barcelona.

Huckle, J. (1989) *Our Consumer Society*. Godalming: WWF.

Lang, T. (1991) 'Consumers or citizens?' *The Ecologist 21*, 4, 154–56.

PART SIX

Children's Voices in Learning Materials

CHAPTER SEVENTEEN

Speaking for Ourselves, Listening to Others
Young Global Citizens Learning through the Study of Distant Places

Julia Tanner

INTRODUCTION

Children in primary schools today face an uncertain future. They are growing up in a world which is characterised by unprecedented technological, economic, political and social change and in which the future is, more than ever before, an 'unknown country'. One urgent task for schools and teachers is to prepare pupils for the opportunities and challenges they will face as citizens of this unknown future. I believe that education for citizenship should be concerned with helping children to become informed and active citizens who are interested not only in their own well-being, and that of their local area and nation, but also in that of the rest of humankind and our communal home, planet Earth. Nurturing this sense of global citizenship involves developing children's knowledge and understanding of the wider world and providing opportunities for them to acquire a range of critical skills and attitudes.

The purpose of this chapter is to show how the study of an overseas locality, as required by Key Stage 2 (ages 7–11 years) of the English National Curriculum can provide an excellent context for nurturing young global citizens. I describe an international project 'Speaking for Ourselves, Listening to Others'[1] which involved children and their teachers producing materials about their own local area and using resources similarly created by other children to find out

---

1 'Speaking for Ourselves, Listening to Others' is available from Leeds Development Education Centre, 153 Cardigan Road, Leeds LS6 1LJ. Tel: 0113-278 4030.

about a distant place and the people who live there. The active involvement of children in both producing and in using learning resources was a key feature of the project, which particularly focused on helping pupils to develop communication skills and also skills in the critical interpretation of visual and written sources of information about other places. I show how three fundamental principles – adopting active and reflective approaches, starting from what children already know, and enabling children to speak for themselves – were embedded in the work of the project. I illustrate these by reference to a range of activities which teachers can adapt for use in their own classrooms, and discuss the potential of this sort of work in helping children to develop the knowledge, understanding, skills and attitudes they need in order to become informed, concerned and active global citizens. I shall start the chapter, however, by considering the current debate about citizenship education in schools, arguing that it needs to incorporate a global dimension if pupils are to be adequately prepared for adult life in the next millennium.

EDUCATION FOR CITIZENSHIP

The start of the 1990s saw renewed interest in education for citizenship, following its designation as one of the five cross-curricular themes of the National Curriculum for England (National Curriculum Council 1990a). In the first year of the decade both the Speaker's Commission on Citizenship Report (House of Commons 1990) and the NCC guidance on education for citizenship (National Curriculum Council 1990b) were published. Although criticised as largely concerned with notions of local and national citizenship (Machon 1991; Marsden 1995), both these documents acknowledge the need for young people to be prepared to play a full part in a multi-ethnic and culturally diverse society, and both emphasise the critical importance of developing skills and attitudes as well as knowledge and understanding. The publication of these two documents could have provoked discussion and debate about the fundamental purposes of education and its role in preparing pupils for future citizenship but unfortunately the opportunity was lost as schools struggled to implement the National Curriculum and its associated assessment arrangements.

The mid-1990s brought a substantial review of the curriculum and, in the wake of the tragic murders of toddler Jamie Bulger and headteacher Philip Lawrence, a new debate abut the role of schools in shaping children's values and supporting their moral development. Once again, however, the discussion was limited to issues of national citizenship and this was compounded when Nicholas Tate, Chief Executive of the Schools Curriculum and Assessment Authority, insisted in a series of speeches that schools should promote a sense of pride in national identity and in British heritage. Many critics argued strongly that this would intensify the ethnocentric bias of the school curriculum, and that it ignored the pressing need to educate children for life in what will be an increasingly interdependent global community. Pupils who are in school today will be the workers, parents, producers, consumers and politicians of the future, and they need to be equipped to deal with a shrinking world beset by critical environmental and developmental problems.

THE PROJECT

'Speaking for Ourselves, Listening to Others' was one outcome of a three-year project run by Leeds Development Education Centre from 1994 to 1996. This work, for which I was a consultant, was funded and supported by the European Union, OXFAM, Leeds Metropolitan University, the Undugu Society of Kenya and children, teachers and schools in six countries – Kenya, Greece, Ireland, Denmark, Nigeria and England. This part of the project had four main aims, which were formulated in response to two imperatives – a desire to promote the development of children as active and informed global citizens and the need to work within the National Curriculum framework.

Project aims

The first aim was to develop a model of good practice for teaching about a locality in a country in the south. This is a part of the Geography National Curriculum for Key Stage 2, which requires that children study a locality in a country in Africa, Asia (excluding Japan), South America or Central America (including the Caribbean). The details of what they are to learn about these places are also specified. In studying localities, pupils should be taught:

- about the main physical and human features, such as cliffs, valleys, housing estates, reservoirs, and environmental issues, such as water pollution, proposals for a new supermarket, that give the localities their character

- how the localities may be similar and how they may differ, for example two localities may both be in valleys, but one valley is narrow and steep-sided, while the other is wide and gently sloping

- how the features of the localities influence the nature and location of human activities within them, for example roads following valleys, multi-storey car parks near city centres

- about recent or proposed changes in the localities, such as the closure of a corner shop

- how the localities are set within a broader geographical context, such as within a town, a region, a country, and are linked with other places, for example through the supply of goods, movement of people.
(Department of Education 1995, p.5)

This requirement of the National Curriculum has great potential for developing children's knowledge and understanding of a distant place and the lives of the people who live there, and for developing many of the geographical skills required at Key Stage 2. These include geographical vocabulary, making and using maps and using secondary sources. The potential danger of such work is that it could also promote stereotypical images or confirm children's existing perceptions of southern countries, which as both Bale (1987) and Wiegand (1992; 1993) have shown, are frequently inaccurate and often negative.

The second aim of the project then was to experiment with a range of strategies for challenging children's partial, limited and/or negative perceptions of and attitudes towards people and places in these countries. Although research has shown that primary children do tend to have limited and often stereotyped ideas about distant places (Bale 1987; Weigand 1992) it also seems that during the later primary years, children are open to new ideas about distant places and peoples, and generally demonstrate more tolerant and unprejudiced attitudes than adolescents or younger children. This suggests that Key Stage 2 is an excellent time for the detailed study of overseas localities.

The third aim of the project was to develop a range of approaches and activities which would provide opportunities for children to be actively involved in their own learning. In doing this the project drew and built on the participatory and experimental approaches to learning advocated by development educators (see for example Fisher and Hicks 1985; Greig *et al.* 1987; Pike and Selby 1988; Fountain 1990; 1995; Osler 1994). These approaches acknowledge that how children learn is just as important as what they learn. They foster pupil motivation, engagement, autonomy and critical thinking skills. David Hicks has succinctly described the underlying philosophy:

> Effective learning is seen as arising out of affirmation of each pupil's individual worth, the development of a wide range of co-operative skills, the ability to discuss and debate issues, to reflect critically on everyday life and events in the wider world, and to act as responsible citizens. (Hicks 1994, p.25)

The fourth, rather more practical, aim of the project was to produce a resource pack which would provide English primary schools with teaching materials which would both help them to meet part of the National Curriculum requirements for Geography and English at Key Stage 2 and which would reflect and demonstrate the philosophy of the project. As we say in the introduction, 'Speaking for Ourselves, Listening to Others'

> offers a unique approach to learning about a distant place by providing teachers with source material created by young people who live in Kenya's capital city, Nairobi. It also provides opportunities for girls and boys to speak candidly about their perceptions of themselves and the

locality in which they live...[and] to value their own experience and place equal emphasis on the need to listen and to consider other people's views and opinions. (Leeds DEC 1996, p1.)

Underpinning principles

As noted earlier, three crucial principles underpinned the work of the project. These were, first, adopting active and reflective learning approaches, second, starting from what children already know, and, third, enabling children to speak for themselves.

Both active and reflective learning approaches are important in fostering the development of global citizens. Active approaches encourage pupil motivation and engagement with content, and provide a meaningful context for the development of intellectual skills and social skills. These include written and oral communication, and the ability to work in co-operative ways and make decisions. Reflective approaches encourage the development of 'metacognitive skills', that is skills which are concerned with learning about the processes of thinking and learning. In order to encourage children to reflect on their own learning we used a model developed originally by the National Oracy Project. This process involves pupils first recording what they already know (or think they know!), so identifying their *pre-view*; then working with a range of new sources of information, so developing their *new view*; and then finally explicitly comparing their pre-view with their new view, so undertaking a *review*. In trialling the published materials and activities, teachers found that the review activities helped children become aware of, acknowledge and value their own learning. The children often recognised that their initial ideas and images (their pre-views) were limited or inadequate, and that they had learnt different things from different sources of information. The ability to interpret and analyse a range of material and to draw fair and balanced conclusions is surely one of the key characteristics of a well-informed citizen.

The second key principle which informed the project was that of starting from what children already know. Applying this principle to the study of distant places means eliciting and working with children's existing knowledge and perceptions. It also requires recognition of the ways in which children develop their knowledge of the world. Brian Goodey's (1973, p.7) model of 'the child in information space' shows how their knowledge and understanding of local and distant places is critically shaped by their individual experiences and by social factors. Each child develops a unique 'personal geography' based on a mixture of first-hand experiences, such as the journey to school or holiday visits, and of information gathered from secondary sources such as the television, newspapers and photographs. In the project, we found that work on children's personal geographies proved to be an effective starting point for work on both their local area and on the distant locality. They were encouraged to create and discuss images of their own local area, through map-making, the use of published sources of information and through taking photographs. An example of one of these activities is shown in Figure 17.1 at the end of the chapter.

The project also used personal geography techniques to elicit the children's perceptions of Kenya. They were asked to draw individual pictures and to brainstorm their ideas in small groups. In addition, they were given opportunities to explore Kenyan children's images of England and Danish children's perceptions of Kenya. Teachers trialling this approach found that the children responded enthusiastically to these activities, and that they began to understand how images of places are produced, and the importance of experience, purpose and audience in generating images of places. In undertaking a survey of coverage of African countries in the British media, they also started to recognise that the information was limited, and to develop skills in analysing and detecting bias.

The third key principle underpinning the project was that of enabling children to speak for themselves. We worked with this principle in two ways – first, by recognising the fundamental importance of oral work in mediating learning in the classroom, and second, by producing resources created by children in one country for use by children in another.

Language, especially speaking and listening, is fundamental to children's learning in the primary classroom. Through discussion, pupils can clarify, elaborate and extend their ideas, drawing on each other and the teacher as they try to make sense of and interpret their experiences and new information. Although many classrooms have established guidelines for speaking and listening, in trialling, teachers found that the activity in Figure 17.2 provided an opportunity for pupils to enhance their oracy skills. By reflecting on, acknowledging and discussing their feelings about talking and being heard, pupils can become more confident speakers and sensitive listeners. As development educators, we were also concerned to promote children's confidence and self-esteem, and to help them recognise their unique value. The activity in Figure 17.3 provided a vehicle for doing this, and for learning to respect differences in the classroom.

We also applied the principle of children speaking for themselves in the creation of the published resource pack. As resource producers, we were conscious that most of the available 'locality packs' had been developed by adult outsiders, and felt that there was a need for source materials created by children for children. Putting this principle into practice proved to be a lengthy, complex and difficult task, and we grappled with many practical and ethical problems along the way. The process by which the final resource pack was produced is described in Figure 17.5. Much of the pack consists of material produced by eight of the young Kenyans with whom we worked in Nairobi. They drew self-portraits, wrote about themselves and their home area, and recorded three wishes – for themselves, their country and the world. In addition they drew free-hand maps of the areas in which they live, and took photographs to illustrate the reality of their lives in Nairobi. In the pack we suggest ways in which pupils can produce their own equivalent resources, and provide ideas for making good use of the materials about Nairobi. An example of this is the activity shown in Figure 17.4, which partly mirrors 'Is this who I am?' (Figure 17.3), described above. In trialling these materials, we found that children responded positively to this approach, displaying great interest in and empathy for the Kenyan children. As the School Links International Project discovered in the 1980s, the focus on named individual children provides a sense of realism and actuality which fascinates primary children (Beddis and Mares 1988, p.9). A particularly important aspect of this in relation to fostering global citizenship is the ability to recognise and value similarities and differences, and to empathise with children who live in distant places.

CONCLUSION: NURTURING YOUNG GLOBAL CITIZENS

I argued earlier that there was an urgent need to educate primary children to be informed and active global citizens. I want to conclude now by discussing the ways in which this project and the associated publication, which represents only a small part of the work undertaken, sought to develop the knowledge, skills and attitudes which such citizens will need.

One important aim of geographical education, recognised in the first paragraph of the Programme of Study for Key Stage 2, is that children learn about their own locality and people and places in other parts of the world. This project provided opportunities for them to actively develop knowledge and understanding of their school's local environment and to find out about a contrasting locality through a parallel process. They learnt something of the people, neighbourhoods and ways of life of children growing up in Nairobi, one of Africa's fastest-growing cities. In particular, they learnt that Kenyan children from different social backgrounds have different life experiences, perceptions and opportunities. Study of the photographs, in particular, demonstrates that Nairobi, like cities in England, is a very diverse and varied place.

Children developing their knowledge and understanding of the variety of places, local and distant, is one important aspect of becoming an informed global citizen. Another is becoming aware of the ways in which images of places are created and sustained, and of the ways in which these images affect our perceptions of places and the people who live in them. Many children involved in the project came to realise that their own original perceptions, that is, their previews, were distorted by the limited and partial information they had received from the media. They initially expressed surprise at pictures of urban Africa, of children buying familiar chocolate bars, watching television and enjoying themselves at an open-air leisure complex, but proved both willing and able to incorporate this unexpected information into their 'new view'. In so doing, they developed deeper knowledge and understanding not only of the realities of Nairobi, but also of the images of people and places which surround them in everyday life.

Informed global citizens need not only knowledge of the wider world but also a range of critical, intellectual and social skills. Good communication skills, including clear written and oral expression, the ability to listen and discuss, and to defend one's position are essential for active participation in democratic processes. Equally important are skills involving judgement, including the collection and analysis of many types of information, the ability to draw balanced conclusions, and skills in identifying bias, prejudice and stereotypes. Many of the activities developed by the project were designed to develop these skills, in the context of interpreting information and images of known and relatively unfamiliar places. Teachers who used these activities found that some children developed quite sophisticated skills in using secondary sources of information. This replicates the experience of the Schools Linking International Project, which found that pupils quickly 'became sensitive to the subtleties of cultural similarities and differences, and the crudeness of stereotyping' (Beddis and Mares 1988, p.16). Citizens of the twenty-first century are likely to be bombarded with huge amounts of information, and it is therefore of critical importance that they develop sound skills in judging its quality and providence.

All children need to develop good interpersonal skills if they are to become successful adults who contribute to social, economic and political life. The project aimed to promote children's social skills through its emphasis on speaking and listening, co-operative group work and collaborative enquiry. Teachers trialling the materials reported that they were very effective in promoting personal and social education, especially pupils' sense of self-worth, respect for others, ability to work together productively and their understanding of issues of bias and stereotyping.

While the knowledge and skills discussed above are clearly important in nurturing informed global citizens, it could be argued that it is attitudes that are likely to be critical in fostering commitment to action. In other words, people need to care enough to want to do something. Recent research shows that children are very aware of and concerned about global issues and that they wish for a better world (Hicks and Holden 1995). Many of the hundreds of children who were involved in our project were invited to formulate a wish for the world. Children from all six countries made remarkably similar wishes, very largely concerned with the cessation of war, eradication of hunger and illness, protection of the environment and particularly animals at risk from extinction, and with the elimination of poverty and inequality. The evidence is, then, that children already do care about the future and the fate of the world. The project sought to build on this by encouraging pupils to develop empathy for children living in distant, and in some ways very different, places. The emphasis on children communicating almost directly with other children was part of this strategy, as was the focus on developing critical thinking and interpersonal skills, and the importance given to children reflecting on and recording their own learning.

The development of 'Speaking for Ourselves, Listening to Others' raised as many questions as it posed solutions, and confronted us, as resource producers, with a range of practical problems and ethical issues. While the practical problems of working in six countries, several languages, and in an overcrowded curriculum, were eventually overcome, other more substantive issues remain unresolved. What for example is the relationship between children engaging in active learning in the classroom and becoming active citizens in their lives beyond school? How should teachers respond when children continue to see different lifestyles as inferior, or alternatively recognise injustice but feel powerless to act? How confident can we be that knowledge and understandings acquired in primary schools will persist into adult life, or be acted upon?

In a democratic society, we have to believe that individuals can and do make a difference. History is replete with stories of individuals who have campaigned and fought for social justice and environmental protection. As Margaret Mead famously noted, we should 'never doubt that a small group of committed citizens can change the world...[for]...indeed, it is the only thing that ever has' (Friends of the Earth 1992). The project I have described sought to contribute to the development of informed, active and committed young global citizens who will be both willing and able to play their part in creating a better world.

HIGHLIGHTS AND EYESORES

Objectives
- For pupils to discuss a range of images of their local area.
- For pupils to recognise how these images can convey a positive or negative impression of a place.
- For pupils to consider recent or proposed changes to the area.
- For pupils to consider how localities are set within a broader geographical context.

Materials

Selection of photographs of the local area produced for different purposes, for example photographs cut from local newspapers; from tourist brochures; from local businesses or local authority booklets.

Selection of sticky coloured dots in three colours (enough for each pair or small group to have one dot of each colour).

Organisation

Pupils working in pairs or small groups moving around the room. Coloured dots should be placed in a corner of each photograph so that each image can be re-used in the next activity. If small pictures are being used, which would be obliterated by dots, then each image can be mounted on paper and the dots placed on the border.

Activity
- Display the photographs round the classroom
- Tell the pupils that they are going to move round the room and that each pair will choose a photograph which shows:
  - something that would encourage someone to visit the area (a highlight)
  - something in the area that needs to be improved (an eyesore)
  - something that helps to give the area its character.
- As each pair makes their choice they can identify it with a dot of a specified colour.
- When each pair has completed the task, ask them to return to their seats and for one member from each pair to give the reasons for their decisions.
- Ask pupils to consider where all the dots have been placed.
- Did every group choose the same photographs for each purpose?
- Discuss with the pupils how photographs can portray an area positively or negatively. For example: can the pupils think of any examples of areas that are usually portrayed positively or negatively to outsiders? If a person lives in an area that is usually portrayed negatively, what effect might this have on them?

Differentiation and extension

Additional categories can be suggested. For example:
- Who or what is left out of the pictures chosen by the image makers.
- How the locality has changed or is going to change.
- How the locality is linked to other places in the country or other parts of the world.
- Something about the area of which the pupils are proud.

Figure 17.1 Highlights and eyesores
Source: Leeds DEC (1996)

SPEAKING AND LISTENING IN THE CLASSROOM

Objectives

For pupils to think about how they can help themselves and others to talk and listen with confidence. For the class to decide on guidelines to aid speaking and listening work.

Materials

Four large sheets of paper, each headed with one of the following sentence stems:
- When somebody really listens to me I feel...
- When people don't listen to my opinions I feel...
- I feel confident about saying what I think when...
- We can sort out any disagreements by...

Four slips of paper per pupil with Blu Tack, sticky tape or glue.

Group work

Pupils working in single-sex groups, leading to whole class discussion.

Activity
- Pin up the four large sheets of paper and explain the sentence stems to pupils.
- Encourage pupils to talk within a group about their responses to the sentences and the feelings they associate with each one.
- Ask pupils to write a word or phrase on each slip that they would use to complete each sentence stem in a collecting box passed round the groups. The slips collected in this way can be stuck on by an independent person to aid confidentiality.
- Taking one large response sheet at a time, read out the answers the pupils have given to that sentence.
- Encourage the whole class to discuss the feelings and emotions that have been expressed.
- Help the pupils to use the responses to draw up some class rules to help speaking and listening in the classroom.

Differentiation and extension

The guidelines can be produced in poster form for classroom display to remind pupils what helps and what hinders speaking and listening work. This poster can be referred to, and its effectiveness evaluated at the end of each session.

Information for teachers

The class guidelines for speaking and listening can be reviewed at the end of each section to see if they have been adhered to, whether they remain a helpful remainder or whether they need to be renegotiated.

Figure 17.2 Speaking and listening in the classroom
Source: Leeds DEC (1996)

Is this who I am?

The name I like to be called is _____

Four words which describe me are _____
_____

Last Saturday I _____
_____

I like being a boy/girl because _____
_____

Things that make me feel good are _____
_____

When I am an adult I will _____
_____

The most beautiful place I can imagine is _____

If a girl/boy from another country came to visit I would take them to because _____

The best thing about my neighbour is _____

One thing I would like to see changed where I live is ___
_____

To help improve my area I could _____
_____

To make the world a better place, I think adults could ___
_____

Three wishes

If you had three wishes – one for yourself, one for your country, one for the world – what would they be?

_____
_____
_____

Figure 17.3 *Is this who I am?*
Source: Leeds DEC (1996)

JOHN

The name I like to be called is Mbuthia but my first name is John. Words which describe me are good, shy, brown and short.

Last Saturday I washed my clothes, played volleyball, listened to stories, helped my mother and watched a play.

I like being a boy because I'd like to be a soldier. Things that make me feel good are laughing, playing and joking.

If a girl or a boy from another country came to visit me I would take them to my home.

The most beautiful place I can imagine is the City Sports Stadium.

I live at a place called Mathare Phase 1. It is heavily populated.

Our house is just inside the slums, and where I live is situated between the church and the Chief's camp. Beside that is the primary school.

The main road passes just next to our house. Opposite the house there is a small kiosk.

Three wishes

My wish for myself, if I could manage to do it, would be to have a vehicle.

I wish that the people in my country can have peace, employment, love, happiness and knowledge.

My wish for the world is for everyone to live in harmony and with love and unity.

Figure 17.4 John
Source: Leeds DEC (1996)

HOW THIS RESOURCE WAS PRODUCED

This resource has been produced as part of a three-year Gender and Development Project managed and supported by Leeds Development Education Centre.

We worked closely with teachers and pupils aged 9–11 in a range of primary schools throughout West Yorkshire. Some of this work we were able to take to Nairobi so that the Kenyan young people had a sense of the audience for whom they were producing materials.

We spent time in 1994 and 1995 with young people, their parents and teachers from different socio-economic backgrounds in Nairobi city centre through our links with OXFAM and the Undugu Society of Kenya. We worked with teachers and learners at the Undugu school in Pumwani and heard from them about their experience of being young and poor in East Africa's largest, most modern and fastest-growing city.

Oxfam's Kenya Programme is based near Westlands, a contrasting area of Nairobi. We worked with Oxfam staff, and their children, to gain a different perspective from that provided by the Undugu learners. In order to maintain the principle of girls and boys 'speaking for themselves' we tried to work in ways that minimised the impact that we, as white European women, had on the responses of the Kenyan young people. This was achieved by working through adults with whom the young people were familiar.

To introduce a European dimension we used the activities in this resource to collect source material from primary school pupils in Greece and Denmark. Again, we worked through adults who used the first language of the pupils, recorded their responses and translated them into English.

Producers:

Julia Tanner
Chrys Ritson

Figure 17.5 How this resource was produced
Source: Leeds DEC (1996)

REFERENCES

Bale, J. (1987) *Geography in the Primary School*. London: Routledge and Kegan Paul.

Beddis, R. and Mares, C. (1988) *School Links International*. Brighton: Avon County Council/Tidy Britain Group Schools Research Project.

Department for Education (1995) *Geography in the National Curriculum*. London: HMSO.

Fisher, S. and Hicks, D. (1985) *World Studies 8–13*. Edinburgh: Oliver and Boyd.

Fountain, S. (1990) *Learning Together: Global Education 4–7*. Cheltenham: Stanley Thomas.

Fountain, S. (1995) *Education for Development: A Teachers' Resource for Global Learning*. London: UNICEF/Hodder and Stoughton.

Friends of the Earth (1992) Postcard produced for Rio Conference.

Goodey, B. (1973) *Perceptions of the Environment*. Occasional paper 17. Centre for Urban and Regional Studies, University of Birmingham.

Greig, S., Pike, G. and Selby, D. (1987) *Earthrights: Education as if the Planet Really Mattered*. London: WWF/Kogan Page.

Hicks, D. (ed) (1994) *Preparing for the Future: Notes and Queries for Concerned Educators*. London: Adamantine Press/WWF.

Hicks, D. and Holden, C. (1995) *Visions of the Future: Why We Need to Teach for Tomorrow*. Stoke-on-Trent: Trentham.

House of Commons (1990) *Report of the Speakers Commission on Citizenship: Encouraging Citizenship*. London: HMSO.

Leeds DEC (1996) *Speaking for Ourselves, Listening to Others*. Leeds: Leeds Development Education Centre.

Machon, P. (1991) 'Subject or citizen?' *Teaching Geography* 16, 3, 128.

Marsden, B. (1995) *Geography 11–16: Rebuilding Good Practice*. London, David Fulton.

National Curriculum Council (1990a) *The Whole Curriculum: Curriculum Guidance 3*. York: NCC.

National Curriculum Council (1990b) *Education for Citizenship*. York: NCC.

Osler, A. (ed) (1994) *Development and Education: Global Perspectives in the Curriculum*. London: Cassell.

Pike, G. and Selby, D. (1988) *Global Teacher Global Learner*. London: Hodder and Stoughton.

Wiegand, P. (1992) *Places in the Primary School: Knowledge and Understanding of Places at Key Stages 1 and 2*. London: Falmer Press.

Wiegand, P. (1993) *Children and Primary Geography*. London: Cassell.

CHAPTER EIGHTEEN

Children's Voices from Different Times and Places

Margot Brown and Don Harrison

Once when I was six years old I saw a magnificent picture in a book, called *True Stories from Nature*, about the primeval forest. It was a picture of a boa constrictor in the act of swallowing an animal... In the book it said: 'Boa constrictors swallow their prey whole, without chewing it. After that they are not able to move, and they sleep through the six months that they need for digestion.'

I pondered deeply, then, over the adventures of the jungle. And after some work with a coloured pencil I succeeded in making my first drawing. My Drawing Number One. It looked like this:

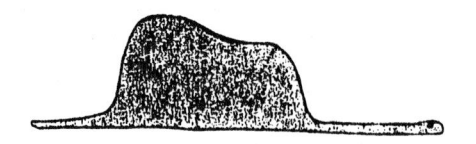

Figure 18.1 'My Drawing Number One'

I showed my masterpiece to the grown-ups, and asked them whether the drawing frightened them.

But they answered: 'Frighten? Why should any one be frightened by a hat?' My drawing was not a picture of a hat. It was a picture of a boa constrictor digesting an elephant. But since the grown-ups were not able to understand it, I made another drawing: I drew the inside of the boa constrictor, so that the grown-ups could see it clearly. They always need to have things explained. My Drawing Number Two looked like this:

Figure 18.2 'My Drawing Number Two'

The grown-ups' response, this time, was to advise me to lay aside my drawings of boa constrictors, whether from the inside or the outside, and devote myself instead to geography, history, arithmetic and grammar. That is why, at the age of six, I gave up what might have been a magnificent career as a painter. I had been disheartened by the failure of my Drawing Number One and my Drawing Number Two. Grown-ups never understand anything by themselves, and it is tiresome for children to be always and forever explaining things to them. (Saint-Exupéry 1974, p.7)

This chapter aims to show the value of using personal experiences – as expressed by children themselves – as a powerful motivating force for learning social subjects in primary schools (for the purpose of this chapter we define social subjects as history, geography and personal and social education). Getting access to the voices of children who have lived in different times or who live now in different places can be difficult – especially given that children's voices in the here and now are not always heard. It is important therefore for teachers to include the perspectives of children, not only because they are part of all societies today but also because they are and will be significant players in the process of social change. Today's children are tomorrow's adults and the decisions they make as adults may well be affected by their childhood experiences.

CHILDREN'S VOICES IN THE CURRICULUM

A useful framework for considering children's experience is the United Nations Convention on the Rights of the Child, as adopted by the United Nations in 1989 and ratified by the United Kingdom government in 1991. The Convention adds to previous international agreements by including children's rights to participate in society, particularly the right to freedom of expression:

> this right shall include freedom to seek, receive and impart information and ideas of all kinds, regardless of frontiers, either orally, in writing or in print, in the form of art, or through any other media of the child's choice.

(Convention on the Rights of the Child, Article 13.1)

This right entitles children to speak and be listened to and provides potential for children's voices to contribute to social, geographical and historical education. At one level the curriculum itself can be a vehicle for the voices of children, where children's experiences are a central focus. At another level, children may begin to play a part in determining curriculum design and teaching methods.

The focus of this chapter is on how children's voices can be heard in the curriculum and how children's experience in the here and now can be enhanced by knowledge about other children's experience in the 'long ago and far away'. There is continuing debate about the appropriate age at which to teach about 'distant places' or particular periods of time and also about the effectiveness of different teaching styles. For example, it is often said that very young children are too young to learn about distant places, thus marginalising the real and vicarious experience many children have. However, we rarely question the leaps in understanding we expect children to make routinely because the distant place or distant time is mainly seen from an adult's perspective.

Books used in support of history teaching often purport to see historical events through children's eyes such as the life of a cabin boy in a Tudor ship at the time of the Spanish Armada. This approach can be tokenistic, presenting an adult view of events. If one asks children today, 'What questions would you want to ask a child living at this time?' the answers are rarely to be found in the books. However, such a question can set children and teachers together on routes of discovery to learn what children might have been doing and so help to build a 'history from below' which includes learning about histories of childhood.

It is not always easy to find children's own reflections from times in the past. Children's experiences have rarely been recorded, and where they have survived they usually give us an insight into the wealthier sectors of society. The advent of technology – home videos, television and radio documentaries – makes the more recent past more accessible but children's own writing about their lives, or their reflections on the world of adults, are still relatively rare. When we do have access to it, such as in *The Diary of Anne Frank* (Frank 1989), or more recently *Zlata's Diary* (Filipovic 1995), they are widely used. These of course are just some books that have succeeded in the hands of adult publishers; it would be good to encourage all children to express their experiences in the understanding that some day others may read and learn from them. Teachers have a role in encouraging children to develop the skill of diary-keeping with their own class and to help children value their own writing as a historical record.

CHILDREN IN HISTORY

This section examines the contribution that children's voices can make to the teaching of history, and to meeting the rights of the child in terms of learning about the pasts of other children. It also advocates that children be taught about the rights of children (and adults) in the past as part of the process of preparing them for active citizenship in the future.

Historical learning in primary schools is, like geography, enquiry led. The Nuffield History Project identifies five key principles related to such an enquiry process:

1. Questioning: history is about asking and answering questions, and above all, getting children to ask questions, *for example about the lives of children in the past.*

2. Challenging pupils to persist, to speculate, to make connections, to debate issues, and to understand the past from the inside, *for example the lives of children as we might imagine them.*

3. Using authentic sources with integrity – sources reflecting all sectors of society, *including where possible authentic resources reflecting children's experiences.*

4. Studying real historical knowledge in depth, even at primary level, *for example first-hand accounts of events written by children.*

5. Beginning with what the children can do and building on it by using a wide variety of teaching approaches – making history accessible, *using the children's own experiences as a starting point.*

(Adapted from Fines and Nichol 1997)

An enquiry-led approach to history, following the above guidelines, allows the child to participate fully in the learning process. Furthermore, when used in conjunction with history topics which look at rights as a central concept, children may learn about the rights of people in the past and compare these to the present day. A study of citizenship in Ancient Greece or Victorian Britain or Britain since 1930 can be used as a basis for understanding citizenship. The members of society who would be deemed 'citizens' have changed over time, with different rights being accorded to different groups. It is safe to assume that concepts of citizen, citizenship and democracy will continue to change in the future. An understanding of how current thinking is specific to our time, place and cultural context needs to be part of the social studies curriculum.

Children can also experience democracy in the classroom through listening to and valuing the voices of others. Hearing the voices of different groups within society contributes to learning *about* democracy and experiencing their own voices being heard contributes to learning *through* democracy.

In the world of children all adults are a powerful group. If we believe it is essential for voices from all sectors of society to be part of history teaching then this must include those of children.

> Increasingly, critical historians have exposed the ways in which the discipline of history itself has tended to privilege the experiences of certain powerful groups and to construct an 'approved' version of the past that marginalised, trivialised or silenced the voices of the less powerful. (Hoepper 1993, p.1)

Changing Childhoods – Britain since 1930 (Brown and Harrison 1996) is an example of a teaching resource for primary schools in both Scotland and England, which focuses on the experience of children, either in the words of the children themselves or in the words of adults reflecting on their own childhood. In addition sources are included which throw light on how national events affected children's daily life in their own locality. It includes the experiences of children from traveller families, children with disabilities and Basque children, seeking refuge from the Spanish Civil War, in addition to family life in different parts of the United Kingdom. This latter includes the experience of an Irish family settling in Rochdale in the 1930s. The book, subtitled as *A Source Book for Learning about Children and Social Change with 8–12-Year-Olds*, is structured in three areas of children's historical experience: children observed (at play, at school, at work); children at home (family homes, family budgets, family routines), and children's rights (children's health, children on the move, children with disabilities). This structure enables teachers to approach learning about rights from more familiar topic areas, or alternatively to focus specifically on learning about rights which can then be related to rights issues in practice at home, at school, at play. As an example activity from the book, the mapping of private and family events beside public events in the history of children's rights along a twentieth-century time-line encourages understanding of how personal and public lives may or may not interact.

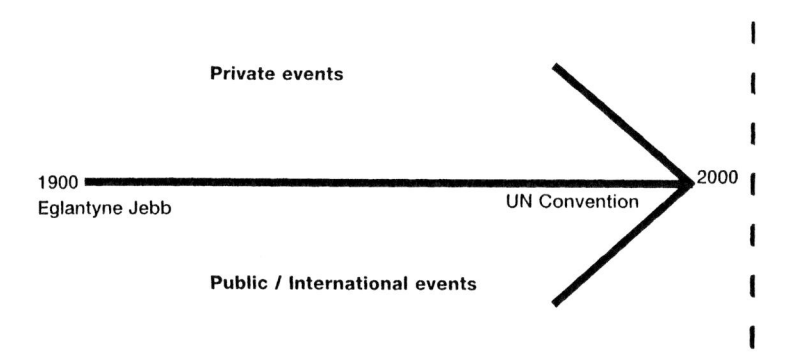

```
                    Private events
                                              ╲
1900 ━━━━━━━━━━━━━━━━━━━━━━━━━━━━━━━╲ 2000
Eglantyne Jebb              UN Convention
                                              ╱
                    Public / International events
```

Figure 18.3 Twentieth-century time-line[1]

This is part of the process of giving voice to children's own experiences and learning from their histories. But it is children's own experience expressed cogently and from the heart which brings alive places and times which are unfamiliar to today's children. Source material in the book shows how Mary Baker, the daughter of an agricultural labourer, was born with a dislocated hip. This caused her to limp, a disability immediately visible to those around her. In 1935, at the age of 12, she was sent to a 'Home for Crippled Girls' in London.

> When I first arrived, the nurse took me into the bathroom, and she stripped me off completely. She cut my hair short, right above the ears. And then I was deloused with powder of some description. They put me in a bath and scrubbed me down with carbolic soap. It was very degrading to me. And I felt as though the end of the world had come and so I cried. I sat in the bath and cried my eyes out. They told me it was no good crying and dried me down. They used such rough towels it felt like they were sandpapering me. [...] The next morning you were given a number and you had to remember it. My number was 29. It was engraved on all my hairbrushes and things with a big hot poker-like thing. I can never forget that number. We were hardly ever called by our first names, only by the other girls. And if Matron wanted you, she called you by whatever number you had. We never had names, we were just numbers there. I felt a bit low about it. I couldn't really put my feelings into an expression, only that I felt very lonely about it. (Brown and Harrison 1996, p.87)

1 Eglantyne Jebb founded the Save the Children Fund in 1919. For further information please contact: Save the Children Fund (UK), 17 Grove Lane, London SE5 8RD.

The thoughts were recorded after Mary had grown up, trained as a nurse, married and had children of her own. Yet the strength of her childhood feelings still survived. By learning about childhood experiences from the past, children today can begin to understand the concepts of continuity and change in addition to empathising with people in the past. Children can also compare their own experience with that of previous generations, 'building on their own experience' as Fines and Nicol (1997) remind us. In this case they can also begin to understand how attitudes to children with disability have changed over time.

Children are experts on play and playthings. Shane, a nine-year-old in a West Yorkshire primary school, has no doubt about how he likes to play.

> I like motor bikes I like having backers. I like going very fast. And I like going in the mud and I like going down the tip it has a lot of mud and bumps and I went up a ramp and it was a big ramp and it was a big bump and it was a big JUMP and it was good and I LIKED it. It was good riding the motorbike. The end. (Brown and Harrison 1996, p.22)

However, when he asked his mother and grandmother what they liked to play with when they were nine years old, the differences of time and gender became clear. Such differences can be explored in the classroom.

Linda McDonald (1960s)

When I was nine I liked to play hide and seek. My favourite toy was a big red-headed walk and talk doll. When I was at school I played with a skipping rope. I enjoyed making a peg bag. My favourite toy was my doll.

Mrs Firth (1930s)

When I was nine I played whip top and marbles. I liked drawing. My favourite game was Ludo. At school I played skipping and hopscotch. My best toy was a doll.

(Brown and Harrison 1996, p.22)

Whether today's children learn about traumatic experiences in the past, (such as that of Mary Baker) or the everyday (like that of Shane), they can better comprehend the similarities and differences of experience. Through the words of yesterday's children they can begin to recognise that people from minority and majority groups within their own nation and from cultures overseas should be presented as individuals with every variety of human quality and attribute. Stereotypes of minority groups, whether expressed in terms of human characteristics, life-styles, social roles or occupational status, are unacceptable and likely to be damaging. Using words from the groups themselves authenticates values and information.

Other source material in *Changing Childhoods* tells us how two Basque children in Ipswich in 1937 wrote to the local newspaper capturing the emotions which they felt as refugees in an uncertain time. This shows well how children can speak across the barriers of time:

> Dear Sir,
>
> Through the cruel war which has beset our country we are protected by yours, which today we call our second country in the affection we have. When the time comes for us to return we shall cry tears of sadness and joy; sadness in leaving this England, which has received us with open arms like a mother when we were forced to leave our homes and country, torn from us by Fascist barbarianism; joy in returning to Spain and to our families, if we are so fortunate as to find them again.
>
> The day, last Friday, which we spent at Felixstowe was a day of very happy memories since we arrived in England, and you do not know how grateful we all are to the Ipswich Cooperative Society for it, because such pleasures have long been prohibited from us Spanish children in our country. The swimming pool and the amusement park helped us to forget, for a time, that our beloved country is at war, and that we have no news whatever of any of our families there. It was one of our happiest days when we were able to make holiday with our schoolmates without having to take refuge or warning from the sirens before the air raids.
>
> When we return to our beloved Spain we will surely leave a great deal of our immense affection here, and we shall never, never forget where we have stayed, where we have been loved so much, and where so many proofs of that tenderness have been given…
>
> How happy we are in England! If only we had good news from Spain and also from our families we should be the happiest children in the world! How lovely it is, and how we admire it all.
>
> We all hope one day to be able to repay you for something that money cannot give.
>
> Yours very sincerely,
>
> Signed:
>
> Isabel Villa Cruz (14 years old).
> Miguel San Martin (12 years old).
>
> (Brown and Harrison 1996, p.83)

CHILDREN IN GEOGRAPHY

There is potential within National Curriculum Primary Geography for children to learn about the experiences of children in different localities. However as a study of such experiences is not explicitly required there is a danger that teachers may overlook this opportunity. Likewise in a study of a local issue such as the construction of a by-pass (Key Stage 2 Programme of Study: Settlement) it is suggested that children look at the 'different views of residents' which could include the perspectives of residents who are children.

Many 'locality packs' for children aged 7–11 produced by non-governmental organisations in recent years have focused on presenting 'communities' or 'families'. Once again while the voice of the child is not always explicit, the potential is there for teachers to incorporate children's experiences. More radically, organisations which focus on children's welfare and rights in global contexts, like Save the Children (UK) and UNICEF-UK have begun to explore what children's right to expression across frontiers could mean in terms of producing learning materials. The photo-pack *Lima Lives* (Harrison 1993), for example, attempts to incorporate children's voices from classroom exchanges between Bristol and Lima. This is a large barrier to cross, because children in a city in Peru may not be interested in issues which are deemed relevant for children in the United Kingdom to learn about. The geography curriculum focuses on 'how people affect the environment', and there is a danger that this can result in presenting Latin American city life through images of shanties and children carrying buckets of water. In *Lima Lives* Edgar and Ericka, both ten years old, speak out (through translation from Spanish to English) to say how they would clear all the rubbish and make the place healthy – if they were in control:

> Lima is an attractive city but it has many kinds of problems... I would like to change everything so there is no more corruption and violence. (Edgar)

> If I were President, I would run water every day... I would give electricity every day to those who could pay and those who could not pay. (Ericka) (Harrison 1993, p.29)

Figure 18.4 Carolina's drawing of playing in the main square

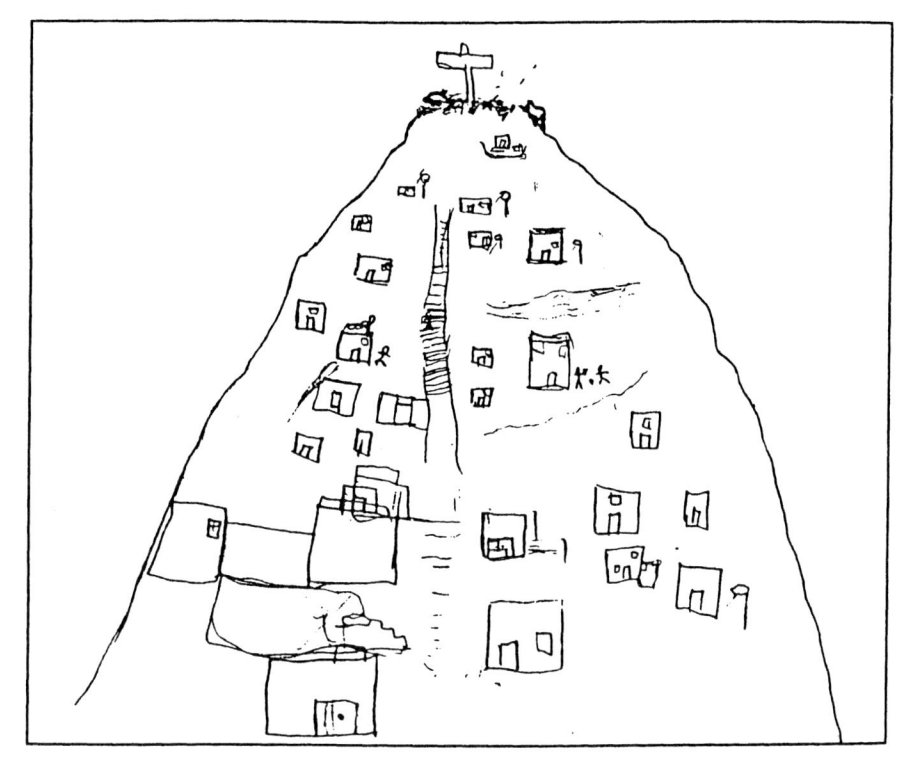

Figure 18.5 Edgar's drawing of his home area

The children draw pictures of their 'barriada' (urban settlement) with the sun shining and children playing football. They describe how neighbours share and help each other with their problems, like sharing water. How much of this tradition of community action will come through if the voices of those most affected are not allowed to be heard – particularly those of children who are least likely to have learnt to present what other people want to hear about them rather than their own direct opinions?

The challenge for a geography curriculum which promotes understanding of global links and action for citizenship is to enable people to meet as equals and exchange ideas, learning from each other. In spite of physical constraints, in this era of electronic communication there is much potential for school-to-school contact. In addition links can be established through friends, relatives or those in the community who have travelled or who have origins in other countries.

Another example of primary classroom experience to realise Article 13 of the UN Convention is the 'Caring and Sharing' project link which took place between schools in urban and rural Scotland and urban and rural Panama during 1996 (Harrison 1997). Pupils on both sides of the Atlantic produced their visual responses to prompts like 'the best people at caring for our needs' or 'children from different countries learning together' annotated in their own language, whether English or Spanish. The pictures were then exchanged with great interest on both sides. The co-ordinator for the project in Darien, Panama, where the participating primary schools have no electricity or tele-visual aids described the initiative as giving the children 'a window on the world'. The co-ordinator for schools in Highland Region, Scotland was fascinated at how pupils picked out *similarities* between young people in Panama and themselves while at the same time focusing on *differences* between lifestyles in urban and rural Panama. The project also enabled direct learning and linking within countries, between a Highland school and a Glasgow school. Teachers set up this learning across distance, but the aim was to enable the maximum possible freedom of expression among children.

This approach aims to exemplify geographical education for citizenship. Through expressing the realities of their own lives and comparing these with expressions from a 'distant' country, children are enabled to be themselves as part of a 'Caring and Sharing' world where lives are linked, both directly through the capacity to share ideas and indirectly through the many lines of economic and cultural contact which bring communities together.

CHILDREN AND VISUAL IMAGES

History and geography books and packs for use in the primary classes rely heavily on the visual image. Views of distant places and past times are key teaching tools in both subjects. Children often appear in the image but their immediate experience is not necessarily included in the text. Some textbooks currently in use in United Kingdom schools present stark images of children staring at a camera, with captions such as 'Children in Bangladesh'. The children themselves appear to have had no role in deciding on the picture or how it is packaged, nor is their view expressed in the text. What is required for real learning with and from real people is to be able to hear their real voices. Happily, some NGOs have begun to address this issue. (eg Sandbach and Fensome (1996), at Leeds Development Education Centre; Dodgson and Midwinter (1992, update 1996), at Manchester Development Education Project).

As well as children's voices being used to illustrate their photographs, children can be given activities which help them to understand the power of the visual image. Again, educating for citizenship would seem to require an education which encourages children to be critical consumers of the visual image, able to distinguish between media manipulation and truth, stereotype and reality.

Such visual literacy activities are now part of many classrooms and are used to support children's learning about periods in history or distant places. These activities first came through media studies but have been adapted by those working in development education, world studies and global education as an important way to build skills in learning about the wider world (Davies 1989; Steiner 1993). They aim to encourage critical analysis of visual images and allow the teacher to understand the children's current perceptions and knowledge base.

Children and adults are also susceptible to images of children from countries in the south such as those used by development agencies. Although the quality of representation has become less negative over the past years, images of children are still to be found as fund-raising stimuli.

> Pictures have power. They can convey information and leave a lasting impression. The right pictures can mobilise people and change the course of events. It's a power that can be used for good or bad. (Regan 1996, p.16)

Children need to be given the opportunity to examine such images, to question the motive behind the photographer and to try to understand the photographed child's perspective. As children's understanding of the world is built up from experience, image and text, this visual aspect deserves the teacher's attention.

CONCLUSION

In conclusion, we believe it is important for teachers to enable children to learn from each other. For social subjects, including history and geography, this means looking for expressions of children's experiences which are apparently distanced by time and space but which, once made accessible, may well be close to experiences of children in the class. Children themselves should play a key role in this learning process. They should be active geographers carrying out studies of faraway places, through whatever media of communication are available to them. Ideally this would involve communicating with children of the same age, formulating their own questions about life in a different society. They should be active historians, investigating everyday lives of children in past times through interviews with people in the community who can describe their childhood (for a study of, for example, 'Britain since 1930') or through searching for evidence of the role and status of children in communities in the distant past.

The rights of the child are met by such an approach to humanities learning where the focus is on the experience of children and where children are required to develop their own investigations. The right to speak and be listened to, and the freedom to receive, seek and impart information are part of the processes described in this chapter. Such an approach promotes active citizenship as children are encouraged to co-operate and to find out the views and concerns of those in the wider world. The learning methods which teachers choose to employ in their classrooms – and the ethos exemplified by the whole school – can support such learning for citizenship, because belief in the importance of listening to 'distant' children is directly related to classroom methodologies which encourage learners to listen to each other.

The examples from primary school projects described in this chapter all come from classrooms where teachers work collaboratively with their pupils, learning to understand the outside world together. Now, with the Convention on the Rights of the Child as backing, it is time for teachers to learn with children about children's worlds through listening to their varied voices.

REFERENCES

Brown, M. and Harrison, D. (1996) *Changing Childhoods – Britain since 1930*. London: Save the Children (UK).

Davies, M. (1989) *Get the Picture*. Birmingham: Development Education Centre.

Dodgson, R. and Midwinter, C. (1992, update 1996) *Living and Learning in a Tanzanian Village*. Manchester: Development Education Project.

Fines, J. and Nichol, J. (1997) *Teaching Primary History*. London: Heinemann.

Filipovic, Z. (1995) *Zlata's Diary: A Child's Life in Sarajevo*. Harmondsworth: Penguin.

Frank, A. (1989) *The Diary of Anne Frank*. London: Pan Books.

Harrison, D. (1993) *Lima Lives*. London: Save the Children (UK).

Harrison, D. (1997) *Caring and Sharing – A Link Project for Primary Social Education and Panama*. Glasgow: Save the Children (UK).

Hoepper, B. (1993) 'Seeking global citizens in the history classroom.' In D. and H. Dufty (eds) *We Sing of a World Reshaped*. Brisbane: Social Education Association of Australia.

Regan, C. (1996) *Images and Impact*. Dublin: Comlach.

Saint-Exupéry, A. (1974) *The Little Prince*. London: Pan Books.

Sandbach, T. and Fensome, J. (1996) *Feeling Good About Faraway Friends*. Leeds: Development Education Centre.

Steiner, M. (1993) *Learning From Experience: Cooperative Learning and Global Education*. Stoke-on-Trent: Trentham.

The Contributors

Geoff Anderson is a Senior Lecturer in Primary Education at Westminster College, Oxford. He teaches professional studies and history on both undergraduate and postgraduate courses. He is working on developing the College's international links, particularly through projects on environmental and citizenship themes with students and teachers in partnership schools.

Martin Ashley taught for 17 years in middle, primary and preparatory schools. He is currently a visiting lecturer in science, humanities and primary education at the University of the West of England, Bristol, where he has recently completed a PhD on environmental education. He also works as a freelance environmental education consultant and has research interests in the public understanding of science and the philosophy of values.

Jean Pierre Branchereau is a Senior Lecturer in Geography at the Institut Universitaire de Formation des Maîtres des Pays de la Loire (IUFM), Nantes. He trains teachers of geography for both primary and secondary schools.

Margot Brown is National Co-ordinator at the Centre for Global Education, University College of Ripon and York St John, York, England. She is currently working with teachers and student teachers on issues of human rights in the primary classroom and the introduction of global issues in the modern foreign languages curriculum. She previously taught in primary and secondary schools, was an education adviser for Oxfam and tutor at the Centre for Urban Educational Studies, ILEA.

Nick Clough has taught for many years in primary schools and is now Senior Lecturer in Education at the Faculty of Education where he is Award Leader for the Primary Undergraduate Teacher Training Programme. He is currently developing a long-standing interest in citizenship education through membership of the World Studies Trust and through work in this field funded by TEMPUS in teacher training institutions in Latvia.

Ian Davies is Lecturer in Educational Studies at the University of York. His previous experience includes ten years as a teacher in a comprehensive school in England. He now teaches undergraduates who are reading educational studies and postgraduate history students. His interests include history education and education for citizenship. Recent publications include *Developing European Citizens* (1997), Sheffield Hallam Press (with A. Sobisch).

Carmen Gonzalo is a Senior Lecturer in Geography at the Faculty of Education in the Universitat Autònoma de Barcelona (Bellaterra Campus). She works in the fields of European studies and environmental education in the training of primary teachers.

Doug Harwood is a Senior Lecturer in Education at the University of Warwick and a member of the World Studies Trust. He has published in the fields of geographical, political and personal and social education.

Don Harrison is Deputy Director of the Council for Education in World Citizenship in London, working on a broad range of materials and learning approaches for global citizenship. Previously he worked for Save the Children's education unit in England and Scotland, developing learning materials about children's rights.

Cathie Holden is a Senior Lecturer at the University of Exeter, having taught in primary schools for many years. She lectures in humanities and educational studies. She is currently involved in research into teachers' perceptions of social, moral and cultural education and how such education prepares children for global citizenship. Recent books include *Visions of the Future: Why we Need to Teach for Tomorrow* with David Hicks (1995, Trentham) and *Teaching Early Years History* with Liz Wood (1995, Chris Kington Publications).

Phil Johnson is a Senior Lecturer in the Faculty of Education at the University of Melbourne, Australia. Prior to that he taught in primary schools in Melbourne. His teaching and research interests are in the areas of values education, anti-racist education and teacher development. He has worked extensively in education with Aboriginal and minority ethnic communities.

Audrey Osler is a Senior Lecturer at the University of Birmingham where she leads the Human Rights and Equality in Education postgraduate programme. She has worked as consultant for the Council of Europe and UNESCO and published widely on development and human rights education in Africa and Europe. Her recent books include *The Education and Careers of Black Teachers* with A. Starkey (1996, David Fulton) and *Teacher Education and Human Rights* (1997, Open University Press).

Rhiannon Prys Owen has worked as a teacher in a wide variety of special and primary schools throughout the United Kingdom. She is currently working for Barnados on an inclusion project which involves two further education colleges.

Hanns-Fred Rathenow is Professor of Education at the Technical University of Berlin. In 1983 he was a visiting professor at the Richardson Institute for Peace and Conflict Research, Lancaster University and in 1989 he was a visiting fellow at the Centre for Global Education, York University. He has edited a number of books and has written articles on Global Education, Peace Education and Holocaust Education.

Micheline Rey teaches at the Faculty of Psychology and Educational Science at the University of Geneva. She also works for the canton of Geneva with responsibilities within the department of public education. Her research and other work is focused upon the reception and education of migrants. Her particular interest is intercultural education. She is a consultant at the Council of Europe where she has worked on a number of programmes.

Chris Spurgeon teaches English at Hartshill School, a 12–16 comprehensive near Coventry. Teaching about human rights and 'race' are his particular interests, and he has published in this area. His doctoral work considers the possibilities and problems involved in teaching about citizenship issues through literature.

Julia Tanner is a Senior Lecturer in Primary Education at Leeds Metropolitan University, where she is responsible for geography within the School of Teacher Education Studies. Her research interests include children's personal geographies, primary schools' approaches to managing the National Curriculum and the changing role of the primary subject co-ordinator.

Jane Tarr taught in special and primary schools in the south-west of England before joining the Faculty of Education at the University of the West of England where she is Senior Lecturer in Education. Her major areas of interest are the creative arts (in particular music) and special educational needs. Her current area of research is the conceptions of parents and professionals of special educational needs.

Marta Utset is a teacher at Bellaterra Primary School. She is the co-ordinator of the COMENIUS project (1995–1998) referred to in the chapter. She teaches English and is an active leader in her school on projects involving environmental and consumer education.

Maria Villanueva is a Senior Lecturer in geography at the Faculty of Education in the Universitat Autònoma de Barcelona (Bellaterra Campus). She teaches European Studies in initial and in-service teacher training. She is the Faculty co-ordinator for European Programmes.

Veronica Voiels is a Senior Lecturer at Didsbury School of Education, Manchester Metropolitan University where she co-ordinates the postgraduate certificate in Religious Studies and is a tutor on the B.Ed in Religious Studies and Humanities. She has worked with colleagues in non-governmental agencies for development education in the areas of global awareness and values education. She runs in-service courses for primary teachers in social, moral and spiritual education.

Norbert H. Weber is Professor of Education at the Technical University of Berlin where he is working on problems of Drug Prevention, General Didactics and Holocaust Education. He has been involved in German-Polish relations for more than 20 years and is the Chairperson of the Berlin-Brandenburg Protestant Academy's committee 'Poland – our neighbour' (Nachbar Polen).

Liz Wood is a Senior Lecturer in Education at Exeter University, specialising in Early Childhood Education. She has published widely on the importance of play in early childhood and the relationship between teachers' theories of play and their classroom practice. She has also researched into the progression in young children's understanding of history.

Subject index

Aborigines 142, 145, 146, 148, 150
active learning 111, 154, 246, 247
alternative view of society 134
anti-racist education 141, 146, 149
assessment 236
assisted participation 17-21
Australia 142-150

biographies 183
brainstorming 96, 156, 157
British traditions 190
bullying 22, 39, 43, 218

Canada 43
challenging behaviour 81
charity work 50, 51
children's newspapers 26, 209-220
children's voices 259-270
circle time 58, 217
citizenship: European 196-204, 228
collaboration 211
community 199, 204
community decision making 230
community involvement 13, 21, 22, 53, 59-61
conflict resolution 35, 211, 212
consumer education 224, 230-239
consumer rights 26
consumer: ethical 25, 50, 51, 228-239
controversial issues 22, 64, 97, 167-169, 210, 218, 219
co-operation 247
critical thinking 72

democracy 69

democracy: learning about 56-59, 262
democratic processes 87-94
democratic teaching 154-169
Denmark 66
development 222
disability 22, 81-94, 119, 120, 263
distant locality 243-251, 265-268

early childhood 20, 21, 33
economic education 24, 25
economic priorities of children 177
economics 171-182
emotion 24, 95, 141-142, 146-149, 152
empowerment 31, 32, 35, 37, 39-41, 44, 219
energy 180
English literature 127-137
environment 171-182, 219
environmental action 49, 50
environmental citizen 171
environmental education 171-182
environmental issues 15, 22, 51, 52, 54, 64
Equal Franchise Act (1928) 70
ethnic minorities 47,117, 119, 120, 124,141,143, 168
Europe 13, 25, 26
European 196, 199, 200, 203, 204, 222, 228-239
evaluation by children 166

field visits 100
Finland 228
food 26, 214, 231, 232, 235
food products 222
France 215, 222, 228
future 21, 47, 53-56, 67, 68, 144, 152

Gambia 209
gender 20, 21, 23, 34, 39, 47, 118, 120, 123,134,187, 214
geography 27, 265-268
global system 222

health education 232
history 23,25, 261-265
history education 188-195
Holocaust 23, 95-111
homosexuality 23,114,117, 119, 120, 121
human rights 14, 23, 82, 113-125, 127-137, 203, 204, 260, 269
human rights education 95-111

Iceland 215
identities
 children 187
 student teachers 183, 196-204
identity 122
inclusion 82
inequalities 225
Information Technology 26, 43, 210, 212
instructor role 158
intention to act 178
intercultural education 183
Italy 216-218, 229

language 248
law breaking 71, 134
literature 202, 261
local area 243

metacognition 41, 142, 147, 150, 151, 247
migration 25, 143,184-186
minorities 184
moral conflict 71
multi-cultural education 141, 149, 150

national identity 199, 205

Netherlands 25, 196, 197, 200, 203
neutral chair 24, 154
nursery/reception 38

Panama 267
participatory skills 84
pedagogy 95
peer pressure 179
personal, social, moral, cultural development 67, 75 136
play 36
playground 38
political education 165
pollution 216
problem-solving 42

racism 13, 21, 122, 130-132, 143, 144, 146, 147, 149
reclaim the streets 65
reflection 105
role of teacher 13, 16, 17, 21, 22, 24, 26, 27, 54, 125, 154-169, 196, 211, 214
role play 102

school councils 22, 56-59, 87-94, 218
school environment 87
segregation 84
social and moral education 122, 123, 197, 16
social class 134
social relationships 89-93
Spain 229
special schools 81-94
stereotypes/prejudice 144, 147, 211, 213, 214, 246
sustainability 63

teachers' beliefs 24, 25, 35, 196, 197
technology 210, 212
time-line 263
trade 26
transport 64-76, 176

under development 223

value-free 172
values 14, 15, 18, 47, 61, 144, 147, 151, 244
  clarification 175
  democratic 70
  ecological 69
  economic 71
  expressed 175
  of children 209, 220
  operative 25, 175
  statement of 72
visual images
  children 268

waste recycling 50, 176
whole class teaching 154
witnesses 101, 108

Youth Start Disability Project 92

Author index

Aboud, F. 142
Abram, I. 101
Adorno, T. 95, 97, 99
Ashley, M. 172, 174
Attfield, J. 37, 41
Baines, B. 154
Bale, J. 246
Beck, V. 15, 16, 64
Beddis, R. 210, 249, 250
Bennett, N. 35, 37, 196
Biott, C. 211
Boal, A. 103
Bonino, B. 230
Bracey, P. 190
Brandes, D. 162
Breit, G. 102
Bristol City Council 66, 69
Brown, A. 150
Brown, L. 53
Brown, M. 262, 263, 264, 265
Bruner, J. 17
Buck, M. 225, 226
Burns, C. 211
Cahill, D. 149
Camus, A. 130, 135
Cantwell, N. 115
Carrington, B 154
Castles, S. 143
Celan, P. 99
Central Bureau 210
Clough, N. 72, 173
Cohen, E.G. 164
Commission of the European Communities 193
Cooper, P. 82
Cordelier, S. 223
Council of Europe 13, 57, 184
Covell, K. 116, 123
Craft, A. 211
Cullingford, C. 213
Curtis, A. 187
Damasio, A. 147
Davies, I. 190, 203
Davies, M. 268

Day, J. 56
DeLoache, J. 150
Denzin, N.K. 148
Department for Education and Science (DES) 83
Department for Education (DFE) 40, 245
Department of Health 82
Department for Education and Employment (DfEE) 71, 82, 83
Dhondy, F. 130, 131, 132
Dodgson, R. 268
Doherty, A. 64
Dolifus, O. 222
Drew, D. 122
Dudek, P. 96
Dunlop, F. 151
Easen, P. 211
Edwards, J. 239
Egan, G. 163
Elliott, J. 127
Feinburg, S. 35, 42
Fensome, J. 268
Fielding, M. 16, 56
Filer, A. 32, 42
Filipovic, Z. 261
Fines, J. 261, 264
Fisher, J. 41
Fisher, R. 42
Fisher, S 155, 246
Fogelman, K. 239
Fountain, S. 246
Fouts, J. 184
Frank, A. 86, 261
Fransecky, M. von 107
Friends of the Earth (F.O.E.) 251
Fuller, S. 86
Gathercole, P. 190
Gilbert, R. 211
Gilligan, C. 119
Ginnis, P. 162
Ginott, H. 108
Gonzalo, C. 239
Goodey, B. 247
Graham, D. 172
Greig, S. 246
Griffith, R. 15, 16, 27
Griffiths, M 171

Guardian, The 13, 47, 58, 220
Haas, G. 98
Hage, K. 97
Harber, C. 164
Harris, M. 175
Harris, R. 175, 211
Harrison, D. 262, 263, 264, 265, 266, 267
Hart, R. 19, 20, 27, 32, 59
Harwood, D. L. 154, 162, 163, 164, 165
Hatcher, R. 130
Heater, D. 184
Heyl, M 101
Hicks, D 15, 16, 46, 47, 53, 67, 68, 70, 155, 246, 250
Higgins-D'Alessandro, A. 59
Hines, B. 86
Hinton, S.E. 130, 134, 135
Hobsbawn, E. 190
Hoedeman, O. 64
Hoepper, B. 262
Holden, C. 15, 16, 46, 47, 70, 72, 173, 197, 250
House of Commons 244
Housego, E. 211
Howe, R. B. 116, 123
Huckle, J. 239
Humanities Curriculum Project 154
Inman, S. 225, 226
Inner London Education Authority (ILEA) 82
Izard, C.E. 148
Jahoda, G. 174
Jeleff, S. 115
Jensen, B. 18, 75
Johnstone, K. 103
Jones, T. 122
King, M. 123
Lane, N. R. 161, 165
Lane, S. A. 161, 165
Lang, T. 239
Lansdown, G. 44, 115
Lavisse, E. 223
Leeds DEC 247
Lewis, A. 82

Lipman, M. A. 152, 161, 165
Lister, I. 127
Lowenthal, D. 190
Machon, P. 244
Mares, C. 210, 211, 249, 250
Marsden, B. 244
Mathieson, N. 127, 136
McCormick, J. 193
McLaughlin, T. H. 184
McNaughton, A. H. 165
McNeish, D. 123
Meighan, R. 164
Midwinter, C. 268
Mindess, M. 35, 42
Ministere de L'Education Nationale 224
Moore, M. 82
Morrison, K. 211, 219
Moscovici, S. 174
Mueller-Ott, D. 99
Nader, R. 230
Naidoo, B. 130
National Curriculum Council (NCC) 129, 190, 191, 210, 212, 214, 244
National Primary Centre (NPC) 210, 212
Northern Examination and Assessment Board (NEAB) 127
Newell, P. 115
Newman, T. 121
Newspapers in Education 212
Newton, J. 212
Nias, J. 197
Nichol, J. 261, 264
Noctor, M. 154
Nutbrown, C. 35
OFSTED 92, 129
Organisation for Economic Co-operation and Development (OECD) 83
Orr, D. 15, 72
Orwell, G. 130, 132, 134
Osler, A. 16, 32, 115, 124
Pike, G. 149, 188, 246

Pollard, A. 32, 42
Porter, J. 93
Potts, P. 82
Ranger, T. 190
Rathenow, H.F. 109, 110, 111
Rauner, M. 184
Regan, C. 269
Rey, M. 183, 185
Richardson, V. 196
Roberts, H. 116
Roebben, B. 147
Rogers, C.R. 102
Rogers, S. 35, 37, 196
Roszak, T. 72
Rowe, D. 212, 219
Rudduck, J. 15, 17, 56, 154
Rutland, A. 174
Sachdev, D.116, 122
Saint-Exupery, A. 258, 259
Sandbach, T. 268
Schnack R. 18, 75
School Curriculum and Assessment Authority (SCAA) 13, 40, 190, 191, 205
Schulz-Hageleit, P. 104
Selby, D. 149, 188, 246
Sen, A. 172
Shennan, M. 230
Shlyakhter, A. 180
Singh, B. 212
Siraj-Blatchford, I. 40
Slater, L. 211
Smucker, B. 130, 131
Starkey, H. 16, 84, 115, 124
Steiner, M. 162, 268
Stenhouse, L. 127, 161, 164
Stevenson, R.L. 86
Stradling, R. 154, 162
Swindells, R. 130, 132, 133
Talbot, M. 72
Tappin, M. 53
Tate, N. 72
Taylor, M.D. 130, 131
Theissen, D. 32, 42
Thomas, G. 82

Thompson, A.G. 197
Times Educational Supplement (TES) 13, 23, 32, 203
Trafford B. 18
Troyna, B. 130, 154, 171
Tudor, I. 154
Tytler, D. 172
United Nations (UN) Convention on the Rights of the Child 14, 83, 260
United Nations Declaration of Human Rights (UNDHR) 14
Uzzell, D. 174
Vasta, E. 143
Vidal, J. 69, 70
Villaneuva, M. 239
Voiels, V. 197
Vygotsky, L. 17
Wade, B. 82
Walker, D. 93
Wallace, G. 56
Watson, B. 175
Weber, N. 109, 110, 111
Weizsaecker, R. von 95
Wellington, J.J. 154
Whistance, D. 174
Wiegand, P. 246
Williams, C. 85
Williams, R. 190
Wilson, R. 180
Wolf, C. 96
Wood, E.A. 37, 41
Wood, L. 35, 37, 196
Wright, D. 175
Zych, A. 99

Printed in the United Kingdom
by Lightning Source UK Ltd.
105466UKS00001B/82-117